THE WORLD'S STORY 2

THE MIDDLE AGES

THE FALL OF ROME THROUGH THE RENAISSANCE

ANGELA O'DELL

MASTERBOOKS®
—CURRICULUM—

Author: Angela O'Dell

Master Books Creative Team:

Editor: Shirley Rash

Design: Diana Bogardus

Cover Design: Diana Bogardus

Copy Editors:
Judy Lewis
Willow Meek

Curriculum Review:
Kristen Pratt
Laura Welch
Diana Bogardus

First printing: August 2018
Fourth printing: May 2022

Master Books, P.O. Box 726,
Green Forest, AR 72638

Master Books® is a division of the
New Leaf Publishing Group, Inc.

ISBN: 978-1-68344-094-9
ISBN: 978-1-61458-673-9 (digital)
Library of Congress Number: 2018933110

Printed in the United States of America

Please visit our website for other great titles:
www.masterbooks.com

Author Bio:

As a homeschooling mom and author, **Angela O'Dell** embraces many aspects of the Charlotte Mason method yet knows that modern children need an education that fits the needs of this generation. Based upon her foundational belief in a living God for a living education, she has worked to bring a curriculum that will reach deep into the heart of home-educated children and their families. She has written over 20 books, including her history series and her math series. Angela's goal is to bring materials that teach and train hearts and minds to find the answers for our generation in the never-changing truth of God and His Word.

INTRODUCTION

Most of us think about castles and knights when we hear the words the *Middle Ages*. Although these images *are* representative of this time period, there are also many other interesting events, influential historical figures, and world culture changes to study in order to see more of the whole picture. As we work our way through this volume covering what history calls the Middle Ages, you will discover that the Christian Church was one of the most influential powers of this era. This power is what I want to focus on in this introduction.

In the first volume of this series, *The World's Story 1, the Ancients,* we learned about the beginning of the world, how God created everything, including the first man and his wife, and how sin first entered into the picture. We studied the civilizations that rose and fell, and we followed the story of God's chosen people, the Israelites. We spent time learning the historical facts surrounding the culmination of the redemption story. We watched our Savior and friend, Jesus Christ, dying a terrible death to take the penalty of our sin, and finally bursting forth from the grave, conquering the power of death on our behalf.

As Jesus left His followers to return to His Father's right hand, He sent two angels to give this promise to His disciples who were standing with their mouths ajar in wonder at the sight. Acts 1:9–11 says this: "After saying this, he was taken up into a cloud while they were watching, and they could no longer see him. As they strained to see him rising into heaven, two white-robed men suddenly stood among them. 'Men of Galilee,' they said, 'why are you standing here staring into heaven? Jesus has been taken from you into heaven, but someday he will return from heaven in the same way you saw him go!' " (NLT). After the Holy Spirit that Jesus had promised came to the disciples, they all went out preaching and praising God, and the Scriptures said that many were added to the Church.

As months turned into years and years into centuries, the Christian Church gained powerful influence and prestige. This power was often abused by men who wielded the name of Christianity like a lethal weapon, beating those under their authority into submission. In this volume, you will come across many instances where I have written these words: *forced to convert to Christianity.* I cannot tell you how many times, as my fingers tapped out those words on my keyboard, my heart shivered. Each and every time I saw those words form on my computer screen, I felt the sadness of the Holy Spirit within me, and I knew that I needed to write to you about it.

The very essence of Christianity, or Christ-following, is based on the premise of personal relationship with God — a relationship based on free will. When Christ allowed Himself to be crucified on that Cross, His blood became the atonement needed to wash away the sins of the world. Through His death and Resurrection, we have access to the very throne room of Almighty God. We each have to decide that we want to put God on the throne of our life and live to please Him. *This* is being a Christian, and it is an extremely personal choice. No one can force someone to kneel their hearts and souls before their Maker. God Himself does not force us to worship Him; He asks us to do so and pursues us with His redeeming love because He knows He made us to be satisfied by only Him. It really is as simple as that.

When rituals replace relationship, religion becomes dead, empty, and potentially dangerous. Jesus said this to the Pharisees in Mark 7:6–8: "Jesus replied, 'You hypocrites! Isaiah was right when he prophesied about you, for he wrote, "These people honor me with their lips, but their hearts are far from me. Their worship is a farce, for they teach man-made ideas as commands from God." For you ignore God's law and substitute your own tradition'" (NLT).

When you are reading the stories in this volume, I want you to remember that there have always been — and still are — humans who try to use the mighty name of Christ to gain control over other humans and to greedily gain worldly wealth. I also want you to remember that throughout history, from the time of Christ's gift of redemption, there have been true followers of Christ. You will read about many of these true followers in this volume. It was an honor and a privilege to tell you the stories of some of my favorite heroes of the faith who lived in the Middle Ages. In writing this section of our world's story, I have worked diligently and prayed fervently that God would guide me in teaching about this time period, which involves many difficult events, as well as wonderful world-changing happenings and characters. I understand that there are many types of families reading this story together, and I will do my best not to portray Christian church history from any particular angle or bias.

C.S. Lewis, the author of the beloved *The Chronicles of Narnia,* once said this in his book *Mere Christianity,* "[H]uman history [is] . . . the long terrible story of man trying to find something other than God which will make him happy" (Lewis 2009, Book 2, Chapter 3). I couldn't agree more. Humanity — what an indescribable jumble of all things good and terrible, so much so that I reach out to you with the comfort of this reassurance from our God and King: "I have told you all this so that you may have peace in me. Here on earth you will have many trials and sorrows. But take heart, because I have overcome the world" (John 16:33; NLT).

I pray that you will see the hand of God as you learn about the Middle Ages.

All dates are A.D. unless specifically noted as B.C.

01

START HERE

The time period that we know as ancient history had come to a close. Christ Jesus had come and fulfilled His divine purpose here on this earth. He had died, resurrected, and ascended back to His place at the right hand of His Father. In the decades after these miraculous and prophecy-fulfilling events, the disciples and followers of Christ spread the good news of the gospel, and the Early Christian Church was formed. A few centuries later, Rome, the world power that reigned supreme during the time of Christ, was teetering on the brink of destruction. Generations before, the famous Babylonian king, Nebuchadnezzar, had dreamed about the rise and fall of the major world kingdoms; his dream depicting history as a giant statue, which comprised various types of metals, had thus far come to fruition. The iron legs of the statue depicted an incredibly powerful kingdom that would stand for an extended length of time and leave a lasting influence on future empires. This kingdom, the Roman Empire, would split before it fell. In this chapter, we will look closely at this devastating crash that would set the tone for centuries to come. After the fall of Rome, humankind had stepped into the Middle Ages, which is the time period we will study together in this volume. It spans from the fall of Rome in 476 to the end of the Renaissance in about 1600.

If you have studied ancient history like we did in the first volume of this series, you'll remember that Rome was a mighty empire. It included large portions of the continents of Europe, Asia, and Africa and ruled millions of people. In fact, the empire was so big that it was eventually divided between a western half of the empire and an eastern half. The Eastern Roman Empire was ruled from a city in modern-day Turkey called Constantinople. This city was made the capital by an emperor named Constantine in 331. The western half of the Roman empire included the ancient city of Rome, though it was no longer officially the capital. Nevertheless, Rome remained an extremely important city.

Though the Roman Empire was still large, it had an abundance of problems. One problem was its size; it was so big that there really wasn't a good way to protect it. The very size of the empire became its downfall. There were many additional problems plaguing the Roman Empire at this time, however, including diseases the Roman army brought back from other places in the ancient world. These terrible epidemics killed thousands upon thousands of people, therefore weakening the army and the civilian population. Another problem was the Roman army stopped relying on Romans to fill their ranks. They instead began recruiting foreign mercenaries — soldiers who fight for money. These mercenaries were not as loyal to the Roman Empire as Roman armies in the past had been simply because they were not Roman. In fact, many members of the so-called barbarian tribes that helped bring the Roman Empire down had previously served in the Roman military!

Roman society and the economy were a mess, as well. The government was unstable and extremely corrupt, with many of the emperors only ruling for a matter of years or months before being overthrown and replaced by someone else. For the most part, these emperors were not sincerely concerned with taking care of the people under their control. Instead, they were more interested in how much money they could get from their position. The government had also unwisely overspent its money on wars and other expenses. The people of the empire were heavily taxed to help make up for this, but the result also made the financial gap between the rich and the poor even worse.

1920s illustration of Visigoth King Alaric entering Athens, Greece

Another consequence of the economic problems was that the empire no longer had the money to maintain its infrastructure. In its early history, Rome was justifiably famous for the quality of its roads, which spanned the entire empire. Its later economic difficulties meant there was no longer enough money to maintain these roads, so they fell into disrepair. In years past, Rome's excellent roads had aided trade and the mighty Roman army, but now, its crumbling conditions made it harder to transport goods and soldiers long distances.

Another significant issue was recurring invasions from barbarians. This was the term Romans used for people who were not Roman citizens. If you read Volume 1 in this series, you might remember reading about Attila the Hun, who led his army of barbarians against Rome. Attila was defeated before he could reach Rome, but other barbarians did successfully attack the city of Rome. At the height of the Roman Empire in centuries past, such an attack would have seemed unthinkable, but now, they became a recurring issue. Each time, the city was sacked, which meant that its valuables were looted and taken away.

In 410, a Germanic tribe called the Visigoths sacked the city. Forty-five years later, the city was sacked by another Germanic tribe called the Vandals. Finally, in 476, the city of Rome was sacked by still another Germanic tribe, the Ostrogoths. The fall of Rome is usually dated to this event because Rome fell into

The Visigoth king, Alaric I, leads the first sack of Rome in 410.

Juan de la Corte's depiction of a Roman siege, 1600s

a period of Germanic rule. Other times when Rome was sacked, a Roman emperor remained in charge, but that was no longer true after 476. There was never another Roman emperor ruling the western half of the empire after this point. The once mighty empire had fallen.

As you can probably imagine, the last days of the Western Roman Empire were very difficult for the people who lived there. Even though life was always hard, it was still a great shock when the once-powerful empire collapsed, especially at the hands of barbarians, whom most Romans considered inferior and uncivilized. When the dust settled after the collapse of the Western Roman Empire, panic began to set in. The conquering barbarians had excellent sacking skills, but they lacked the ability to set up a functioning replacement government.

There was no longer a central government; therefore, there were no schools or law enforcement officers. No one knew who would lead them, teach them, or protect them. Roman money was no longer issued, and the old Roman coins were worth nothing more than the metal they were made of. Suddenly, even people who had been rich became poor overnight. Can you imagine how frightening and uncertain this would be? It was a very difficult time, and we'll learn more about what happened because of the fall of Rome in the next chapter, but first, we'll check in with the eastern half of the Roman Empire.

19th century Dutch painter Charles Rochussen's scene showing Romans interacting with the Germanic Batavi tribe. The Batavi were barbarian allies of the Romans.

NARRATION BREAK:

Discuss what you learned about the fall of Rome.

The Eastern Roman Empire had also been subject to the attacks, but they had managed to ward off the barbarians. Even though they lost a large portion of land to the barbarians, and their empire shrank to the area directly surrounding Constantinople, the Eastern Empire survived.

We call this surviving part of the Roman Empire the Byzantine (BIZ-in-teen) Empire. It was called that because Constantinople's ancient name was Byzantium. The Byzantine Empire may have started out small, but it certainly did not stay that way. Eventually, strong emperors came to the Byzantine throne. These emperors fought and conquered sections of the surrounding area until the Byzantine Empire was soon spreading far beyond Constantinople.

Valentine Cameron's 19th century painting of Empress Theodora

One of the most powerful Byzantine emperors was Justinian. Emperor Justinian was not born into a royal family in 483; in fact, he was not even from a rich, influential family. Justinian grew up as a poor country boy. His parents were farmers, and they worked hard to feed their family. Justinian's mother had a brother named Justin, who was a high-ranking officer in the imperial guard. Uncle Justin knew that his nephew needed an education to have a good future. So, it was that Justinian was taken to Constantinople, where there were many renowned institutions of education. After he finished school, Justinian decided to go into the army. Everyone liked this bright, organized young man. He was helpful to his officers, and he gained respect for his bravery. As you might expect from such a young man, he moved quickly up through the ranks in the army.

It just so happened that there was a lovely young woman named Theodora who lived in Constantinople. Theodora had grown up in a family who owned a circus. From a very young age, Theodora worked with the animals in the circus. She led a wild and ungodly life, but when she grew up, Theodora became a Christian. She decided to move to Constantinople to live a quiet, useful life.

CONNECT

If you were to travel to the beautiful Old City part of modern-day Istanbul, you would be visiting the city once called Constantinople. There are many awe-inspiring aspects of this city, with one of the most obvious being the architecture. The structures of Constantinople that were built in the early years of the Byzantine Empire are varied in style. Many of them have a flavor of the Roman style of building, while others are more reminiscent of other nearby civilizations of Asia Minor, which were uninfluenced by Roman architecture.

You and I are quite accustomed to the style of buildings popular in our time and country. Much of the architecture we are exposed to is only a couple of centuries old at the most, and although there are many different styles of houses and buildings in our cities or neighborhoods, they all have somewhat similar lines and layouts. This is not the case with the buildings of the Byzantine Empire! Their mix of traditional Roman or Greek-influenced architecture with more interesting and individual styles creates a unique skyline. One of the most amazing architectural examples is the Hagia Sophia. This gorgeous cathedral was built during the 6th century, while Justinian I was emperor, for Eastern Orthodox Christians to worship in, and it is still considered the most important Byzantine architectural structure. Byzantine cathedrals like the Hagia Sophia were specifically designed to be ornate and magnificent because Eastern Christians believed that was one way to honor God.

If we were to walk into this fabulous architectural wonder, we would be awestruck. The building's architects were also well known for their mechanical skills and mathematical knowledge (Brooks 2009). These ingenious architects designed the cathedral to combine a long, rectangular central building with a huge 32-meter (nearly 105 feet) dome roof. Study the illustration to see how they supported a circular dome roof over a rectangular building.

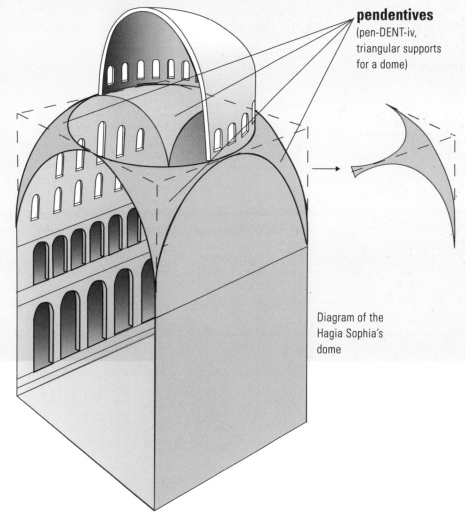

pendentives
(pen-DENT-iv, triangular supports for a dome)

Diagram of the Hagia Sophia's dome

Byzantine mosaic of Jesus in the Hagia Sophia

One day, Justinian, who was at this time a soldier in the army, rode through the streets of Constantinople. He saw Theodora standing by the side of the road. He was enthralled by her beauty and asked about her. No one knew who she was, so Justinian searched and searched until he found out where her home was. When he had finally found her, Justinian asked her to marry him.

Justinian's uncle eventually became the emperor, and when he died, Justinian became ruler in his place. Theodora then became the empress of the Byzantine Empire. Empress Theodora is thought by many to be the most powerful woman in the history of the Byzantine Empire.

After he became emperor, Justinian did not like the fact that his empire was so small, so he decided to do something about it. After building up his army, he set out to conquer the lands that used to belong to the empire but had been lost. This increased the size of the empire, and soon, the Byzantine Empire was the leading power in the world. He also increased taxes, though, and that made many people unhappy.

Justinian also worked to remove corruption from the government. One of his most famous achievements was the Code of Justinian. Shortly after becoming emperor, Justinian ordered the laws of the empire to be written down. This would be a good way to make sure everyone living in the empire knew what the laws were. In the process, the laws were also updated and revised. This was a huge undertaking that required several years to complete. Even though many of the laws were not new at all, the result of this project became known as the Code of Justinian. For centuries afterward, these laws (known as Roman law) formed the foundation of the legal system of most European kingdoms. Even modern American law is still influenced by Roman law and, by extension, the Code of Justinian.

Things did not always work out smoothly, however. Chariot racing was very popular in Constantinople, and the fans could be unruly, to say the least. When some of them got in trouble, their friends became angry and started a terrible uprising in the city. The uprising was called the Nika Riots and was so bad that it almost forced Justinian to flee Constantinople; however, Theodora convinced him to stay.

There was so much wealth in the Byzantine culture that the glory that was Rome paled in comparison. The Byzantine children attended school to learn from the philosophers of the day. They were taught by strict professors, who oversaw the educational process with a watchful eye. The architectural glory in the city of

Constantinople was astounding; there were beautiful palaces, schools, and churches in abundance. Homes were emblazoned with mosaics made of precious stones, gold, and colorful glass.

As we will learn more about in the next chapter, both the Western and Eastern Roman Empires eventually became Christian. The most famous and beautiful church in Constantinople was called the Hagia Sophia (HAZSH-ee-uh so-FEE-uh). This church was actually a great cathedral, with huge, open spaces, beautiful windows, intricate mosaics, and huge domes. Indeed, it is considered an architectural wonder of the world.

NARRATION BREAK:

Talk about what you read about the Byzantine Empire.

Aus der Zeit des Bilderstürmes.

There was a great controversy among the Christians of the Byzantine Empire over whether or not to use icons (depictions of saints and religious figures that are revered). Some—called iconoclasts (eye-con-uh-CLASTS) —saw the practice was not scriptural and destroyed the icons. This is one of many disputes over doctrine and practice that affected the Christian Church during the Middle Ages.

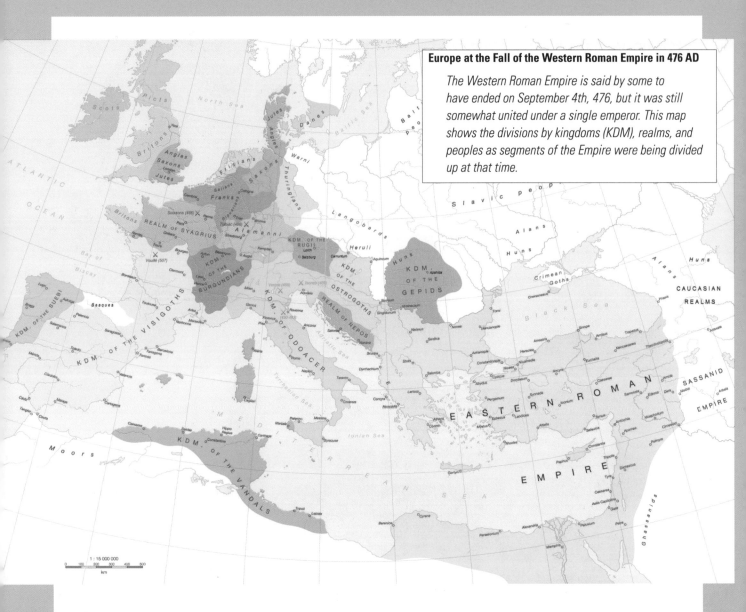

This map shows Europe at the Fall of the Western Roman Empire in 476 A.D. After the Western Roman Empire collapsed, barbarian kingdoms rose in many parts of Europe. The barbarians had migrated there from Eastern Europe. "Barbarian" was the term the Romans used to describe anyone who was not a Roman citizen. The people they were describing as barbarians did not call themselves barbarians. They instead considered themselves members of their individual tribe. For instance, members of the Visigoth tribes would think of themselves as Visigoths, not as barbarians. It is also important to remember that even though the Romans looked down on the barbarians for their different customs, many of these barbarians adopted Roman customs. In fact, within a couple of centuries, most of the formerly pagan barbarians had become Christians! We will be learning about several of these kingdoms that rose after the fall of Rome throughout this book, including the Angles, the Saxons, the Jutes, the Franks, the Vandals, and the Visigoths.

ANALYZE	How much of Western Europe was under the control of the barbarian kingdoms? (Hint: Only the Eastern Roman Empire on the map is not barbarian.)
CONNECT	How many different barbarian kingdoms can you see on the map?

If you were with me in the first volume of this series, you will remember how we learned about the Early Christian Church — the brave men and women who were either eyewitnesses of the resurrected Christ or had heard the gospel from another early follower of the faith and placed their trust in Christ. The Early Church faced incredible persecution from the outside and turmoil from within. Those who did not understand them or outright hated them for this new religion sought to hurt or kill them, and there were also those who attacked it from within by wanting to change the gospel to what they wanted it to be. God knew that the Early Church needed strong leaders to help guide them through these difficult times. These Early Church leaders have become known in history as the Church Fathers.

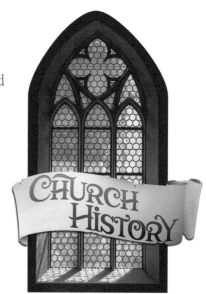

CHURCH History

One of these church leaders, Polycarp, who lived about a century after Christ, taught that every believer should protect the Apostles' teachings. This reminds me of the Apostle Paul's words in 2 Timothy 1:5–7: "I am reminded of your sincere faith, which first dwelt in your grandmother Lois and your mother Eunice and, I am persuaded, now lives in you also. For this reason I remind you to fan into flame the gift of God, which is in you through the laying on of my hands. For the Spirit God gave us does not make us timid, but gives us power, love, and self-discipline" (NIV). We each have the duty to guard the gift of the gospel. Polycarp endured much persecution in his life, which ended in martyrdom (Jones 2009, 28–29) when he was burned at the stake.

Another Early Church leader who made a deep impact on the medieval church was Augustine in the late 300s and early 400s. Augustine is a wonderful example of how God uses His redeeming love to chase people down. As a young man, Augustine's mother prayed faithfully for her son to turn from the rather wild and sinful life he was so attracted to. God brought the wayward Augustine to His heart and taught Him the power of forgiveness. Augustine founded a monastery, became the bishop of Hippo, and became known in history as a brilliant theologian.

Polycarp

Saint Augustine by Philippe de Champaigne

BYZANTINE CONSTANTINOPLE

The Hagia Sophia is nearly 1,500 years old and has been a focal point of the city's architecture ever since it was built. For centuries, it was the city's main cathedral. (A cathedral is the seat of an area's bishop and is the most prestigious church in the area.) After the fall of the Byzantine Empire, it became one of the city's chief mosques (MAWSK). Now, it is one of Istanbul's most popular museums.

Turkey

The Grand Palace was where the Byzantine emperors lived for centuries; however, the site is now in ruins. But its mosaics, such as this one, have been preserved. Byzantine mosaics were unusual because they usually went on walls rather than floors.

Though the Hagia Sophia is the most famous of the city's churches, it is not the only one. The Hagia Irene remains one of the few Byzantine-era churches that was not converted into a mosque, though it eventually was turned into a museum.

The interior of the Hagia Sophia

Justinian also built the Basilica Cistern. It stored water for the city and Justinian's Palace, but it was forgotten for many years before being rediscovered in the 1600s. Though it is empty now, the cistern can hold hundreds of tons of water.

The Byzantine Empire is noted for its mosaics. The Hagia Sophia includes many of these artworks, as well. It was common for the mosaics to include images of the emperors alongside religious figures. This one shows Jesus and Mary with the emperors Justinian and Constantine on either side. On the left, Justinian is showing them the Hagia Sophia. On the right, Constantine presents them with the city of Constantinople.

02

START HERE

As we learned in our last chapter's Church History section, God gave the Early Church strong leaders to help them through their beginning growing pains. In this chapter, we will learn more about the role of these leaders in the society that was established after the fall of Rome. You will see that as the centuries passed, the Church became more powerful. This was the beginning of the feudal system, the societal and cultural structure that would remain dominant throughout Europe for centuries. As the Church's affluence grew, the struggle to remain faithful and unswayed by power grew also. Throughout it all, God raised up men and women who willingly stepped forward to be His hands and feet to those in need.

THE RISE OF THE CHURCH

As we learned in the last chapter, the collapse of the Western Roman Empire was a scary time. People were frightened and looking for strong leaders, and at this time, they tended to come from either the Church, which was already a powerful entity, or from landowners, who maintained their wealth even as the currency system crashed. We will study both in this chapter. To learn about the importance of the Church at this time, though, we need to go back even further in history to when the Western Roman Empire was still around.

Constantine, who founded Constantinople, was the first Roman emperor to be a professing Christian. At this time in history, there were no separate, official denominations. The Christian Church was just the Church. Although the Early Church is not the focus of this history volume, I do believe it is necessary to show how the Church was so closely and intricately intertwined with the Roman culture of this time. It would be impossible to understand the flow of history if one or the other was left out of the story.

At this time in history, the Christian Church, as it was called then, was relatively new. The Church believed that Christ had come to earth as a baby, died, risen, and ascended into heaven. His followers had written down their accounts of His healing, walking on water, and making the final sacrifice on the Cross. The Church was surprisingly still united on most of the important issues; however, little by little, the leaders in charge of the Church had, in some ways, overstepped their authority. In trying to protect the original teachings and writings of the apostolic elders, they went through great pains to trace their teachings back to the Apostles. There was nothing wrong with that, but when they started tracing their authority back to the Apostles as well, their roles in the Church started to shift ever so slightly.

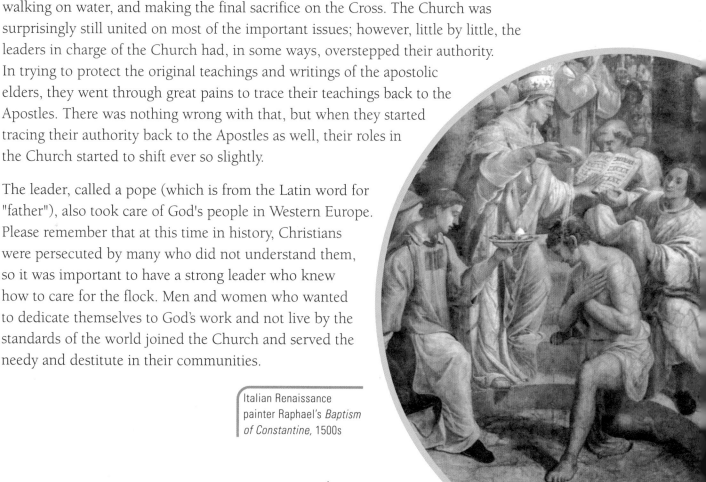

The leader, called a pope (which is from the Latin word for "father"), also took care of God's people in Western Europe. Please remember that at this time in history, Christians were persecuted by many who did not understand them, so it was important to have a strong leader who knew how to care for the flock. Men and women who wanted to dedicate themselves to God's work and not live by the standards of the world joined the Church and served the needy and destitute in their communities.

Italian Renaissance painter Raphael's *Baptism of Constantine*, 1500s

By this time in history (the mid to late 4th century), the Church had gained a powerful position in politics, but what happened after the fall of Rome? You might think the Church would also fall, but Christianity is not based on who is in power or who is the ruler on earth. God is in control over all the rulers and countries in the world. The Roman citizens were frightened, though. They did not know who was in charge because of the barbarians' lack of governing skills. Many Roman citizens turned to the Church because they knew they could at least receive help there.

It is not surprising, then, that after the Western Roman Empire collapsed, many people also looked to the Church for protection and leadership. The Church became extremely politically influential and powerful. This was also true of the popes. Each pope was elected to lead the Church after the previous pope's death. Leading the Church made the pope an extremely powerful ruler in Western Europe at this time. Even as other rulers gained power, they had to be mindful of the Church's position and respect it if they wanted to maintain their control.

The Christian church in the East was different than the church in the West. Though the Western Church was mostly run by the pope, the Eastern Church did not agree with this. They still considered themselves brothers in Christ with their fellow believers in the West, but they did not consider themselves part of the same type of church. There was much division creeping into the Christian Church.

NARRATION BREAK:

Discuss what you read today.

Peter
(Circa 30s-60s)

During the time of the Early Church and through the Middle Ages, the pope was regarded as the leader of the Western Christian Church. The Apostle Peter was considered the first pope, and the popes who followed were seen as his successors, with his authority and prominence. Though Eastern Orthodox and Protestants do not accept the authority of the pope, Roman Catholics still do. These images show depictions of some of the early popes.

Anacletus
(79-88)

Pius
(140-155)

Fabianus
(236-250)

Caius
(283-296)

 Education was not a strong focus for most people in Europe during the Middle Ages. The lack of general education century after century had a negative effect on the culture. However, this does not mean that there was absolutely no discovery or scientific growth; there were simply far fewer and a much slower rate of growth than in previous eras. The practice of medicine was advanced by religious foundations, convents, and monasteries establishing great hospitals, and it was common for spiritual and physical healing to be administered together.

In the early to mid-Middle Ages, the studies of astronomy, biology, and chemistry were mostly stagnant, with even the ancient writings largely unread and unstudied. It wasn't until the 8th century that there was some progress made in the field of astronomy when ancient astronomer Ptolemy's writings were translated and studied. The study of chemistry was dominated by those who held to the writings and theories of Aristotle, a student of the ancient philosopher Plato. This was not chemistry as we know it, with the table of elements or the scientific study of chemical reactions; instead, it was a highly experimental study called alchemy, which was centered around the early Greek theory of matter. According to this theory, metals like iron or lead could be changed into more valuable silver or gold (Usselman and Rocke 2017). Of course, gold and silver are not created this way, but it would take centuries before alchemy was replaced with a more scientific understanding of these elements.

Pietro Longhi's *Alchemists,* 1757. This painting depicts medieval alchemists at work.

The Church was not the only source of power and leadership at this time. It soon became apparent that those who owned large amounts of land were the new "top dogs." Since their wealth was in land, the collapse of the currency system with the fall of Rome did not cause these people to lose their wealth. Instead, these landowners became powerful men very quickly because their land produced food on which everyone depended. It seemed the rest of the population was at the mercy of these men.

Many times, these newly powerful landowners funded the churches if the church leaders did what they were told. A new cultural and government system was starting to emerge: the feudal system. This new way of life was truly based on the principle of "survival of the strongest." The richest were at the top of the status ladder, with everyone else jostling for position under them.

The poor people, who did not own land, worked for the landowners. These people were called serfs, and their wages were enough food to keep them alive, a rundown cottage or hut to live in with their families, and a job. There was not much hope of improving their position. This was a time of desperation for many common folks, as they eked out a living from the hard ground of the masters' fields. Every family

Kings

Nobles

Knights

Peasants

In American history, it is very common to hear about people who were born poor but worked hard and became wealthy or powerful people in society. Many American presidents, business people, and generals come from this sort of background where they worked their way up to a higher social class.

This sort of life was virtually impossible to have in medieval Europe. People almost always lived in the social class they were born into. For instance, kings and queens were the children of other kings and queens, and peasants were the children of other peasants.

Because of how society operated at this time, it is essential to understand this system to understand the history of the Middle Ages. It is often shown as a pyramid. The king was at the very top. Below him but above everyone else were the nobles. Below them but above everyone else were the knights. If a knight could work hard enough to be promoted to a higher position, he might receive a piece of land as a reward from his king. This land, along with its accompanying manor or castle, was called a fief (FEEF). Below them were the peasants, who farmed the fief. Church officials were not usually included in the pyramid, but they generally occupied the same place as nobles.

member was expected to work long, hard hours; they were more slave than servant. While the serfs lived in shacks, the landowners lived in manors — huge houses or castles.

Some of these landowners became so powerful that they were given the titles that royal families use, such as lord, sir, lady, baron, or your lordship. They became the local nobles and rulers. Soon, the landowners were building up their own little kingdoms. The profits from their lands were huge, and trading with surrounding landowners made them even wealthier. The landowners also built up their holdings by conquering the land of others around them.

Some of these landowners conquered enough that they became the king of their own kingdom. These kings ruled over the other landowners, even though they were almost equal in power. The landowners had their own armies of knights to protect their lands and to fight with the other lords around them. (We'll learn more about knights in a later chapter.) Sometimes the landowner would divide the land out among his loyal knights and make them his officers. These knights would sometimes work hard to move up in rank, and if the lord of the manor did not have a son, these knights might be named to inherit the lord's holdings. Study the diagram on the left. Can you see how the feudal system is arranged? How would you like to be stuck at the bottom of such an arrangement?

As you can see, the king is at the top, peasants are at the bottom, and the knights are in the middle. The fief was farmed by the peasants (farmer serfs), who produced enough to pay the taxes and support the landowner and his family. In turn, the knight and his men fought to protect the landowner and his family. When the king needed to make everyone support an idea or a project that he wanted to do, he called together all the landowners living in his kingdom. At this gathering, he would ask for their support.

All across the land that used to be the Western Roman Empire, a new world culture emerged. There was no longer a huge, powerful empire ruling vast stretches of land. As centuries passed and alliances were made between kingdoms, Europe organized into separate countries. As you can imagine, the feudal system was not a uniform system of government; it varied from place to place and from century to century.

As time progressed through the Middle Ages and the feudal system took hold, the Church took on another role in history. Priests were paid to serve the lords of the manors, and many did this willingly to keep their churches open. As we have learned throughout this chapter, these lords were often the only people who had any money, but it was also in this way that the rich became more and more powerful.

NARRATION BREAK:

Talk about what you read about the feudal system.

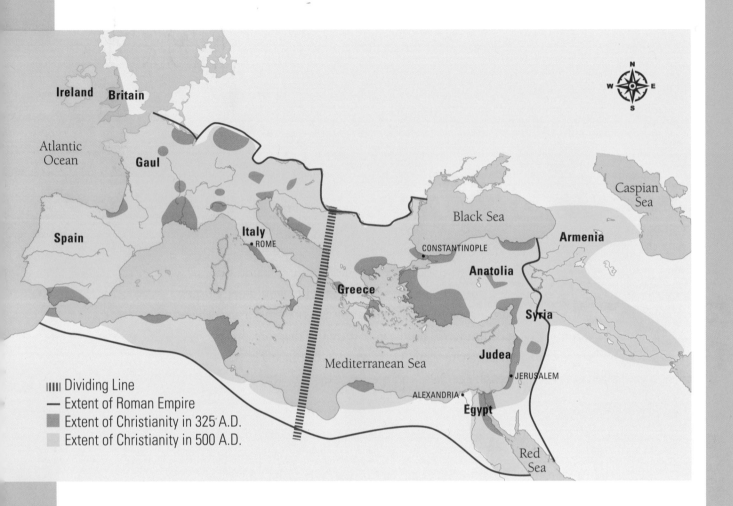

Dividing Line
Extent of Roman Empire
Extent of Christianity in 325 A.D.
Extent of Christianity in 500 A.D.

This map shows the approximate extent of Christianity in 500, a couple of decades after the fall of the Western Roman Empire. It also depicts the approximate dividing line between the Western Christian Church, which became the Roman Catholic Church, centered in Rome, and the Eastern Christian Church, which became the Eastern Orthodox Church, centered in Constantinople.

Throughout the Middle Ages, the Western Christian Church was the dominant Christian faith in Western Europe in what is now England, France, Germany, Spain, and Italy, as well as certain North African countries. The Eastern Christian Church was the dominant Christian faith in Greece, Eastern Europe, and parts of the Middle East and North Africa.

We will learn more about the history of these churches and how they divided throughout this book, but the results are still reflected in Europe today, with Catholics and Protestants (whom we will study later) being far more common in Western Europe and Orthodox being most common in Eastern Europe.

MAPS

| ANALYZE | How far north had Christianity spread by 500 A.D.? |
| CONNECT | Did Christianity spread very far outside the borders of the Roman Empire? |

In this chapter, we learned that the Western and Eastern Churches were different from each other and that these differences caused division. Eventually, in the 11th century, this division would lead to an official split from each other. This breakup began much earlier, however. These two churches could not see eye to eye on several issues that were deemed of great importance. They bickered about which church leader had the authority to lead or decide certain matters, they argued about whether priests should be married, they disagreed about what language should be used in the written Word of God, and they fussed about who was the true leader of the Christian Church on earth — the pope or several patriarchs. The church in the East, for instance, did not recognize the authority of the Western leader, the pope. The Eastern Christians did not think one church leader should have that much power and preferred to have several leaders at a time, called patriarchs.

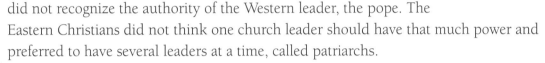

The church in the East also believed priests could marry, while the church in the West did not. The Eastern Christians favored the use of Greek, but the Western Christians preferred Latin. These differences are still reflected in the traditions of Eastern Orthodox Christians (the church of the East) and the traditions of Roman Catholics (the church of the West).

With all this focus on arguing and fussing, it is important to remember that although the churches argued and fussed with each other, God was still always in control. You see, God sees the heart of each and every person who has ever lived, and He saw the hearts of the people who made up these two churches. He saw the individuals who were trying to bring honor to Him, and just like in the present day, God uses imperfect people to fulfill His plan. Psalm 103:14 says, "For he knows how weak we are; he remembers we are only dust" (NLT).

VATICAN CITY

Vatican City is the modern seat of the Roman Catholic Church and is the smallest nation-state in the world. It is less than a square mile in size and fewer than 1,000 people live there. The picture shows a view of St. Peter's Square from St. Peter's Basilica in the Vatican.

Vatican City

Since the 1500s, the pope has had an army of Swiss soldiers who protect him and the Vatican. These guards were first recruited from Switzerland because the Swiss were considered excellent soldiers. They are called the Swiss Guards. Even today, the pope's army still comes from Switzerland and wears traditional uniforms for ceremonies. They are shown here during a swearing-in ceremony. Ordinarily, they wear more modern uniforms and train with modern weapons.

St. Peter's Basilica is the main church in Vatican City, so it is also the pope's main church. It was completed in the 1600s over the site traditionally believed to be where the Apostle Peter was buried. It is still one of the largest churches in the world. We'll learn more about it when we study Renaissance art.

Inside St. Peter's Basilica. When a Catholic church is called a basilica, that means it is recognized as an especially old or important church building. Because St. Peter's in the Vatican is where Peter is said to be buried and is the center of the Catholic Church, it is considered a basilica.

Next to St. Peter's Basilica is the Apostolic Palace. People often gather outside because the pope will often speak to crowds from one of the windows. Here, Pope Benedict XVI addresses a crowd on Easter Sunday in 2009.

03

START HERE

In our previous chapters, we learned about the far-reaching effects the fall of Rome had on the civilized world of that time. In this chapter, we are going to learn about the history of England shortly after the fall of Rome. Although you will learn that the people of that area struggled tremendously to adjust, you will also see that this is a wonderful story about the obedience of a few key missionaries and their influence on the culture of this geographical area. As you read through this chapter, I encourage you to think about how the obedience of these missionaries changed the lives of those they served and how the good news of the gospel came to set all people free. The establishment of the Christian Church in Medieval England still influences us and the world today.

ENGLAND'S ANGLES AND SAXONS

We are now going to turn our attention to England and its northern neighbor, Scotland. The Romans had gained control of England in 43, though they had launched previous invasions into the island. A Celtic-speaking people called the Britons lived in England; however, they had become quite Romanized after being under Roman control for so long. Though Rome governed England for centuries, the Romans left in 410. Rome was in much turmoil then (the city was sacked by the Visigoths the same year), and the Roman government and military pulled out of England, telling the Britons who lived there that they needed to defend themselves. The Romans left because they were over-extended and could not effectively govern a remote part of the empire. They may well have imagined that they would return once things calmed down, but that never happened.

For the Britons who were left behind, the loss of Roman protection was frightening. Rome was not the only place under attack by the barbarian tribes. In fact, this period of history is sometimes called the Migration Period because so many Germanic tribes were moving around Europe. This is one reason why Rome was repeatedly sacked by these various tribes throughout the 400s.

Historians disagree on whether the Western Roman Empire collapsed because of these migrations or if these migrations were just the result of the decline of Roman influence throughout Europe. What is known is that many of these tribes themselves had been displaced from their original homes by invasions from the Huns, who were from Central Asia. There was a lot of turmoil during this time in history — can you imagine what it was like to live near so many dangerous invaders? At the same time, can you imagine what it was like to lose your home and feel like you needed to move far away to find land to start over?

Even though they lived on an island and were not physically attached to the rest of Europe, the Britons also had to worry about invaders. One of the most pressing problems was the Picts, their neighbors who lived to the north in modern-day Scotland. The Romans had built a wall called Hadrian's Wall to keep the Picts out of Roman-controlled Britain. Once the Romans had left, however, the Picts were a continual threat from the north.

19th century illustration of the Romans conquering Britain

The Romans built Hadrian's Wall as a border between England and the fierce inhabitants of Scotland. Much of this wall is still intact.

The Britons likely invited Germanic tribes to come over and protect them after the Romans had left. In the mid-400s, a king named Vortigern (VOR-tih-gern) is said to have asked them to help him fight off the Picts. Instead, they betrayed him, and Vortigern found himself losing his kingdom to the people who were supposed to be protecting it. As we read through this volume, you will notice that this has happened quite often in history — people will disagree over who is supposed to be in charge. Instead of resolving the dispute peacefully, they will fight. Like the Britons, some will even invite other people to help with the fight. They think they are helping themselves win, but many times, the people who are asked to help don't want to be helpful — they see how the situation can benefit themselves by taking advantage of the turmoil. They use this opportunity to overthrow the already weakened kingdom who is trusting them for help and protection.

Within 50 years of the collapse of Roman control in England, the Britons were facing invasions from these Germanic tribes who had been asked to help. They were called the Angles, Saxons, and Jutes. These tribes, who came over by boat to attack and invade the land, were from modern-day Denmark and Germany. The Angles, Saxons, and Jutes largely settled in the eastern half of England, while the native Britons retained some control in the western part of the country. By about 600, the native Britons and Celts were limited to modern-day Wales and the southwest part of England, a place called Cornwall. The Angles also attacked Scotland. Though they gained territory, much of the land remained in control of the Picts and other local peoples.

These Germanic invaders, who are usually referred to as Anglo-Saxons, were not united. There were many groups of them, and each group had its own war chief or

Stories of Vortigern intrigued later artists and writers for centuries. One of the popular legends about him says he traded his kingdom to the Anglo-Saxons to marry one of their daughters, Rowena. This image depicts Vortigern and Rowena meeting.

This medieval manuscript shows King Vortigern watching two dragons fight. In some fanciful stories, he believes the two dragons fighting are why he is having trouble controlling his kingdom.

king. For this reason, they divided England into several smaller kingdoms, and these kingdoms were sometimes at war with each other. Nevertheless, the Anglo-Saxons had a huge impact on the culture of England. In fact, the name England comes from what the country was called during this time: Engla Land (Bosworth 2010). The name means "the land of the Angles" (Bosworth 2010). It was called that because the Angles held a lot more of England (almost all the northern and central parts of the country) than the Saxons and the Jutes, who both were in the southern part.

The English language is another legacy of the Anglo-Saxons. English is considered a Germanic language, which might seem strange since English is not from Germany. However, the Germanic tribes like the Angles and Saxons spoke an early form of the language, which we often call Old English or Anglo-Saxon. In many ways, it is very different from modern English. Anglo-Saxon words only consist of about 30 percent of modern English vocabulary, but you will probably recognize many of these words. For example, did you know the word "dog" is of Anglo-Saxon origin? It comes from the Anglo-Saxon word dogca (Merriam-Webster, "dog," n.d.). The word "gold" is also derived from Anglo-Saxon (Merriam-Webster, "gold," n.d.). Like many Anglo-Saxon words, the English word is similar to the German word. "Gold" is German for gold, too!

NARRATION BREAK:

Talk about what happened after the Romans left Britain.

The Anglo-Saxons were pagans who worshiped false Germanic gods. When they came to England, there were some Christians already in the country because Christianity had spread throughout the former Roman Empire by this point. Other Britons still held to their own traditional pagan beliefs. When the Anglo Saxons took over, Christianity survived in the areas still under Briton's control, but it seemed like the entire country would succumb to the Anglo-Saxon beliefs.

Do you remember what the church leaders were called at this time in history? That's right — they were called popes. This is the story of Gregory ("the Great"), the pope who wanted to evangelize the Anglo-Saxons. One story says that Gregory was walking in the marketplace and witnessed a slave auction. As he approached, he saw men, women, and even children being sold as slaves. As Gregory walked closer, his attention was drawn to a group of young boys. These boys had pale skin tones and blond hair. Gregory had never seen children with such light complexions, so he asked the children what land they were brought from.

The boys answered Gregory that they were Anglo-Saxons from the part of England that was ruled by King Aella. Gregory thought this sounded like "Alleluia," and he

19th century illustration of Augustine ministering to Aethelberht

20th century stained glass depicting Aethelberht and Bertha in a church in Kent

took this as a sign that he needed to tell the Anglo-Saxons about God. He decided that he would send a group of missionaries to the Anglo-Saxons.

In 597, a group of about 40 missionaries arrived in England. To be honest, some of these men were not excited about being missionaries to these "barbarians," but they served anyway. One of these missionaries was named Augustine. (He's a different Augustine than the one we learned about in Chapter 1). He was originally from Italy and had been chosen as the leader of the mission.

History calls this man Augustine of Canterbury because the missionaries who went to Britain to evangelize the Anglo-Saxons settled in a town named Canterbury. This town was the capital of the local king, Aethelberht (A-del-bert). King Aethelberht was a pagan, but his wife, Bertha, was a Christian. Bertha's Christian faith was a big part of why the missionaries were well-received and well-treated. The missionaries were encouraged to stay and experienced great success in their work. On Christmas of that year, thousands were baptized. Eventually, even Aethelberht himself converted to Christianity.

Commemorative statue of Queen Bertha in Canterbury, England

The success of the missionary work led to the arrival of more missionaries in 601. Augustine remained in charge of the missionary efforts in England as they spread far beyond Canterbury, which he had established as his headquarters. One of the highest-ranking positions in the Church at the time was that of an archbishop. Because he was in charge, Augustine was made Archbishop of Canterbury. Even today, that is the highest-ranking position in the Church of England. The good news of the gospel spread quickly into the darkness, and by the end of the 600s, the Anglo-Saxon kings and their subjects had become Christian. Though a small handful may have clung to their pagan ways secretly, the country was deemed Christian.

Within a couple of hundred years of their arrival, the Anglo-Saxons and their way of life became deeply ingrained in the culture of England. Even after they became Christian, many elements of their culture remained the same. For instance, they preferred to live in villages rather than the cities that the Romans had built. Most people lived in thatched-roof houses and farmed for a living. As a result, Roman structures fell into ruin across the country.

An important aspect of Anglo-Saxon culture was storytelling. Many people could not read or write, so stories were part of an oral tradition, passed down from generation to generation from memory. Have you ever played the game "Telephone"? If you have, you know how it goes, but for those of you who may not have played it, I will explain the process. First, ten or more players sit in a circle. Next, one player is chosen to be "it." This person must think of something to say and then whisper it into their neighbor's ear. That person, in turn, whispers what they heard into the next player's ear, and so it goes, player by player, until everyone has heard. The last player, who is sitting next to the player who started the game, repeats out loud what they heard. It is amazing and often hilarious to hear what the original message has become as it moves from person to person!

In the 1930s, the Sutton Hoo burial site was discovered. Though it was an Anglo-Saxon burial site, it followed the Viking custom of using a ship as a grave for the deceased and his possessions. The Sutton Hoo ship contained a treasure trove of Anglo-Saxon artifacts, including this helmet and shoulder clasp.

CONNECT

> Hwaet wē Gār-Dena   in gear-dagum
>
> pēod-cyninga   prym gefrūnon,
>
> hū ðā aepelingas   ellen fremedon (Heaney 2000, 2).

Could you read the passage above? Chances are, no, you can't! That's because it's written in Old English. In fact, it is the opening lines of *Beowulf.*

In modern English, a way of saying what was written above is

> So. The Spear-Danes in days gone by
>
> and the kings who ruled them had courage and greatness.
>
> We have heard of those princes' heroic campaigns (Heaney 2000, 3).

Can you see how much English has changed in the past thousand years or more? Just like you didn't recognize the first passage, an Anglo-Saxon would not be able to understand the second passage.

Today, you can try your hand at the original Old English version of *Beowulf,* or you can instead read it in a modern English translation. Regardless of who translated the edition, most newer versions of *Beowulf* try to keep one aspect of the original — the kennings. This is an aspect of Norse poetry that the Anglo-Saxons brought over to England, and the early English poets continued the tradition.

A kenning is simply a distinctive descriptive word formed by combining two other words. For instance, *hron-rād* is a kenning that literally combines the words for "whale" and "pasture" but means "sea" (Chickering 2006, 6). Most people would never think to describe the sea as a whale pasture, but it is a very descriptive, memorable image. Another kenning is *hilde-lēoma,* which combines the words for "battle" and "flame" to mean "sword" (Chickering 2006, 6). It's another vivid description for the reader or listener. Can you think of some kennings?

This is exactly what has happened with some of these stories. Some of them changed a lot over the years, though the basic elements usually stayed the same. You may have heard one of these tales because it is still told today. *Beowulf,* an old Anglo-Saxon poem, has been passed down for hundreds of years. This story is one of the oldest pieces of literature in the English language and is still enjoyed by readers and listeners today.

NARRATION BREAK:

Discuss how England became Christian.

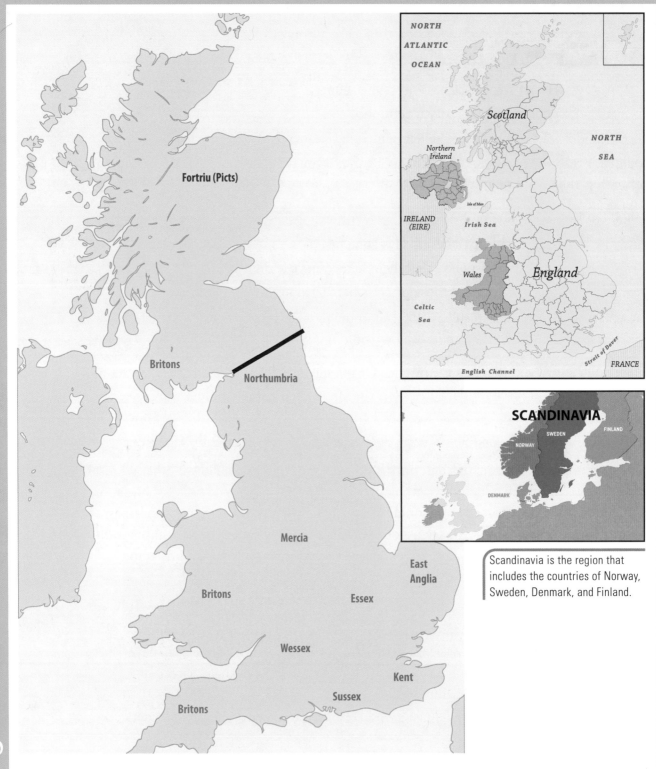

Scandinavia is the region that includes the countries of Norway, Sweden, Denmark, and Finland.

This map shows the seven Anglo-Saxon kingdoms that cropped up in eastern England: Northumbria, Mercia, Wessex, Sussex, Kent, Essex, and East Anglia. To the west are the lands that remained under the control of the Britons. To the north, in what is now present-day Scotland, the Britons and the Picts (Fortriu) lived.

ANALYZE   Which countries are part of the Scandinavian Peninsula, as shown on the small map? (If you're not sure what a peninsula is, look it up.)

CONNECT   Which two countries is the black line on the large map dividing?

In this Church History segment, we are going to learn a wonderful story about a man who worked tirelessly to bring the Bible to the Anglo-Saxons. This man, Bede, was born in 672, a time when many families were so poor that it was common for at least one of the children to be sent away to be raised at a convent or monastery. So it was that Bede was raised from the young age of seven by the priests in a monastery. It was at this monastery that he learned to read and write. It was also here that he learned how much he loved to learn and discover. He was a good student and became a deacon at age 19.

Above all other books, Bede loved the Bible most of all, and unlike many other church leaders of that time, he wanted the common people to have the Bible in their language. Bede was a forerunner of the Reformation in this way. He took great pains to translate the Bible from Greek into the Anglo-Saxon language. He was able to complete the Gospel of John shortly before his death.

Bede was also interested in learning and writing about history and science. His writings about Anglo Saxon English history are extremely well done and are, to this day, viewed as some of the most highly respected works of this time period. In fact, the bulk of what we know about this time comes from Bede; he "is almost our only satisfactory source of historical information on the Anglo-Saxons in England and it is for this work that he is known as the father of English history" (Graves 2010 "Venerable").

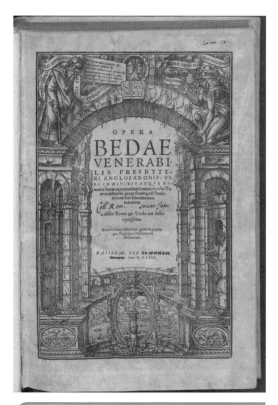

16th century edition of Bede's work. Note that it is in Latin, the language of medieval scholars.

A manuscript illustration from one of Bede's books. This book dates back to at least the early 900s.

CANTERBURY

As we learned in the text, Canterbury is still the center of English Christianity because of its historical significance. The Archbishop of Canterbury's seat is the local cathedral. The Canterbury Cathedral was originally built in the 500s but drastically renovated and expanded in the 1070s. Inside are the tombs of many English kings.

United Kingdom

One of the oldest structures in Canterbury is the monastery that Augustine built shortly after his arrival. Known as St. Augustine's Abbey, it is the burial site of both Augustine and Aethelberht. The abbey was used as a monastery for centuries before it was closed by King Henry VIII. After that, the abbey was used as a royal palace, inn, poorhouse, and school.

The modern city of Canterbury is known for its imposing city gates, which are based on fortifications from Roman times and further developed during the Middle Ages. In the medieval period, the gates were used as a form of protection.

The oldest church in England that is still in use is also in Canterbury. St. Martin's Church was originally Queen Bertha's private chapel.

The Canterbury Cathedral's choir area. The choir has always been an important aspect of worship at Canterbury and is a mixture of professional adult singers and children.

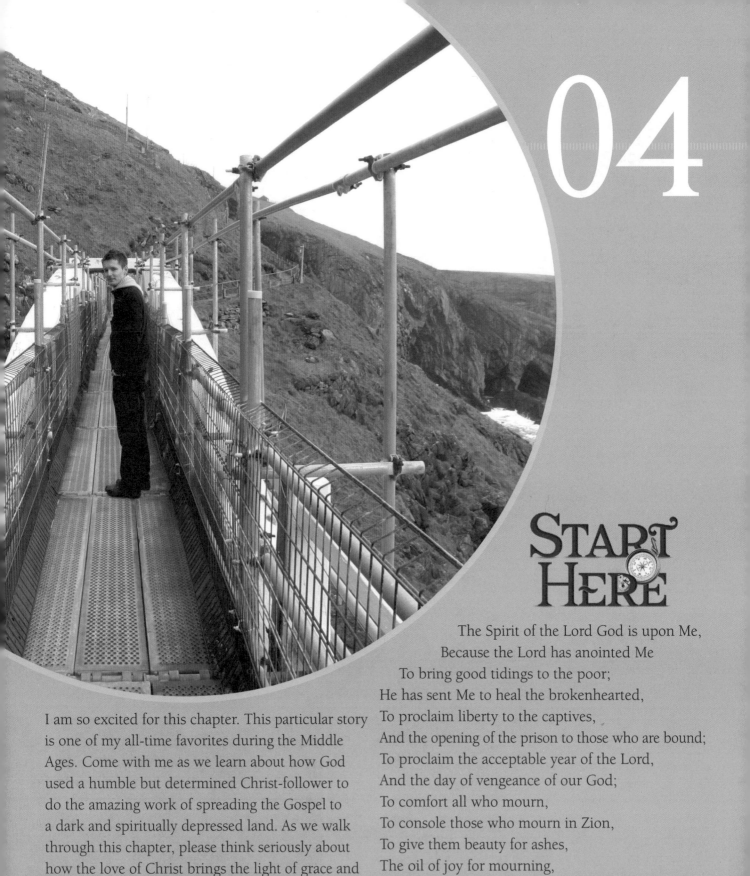

04

START HERE

I am so excited for this chapter. This particular story is one of my all-time favorites during the Middle Ages. Come with me as we learn about how God used a humble but determined Christ-follower to do the amazing work of spreading the Gospel to a dark and spiritually depressed land. As we walk through this chapter, please think seriously about how the love of Christ brings the light of grace and mercy to those who are brokenhearted.

The story of St. Patrick makes me think about Isaiah 61:1–3, which says:

The Spirit of the Lord God is upon Me,
Because the Lord has anointed Me
To bring good tidings to the poor;
He has sent Me to heal the brokenhearted,
To proclaim liberty to the captives,
And the opening of the prison to those who are bound;
To proclaim the acceptable year of the Lord,
And the day of vengeance of our God;
To comfort all who mourn,
To console those who mourn in Zion,
To give them beauty for ashes,
The oil of joy for mourning,
The garment of praise for the spirit of heaviness;
That they may be called trees of righteousness,
The planting of the Lord, that He may be glorified.

Medieval Irish Christianity

Off the western coast of England is a tiny island nation that has made a huge impact on the world. Ireland, known as the Green Isle, has endured a tumultuous history. The Celts were the first known settlers of Ireland. If you were with me for Volume 1 in this series, you might remember that the Celts originally came from Central Europe and spread out across the continent. They first came to Ireland a few hundred years before Jesus was born.

The country never came under Roman control, and its isolation from the rest of Europe also meant that Christianity did not initially reach its shores. It was in the fifth century after Christ that Christianity in Ireland began to grow stronger, thanks in part to the hard work and dedication of one man — a man we know as St. Patrick.

Patrick was born into a Christian, Romanized family living on the west coast of Britain in the early 400s. His exact birth date is unknown, but we do know that he was 16 when he was kidnapped and sold as a slave in Ireland. During his six years of captivity, his faith became stronger and more personal. Upon his return home, he received the call to return to Ireland as a missionary. In his later writings, he remembered this call as a vision of those where he had once lived: "beside the forest of Foclut which is near the western sea, and they were crying as if with one voice: 'We beg you, holy youth, that you shall come and shall walk again among us' " (St. Patrick 2017, 192). Patrick was not a learned man, but he was a man sold out completely to God; he was wholeheartedly dedicated to doing the work that he knew he had been called to do.

Patrick is considered the patron saint of Ireland, as well as the national apostle, but he never considered himself worthy of the high calling on his life. This humble man was initially reluctant to even answer the call to ministry because of his lack of formal education (St. Patrick 2017, 185). But Patrick's two short books are considered beautiful in their simplicity and truth, and although his writing is somewhat incoherent in places because of his poor Latin, his words are soul-reaching and convicting.

Through his words, we see the heart of a humble servant of the Most High God. His certainty of his calling is reflected in these words: "I was like a stone lying in deep mire, and he that is mighty came and in his mercy raised

Briton Riviere's painting of Saint Patrick, 1877

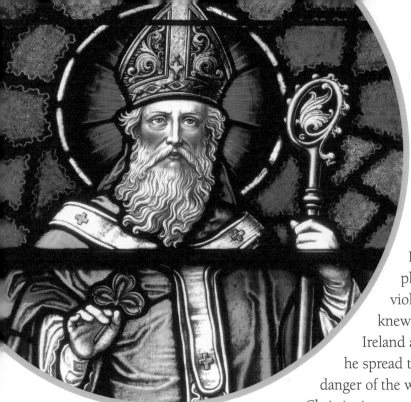

Stained glass depicting St. Patrick in a Catholic church named after him in Junction City, Ohio

me up. . . . Who was it summoned me, a fool, from the midst of those who appear wise and learned in the law and powerful in rhetoric and in all things? Me, truly wretched in this world, he inspired before others" (St. Patrick 2017, 186).

On a personal level, I am one of many who consider Patrick to be a true hero of the faith. Ireland at this time was a very dangerous place. The people followed pagan religions, and violence was a big part of the culture. But Patrick knew the culture because of the years he lived in Ireland as a slave, and that knowledge helped him as he spread the gospel throughout the country. Despite the danger of the work, he successfully gained many converts to Christianity across the entire island. His humble approach to life, his continuous pouring out of thankfulness to his Heavenly Father for choosing him to be the bringer of the joyful tidings of the gospel of Jesus to the lost, and his dedication to the truth of God's Word are a beautiful example for all of us to emulate. This type of devotion and faith in the face of adversity is a wonderful testimony to the saving, redeeming love of our Savior. As I write about this hero of Ireland, the land from which most of my own ancestors came, the words of my personal motto come to mind: Soli Deo Gloria — to God alone be the glory.

Over the centuries, the life and work of the dear Saint Patrick have become legendized. His true work has been almost completely lost in the sea of ridiculous lore about him. One of these legends stars Patrick as a snake wrangler, driving all the snakes out of Ireland and into the ocean. Another legend says that he used a shamrock, which is another name for a clover, to explain the Trinity; each clover leaf represented one of the entities — God the Father, God the Son, and God the Holy Spirit.

You may be familiar with some of these legends because they are commonly told around the middle of March every year. On March 17th, people in many countries around the world celebrate St. Patrick's Day by wearing green clothing decorated with shamrocks and eating traditional Irish cooking. Perhaps the next time St. Patrick's Day comes around, you could gather your friends and family to enjoy some delightful Irish food and tell them the wonderful, true story of the humble, godly, real-life servant of God who helped bring the good news of Jesus to Ireland in the Middle Ages.

SAINT PATRICK,
PATRON OF IRELAND.

This image of St. Patrick repeats the mistaken assumption people have about him driving the snakes from Ireland, ignoring the important missionary work he performed in the country.

NARRATION BREAK:

Discuss what you read about St. Patrick.

CONNECT

In spite of the difficulties it had faced for two entire centuries, the 8th-century Christian Church in Ireland had gained prestige, wealth, and power. Missionaries had done their work of spreading the gospel throughout Ireland, Scotland, and Northumbria, one of the most important kingdoms of Anglo-Saxon England. These three kingdoms shared a common cultural heritage; therefore, many objects from that time share many common elements. One of the most impressive relics for that influential age is the Book of Kells. No one is absolutely sure where it was created, but the first likely mention of it is in the small town of Kells, Ireland, in 1007 (Hughes 1977, 48).

Jesus in the *Book of Kells*

The Book of Kells is a beautiful example of an illuminated script of the four Gospels. Each page of vellum is a work of art. Three hundred forty gorgeous illustrations of the key happenings in those Scriptures, including full-page illustrations of the arrest of Christ and the Crucifixion, are carefully painted to accompany the text. The text of the book is written in Latin and based on the Vulgate text, which was completed in the late 4th century. It is thought that three artists shared the work of creating these illustrations, while four scribes copied the text (Collins et al. 2017, 38).

Ireland's cultural and social history during the Middle Ages is tangled and snarled around the customs and traditions of their mostly pagan society. Historical documentation shows that it took well over a century for Christianity to affect Irish culture enough to triumph over the hold of the pagan traditions (Hughes 1977, 58). The establishment and advancement of monasticism (muh-NAS-ti-cism), the practice of denouncing a worldly life to more fully embrace holiness, is what finally completed the conversion of the Irish religious culture. Monks and nuns practice monasticism. This may be a little difficult to understand because I just used a string of unusual words in my last paragraph, so let me explain it this way…

Monasteries were not uncommon during the time of St. Patrick and the century following his ministry in Ireland (and in other parts of Europe), but they were not embraced wholeheartedly by the Church as a recommended way of life. In the sixth century, two great monastic founders, Finnian of Clonard and Ciaran of Clonmacnoise, died of a horrendous plague that swept through Ireland in 548. Because these two men were considered great leaders, they were elevated to the status of saints, and their way of life was recognized as something holy and desirable (Hughes 1977, 58). The deaths of these two men made becoming a monk or a nun more popular and desirable to Irish Christians.

One of the most famous Irish missionaries besides Patrick is Brendan. He worked in the British Isles and France, though a popular legend says that he also once traveled to America. This sketch is a depiction of him and his men setting sail.

Let's take a look at what life was like in an Irish monastery in the Middle Ages. At this time in Church history, and still in some places today, many Christians believed that denying themselves physical comfort or pleasure would cause them to be closer to God. These monks, as they are called, held their beliefs closely, governing every aspect of life with discipline and strict adherence to their code of conduct. They lived simple lives, with only the barest necessities.

Many people think of monasteries as being cold and silent, with monks living reclusive, silent lives, but nothing could be further from the truth concerning the Irish monasteries of this time period. Irish monasticism was not as strict as the rules followed in other parts of Europe under the Western Christian Church. For example, in most other European countries, monasteries were inhabited by single men who had taken the oath never to get married or have children, while in Ireland, many monasteries were built on family land and were a center of the community. The Irish monks were often married and, along with their families, farmed the land and cared for their neighbors by teaching, preaching, and fellowshipping with them.

The monks had another important job: they wrote copies of the Bible and other Christian literature. Why would they do this? Well, during the Middle Ages, there were no printing presses yet, and there were no bookstores like we have today. As I am writing this book, I am sitting in my office chair, typing away on a computer. If I make a mistake, I can easily hit the backspace key, and voilà, the mistake is gone. I don't have to dip a pen into a bottle of ink and write slowly and carefully on parchment paper — and thank goodness, too! It would take me a very long time indeed to complete a book. The monks did not have ink, paper, or parchment unless they made it. They truly made each book "from scratch."

First, they made parchment by soaking, stretching, scraping, and drying animal skins. Next, they made dyes for their ink by soaking, mashing, and straining certain berries

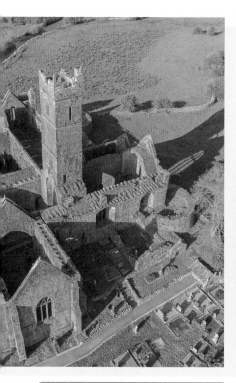

Quin Abbey in west Ireland

The cemetery at Skellig Michael, a monastery on a small rugged island off the coast of Ireland. This medieval monastery was abandoned in the 1200s.

Muckross Abbey is near the town of Killarney in southern Ireland. The current abbey was built in the 1400s, though the original monastery was built centuries earlier.

and fruits. Their inks were also drawn from sources far and wide, including common sources, like chalk for the color white, to rare and expensive ones, like the lovely rock lapis lazuli for blue. They made pens by whittling and sharpening goose quills.

These books they created were not just words written carefully on a page; they were masterpieces! There are still many samples of these monks' handwritten books available to see today, and if you ever get the chance to view them, I am sure you will be amazed at the artwork decorating the pages.

The monks working in the scriptorium, the writing room, were supposed to be silent and not interrupt the writing progress, but many of them wrote little notes to each other on the corners of the books' pages. They would also get bored of spending all day in a scriptorium; this led to them drawing little doodles in the margins. You can still see these notes and doodles of cats and dogs and mice running around on the pages of these well-preserved books. Even though the monks who were copying these texts may have found the work hard, they played an important role in preserving Scripture for countless Christians who followed them.

Narration break:

Talk about what life in medieval monasteries was like.

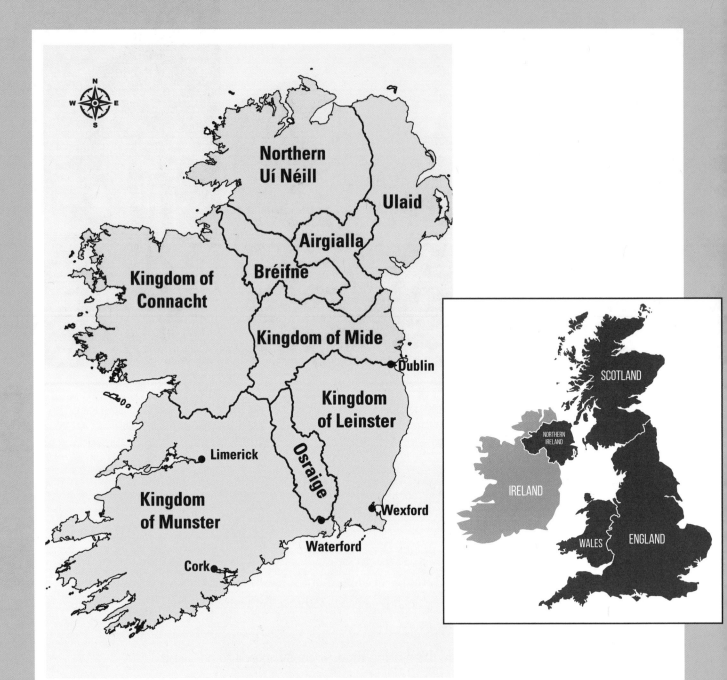

Many of Ireland's ancient cities still exist. In fact, all the cities shown on the map are still in existence. Dublin is the country's capital, and Wexford, Waterford, Cork, and Limerick remain important cities.

Likewise, many of Ireland's traditional kingdoms, though no longer in existence, are the names of modern regions. For example, western Ireland is still called Connacht, eastern Ireland is still called Leinster, and southern Ireland is still called Munster.

The northern part of Ireland remains under British control and is often called either Northern Ireland or Ulster (its traditional Irish Gaelic name). We will learn more about why this happened as we study English and Irish history in this volume and the next.

ANALYZE	In which direction from England and Scotland does Ireland lie?
CONNECT	Dublin, Ireland's capital, lies on the border of which two kingdoms?

MAPS

In this chapter, we learned the beautiful story of Saint Patrick, missionary to Ireland. Similar to Patrick was a missionary that history would call St. Columba — a man dedicated to the Christianizing of Scotland in the 500s. Columba, an Irish monk, exiled himself to a lonely island to focus exclusively on missionary work. Along with his followers, Columba built churches and a monastery on the island of Iona, off the southwestern coast of Scotland. It was from here that they set forth on their great mission work to spread the gospel to the Scottish people. Columba's work, through monks he had trained, also spread to continental Europe and had a great influence on the Frankish nobility's devotional life, as a result.

The Christians of Scotland and Ireland (often called Celtic Christians) did not follow the same practices that other Christians who belonged to the Christian churches of the West did. These differences caused quite a lot of friction between the two groups. They argued about many issues, including whether the pope was leader of the Western Church. The Irish and Scottish Christians did not accept his authority (Jones 2009, 60). They also feuded over when to celebrate Easter, which led to a considerable amount of confusion and trouble (Corning 2006, 4–13). Finally, it was decided that traditional Roman practices would prevail, and the Celtic Christians were required to adopt them (Highley 2008, 120). Some refused, but within a matter of years, the holdouts had also begun to follow Roman customs.

Columba and his horse. Columba was also called Columcille, which means "Dove of the Church."

GLENDALOUGH

One of the most famous medieval Irish monasteries was Glendalough, approximately 30 miles south of Dublin. Many of its buildings are still preserved for visitors to see and experience. Most of the buildings date back to the 900s–1100s, though the monastery itself is even older.

There are several churches at the monastery site. This one is St. Kevin's Church, after one of the most famous monks associated with Glendalough. Some people mistakenly call this church St. Kevin's Kitchen because they incorrectly assume the tower means it was a place where people cooked.

Another site associated with St. Kevin is a cave some distance away from the monastery. Kevin used to live in this cave. Some monks during the medieval period were hermits. That meant that they lived in seclusion from others to focus on their spiritual life.

Experts are not quite sure what the Priest House's purpose was. Based on the types of buildings that are common in other medieval monasteries, it is reasonable to assume that the Glendalough Monastery had places for the monks to cook, eat, sleep, and work.

One of the most prominent sites is the Round Tower. It stands over 100 feet tall and served as a lookout tower, bell tower, and as a landmark for pilgrims to know where to stop and rest.

05

START HERE

In all the world, there is nothing as powerful as words. It was with words that God created the heavens and the earth. It was with words that Christ commanded the raging, stormy Sea of Galilee to be peaceful and still. Words have power to build up and to tear down. A soft answering word can turn away anger. God has promised that His Word will never return void and that He will always protect it. Luke 21:33 says, "Heaven and earth will pass away, but My words will by no means pass away." In this chapter, we will learn how God used people of the Church to protect His Word, the Bible, through the Middle Ages.

THE CULTURE OF THE MEDIEVAL PERIOD

After the collapse of the Western Roman Empire, education became quite limited. In fact, most European people during the Middle Ages could not read. Of the ones who could read, most were monks, priests, or others associated with the Church. Part of the reason for this is that there was much less of an emphasis on education due to the chaos of Roman collapse. In past centuries, great importance had been placed on transmitting knowledge through the written word. This was still accomplished by the work of the monks who diligently copied material to preserve it in Ireland and other places, but it was not a primary concern for most people outside the monasteries. Life was simply too difficult for most people to think about the survival of knowledge when they were preoccupied with ensuring the survival of their own families.

In addition, for most people, these manuscripts were of no immediate use to them simply because they could not read. During the Middle Ages, most Europeans considered themselves Christians, but few who did not work for the Church could read the Bible, or anything else for that matter. In fact, local churches were often the only source for education at this time, but most people did not get an education because they were too busy working on their family farms or in their family shops to be schooled regularly. Another problem was that even if they had been taught to read, many of them could not read the Bible translation that existed — the Vulgate — unless they read Latin.

The Scriptures were originally written in Hebrew, Greek, or Aramaic. The language of the education in Europe, however, was Latin, the tongue of the Roman Empire. Even after the Western Roman Empire collapsed, Latin remained an admired language. Scholarly texts were written in Latin, regardless of where the material was being written. For this reason, only the most educated people could read the Scriptures in their original languages. But most people, if they could read, regardless of whether they lived in Italy or Ireland or England or elsewhere in Europe, could only read in Latin.

If something was not in Latin, it usually was not written down at all. Most stories or poems in these countries were in the vernacular, which means the language that people used every day, like English, German, French, or Italian. Since these stories were told in the vernacular,

Fra Angelico's painting of Saint Jerome, 1400s

Medieval manuscript depicting the famous French troubadour Perdigon. Some of the songs he wrote nearly 1,000 years ago still survive today.

they were not considered as prestigious as something in Latin and were not written down for centuries. They remained preserved through oral tradition, with people telling and retelling the stories to each other. Remember the game of telephone I told you about while learning about *Beowulf?* People had to tell and retell *Beowulf* because it was in Anglo-Saxon, not Latin, and wasn't written down for many years.

This would not be a good way to preserve Scripture, though, so in 382, a monk named Jerome set to work to translate the Bible into Latin. It took him 22 years to complete this monumental project. When he was finished, some people didn't like Jerome's translation because he didn't translate from the Septuagint, the Greek translation of the Hebrew Old Testament. Instead, he translated directly from the original Hebrew. Also, his translation used words that were more easily understood by the average person of the day. Some people thought his translation was "Vulgate," which is Latin for "common" or "vulgar." (To this day, this version of the Bible is still called the Vulgate.) Of course, when people realized that they could easily read this new translation, they liked it!

Because so many could not read, the Church could not use the written word to communicate with most Christians. The Church relied more and more on fine buildings (funded by the wealthy feudal lords), stained glass, and theatrical plays to try to teach the people about God. Have you ever seen stained glass before? To modern eyes, it may just seem like a gorgeous decoration, but that was not its original purpose. Cathedrals and churches in the Middle Ages used stained glass, statues, and paintings as a way of teaching people who could not read about biblical events and Christian doctrine, such as the life, death, and Resurrection of Jesus.

CONNECT

There has been music in the world almost since the beginning of time. During the Middle Ages, music, like visual art, was largely influenced by the Church and was the most prevalent type of music. One of the earliest types of music during this time was Gregorian chant. A chant isn't really a song, but it was used as one during church services and other times of worship. It is believed that Pope Gregory I organized and established uniform usage of the chants throughout the Christian churches of the West, sometime in the late 590s or early 600s.

Don't confuse these chants with what modern music calls "rap." Chants were something entirely different! These chants were more like a drone — a single melody without any harmony or accompaniment. The words were droned slowly and slipped from major to minor scales and back again. Many of these chants were sections of Scriptures, which were memorized in whole chapters.

Not all music was written by and performed at church. Minstrels were entertainers in the Middle Ages. They often performed music for kings and nobles. These songs were not chants at all but more like folk songs. They were usually sung by one person who played a stringed instrument for accompaniment. Some minstrels lived year-round with the king's family or with a noble's family and worked as their

On one hand, this was the only way to educate people who were never going to have the chance to learn to read and write for themselves. However, this also meant the Church and individual priests had direct control over how God's Word was presented and interpreted since most Christians were not able to read the Bible for themselves. In fact, many thought that it was better for common people not to read the Bible for themselves.

Think about this for a moment. How different is this from how you worship? If you hear a pastor say something in a sermon, you can easily look up the Scripture reference for yourself. Most medieval Christians could not and had to accept on good faith that what they were being told was actually what the Bible said. They had no way to independently confirm this on their own unless they were already a well-educated worker for the Church. Many of the priests and monks and other church officials were sincere and tried their best to help the people in their care, but others with less sincere motives knew that it was unlikely they would be confronted by their congregations for teaching things not in accordance with the Bible.

NARRATION BREAK:

Discuss what you read today.

Stained glass of King David in German cathedral. Creating stained glass was an intricate art that also had to factor in the light that would shine through.

13th century manuscript illustration of the famed medieval troubadour Perdigon

personal musicians, but others made their living as troubadours, roaming singers, traveling around from village to village, singing for their supper and lodging. Many of these songs never made it to paper, but we do know that most minstrels had one main tune, to which they changed words to tell the current events of the day.

Each people group and part of the world had their own type of music. The Celts had their own music, as well as the Vikings and the countries of Asia. Their music and songs told the epic tales of how their countries were forming, sad tales of battles, and romantic songs of love. Each type of music had its own type of melody and harmony, and each had its own place in its respective culture. One of the first music composers to become famous was a French musician and poet named Guillaume de Machaut who lived in the 1300s. Before him, composers were usually anonymous. The focus was on the songs, not who wrote them. Machaut was not just famous — he was also highly influential to other musicians and composers throughout Europe, even after his death.

Now, we are going to look at art from the Middle Ages. If you study the artwork from this time, you will notice how different it looks from paintings that were created later. Part of this is how "flat" medieval paintings appear. This is because these artists painted without using perspective. They had not discovered how to make objects look farther away behind the main focus of their picture. In other words, their pictures had no depth. All the characters were simply lined up across the painting, much like the ancient tomb paintings of the Egyptians. The problem of perspective in art was not solved until the time of the Renaissance, which we will study much later in this book.

Robert Campin's 13th century altarpiece showing Gabriel's appearance to Mary. This is a good example of the lack of perspective in medieval art. The people kneeling by the door are almost as large as the door itself and the placement of the table in the room looks unnatural. Medieval art emphasized symbolism over realism.

This 15th century Renaissance painting by Carlo Crivelli depicts the same scene but with a Renaissance use of perspective. The people are in proper proportion to the doors and buildings and the use of perspective is much more complex.

Another difference between the Middle Ages and later times is the role artists had in society. When you think about artists, you might think of rich, influential people who are famous and admired by their peers. It might surprise you to know that many of the artists of the Middle Ages had very different lives. Most artists of this period were not well known. In fact, many were anonymous! That means nobody knew who they were.

In our modern world, we often think of artists as strong individualists with a unique style. In the Middle Ages, individualism in art was strongly discouraged. Part of this was simply because much of the artwork was focused on the life of Jesus, the early saints, or other church-related topics. The focus was supposed to be on what the artwork was showing — Jesus and the Church — not the artist. Because the Church was such an important institution in medieval life, it was only natural that art, like so many other things, was also focused on religion.

Another important influence on art at this time is that artists, like many other professions, were organized into guilds. These were organizations of people who were all in the same line of work. There were painter and sculptor guilds, as well as guilds for merchants, bakers, shoemakers, candlemakers, blacksmiths, weavers, and more. Guilds were formed because individual workers did not have much power in the feudal system that dominated medieval society. An organization of people, though, was in a better position to make sure they were not being unfairly taxed or mistreated by the rulers of the land. Have you ever heard of a labor union? Modern labor unions operate the same way as a guild. Workers join together and bargain as one person rather than each individual asking for something.

These illustrations from the 1400s and 1500s show craftsmen at work. The first picture shows shoemakers while the other one depicts a locksmith. Shoemakers often had their own guild separate from cobblers who repaired shoes. Locksmiths started out as part of blacksmith guilds before branching out and forming their own.

Guilds also served other important purposes. They worked together to ensure that pricing for their goods and services was fair and that all members followed the same trade practices. The guilds also provided one of the few means of support for the community that was not tied to the local church. For instance, they helped fund schools and made sure that sick members and the orphaned children of members were taken care of. This was a very important service because the only resource for help in most locations at this time was the Church, and sometimes local churches did not always have the resources to help everyone in need.

Another way that guilds worked is that becoming a member involved a lot of work! Children in their early teens would become apprenticed to a guild member and would work for several years under that person's supervision. The apprentice would not be paid, though he would live with the guild member he served under and have his living expenses paid for.

The next step was becoming a journeyman. Workers at this stage were still not considered a guild member, but they were more independent than they had been as an apprentice. Even better, they were paid for their work! A journeyman's focus was creating a "masterpiece." This was proof for the guild that the journeyman had become a master of the craft.

If the masterpiece was accepted, then the journeyman would become a master and a guild member. This was the highest level of achievement, and it took many years. After becoming a master, a worker was qualified to open his own shop and take on apprentices of his own.

This might seem like an odd career path for an artist to take, but artists at this time were considered craftsmen, just like a shoemaker or a candlemaker. Being apprenticed to an artist was hard work, and for the youngest apprentices, that often included a lot of chores that had nothing to do with art, like keeping the workshop clean. However, it also provided valuable learning experiences, including preparing surfaces and mixing paints. Eventually, an apprentice painter would be working on paintings and other works with the master painter.

This type of system ensured that craftsmen, from painters to bakers, were well-trained and skilled and made sure that they were treated fairly and that their customers received good-quality service and goods. Another bonus was that since guilds required members to treat customers fairly, they were considered honorable and trustworthy citizens. Guild members were not necessarily rich, but many of them were well-to-do, especially compared to others in the feudal system, and they had the added benefit of being respected by their neighbors.

Medieval monks at work in a scriptorium. Though the monks were not part of the guild system, they still followed an apprentice model, with younger monks learning from older, more experienced monk scribes.

The scriptorium in a French monastery, preserved to look as it did during medieval times.

Guilds and apprenticeships were such major aspects of medieval life that it often became a tradition for families to stay in the same line of work for generations. Though the guild system is no longer in place, some trades like plumbing and electrical work still require people to serve an apprenticeship to this day. The requirements, of course, are different than they were during the Middle Ages, but it still involves learning on the job under a more experienced person.

The guild system worked to many people's advantage, but it was also another reason why art at the time didn't seem very individualized. Most works were commissioned by either churches or nobles, and the expectation was that the artists would create work that met the requirements of the job, not their own personal vision for the task. Likewise, when apprentices were being trained by master painters, the emphasis was on making sure their use of technique was good, not how lifelike or artistic the painting was. Just like with the issue of perspective in paintings, this would not change until the Renaissance, which we will study in-depth later.

NARRATION BREAK: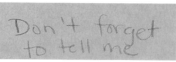

Discuss what you learned about medieval guilds and art.

This is the floor plan of St. Canice's Cathedral in Kilkenny, Ireland.

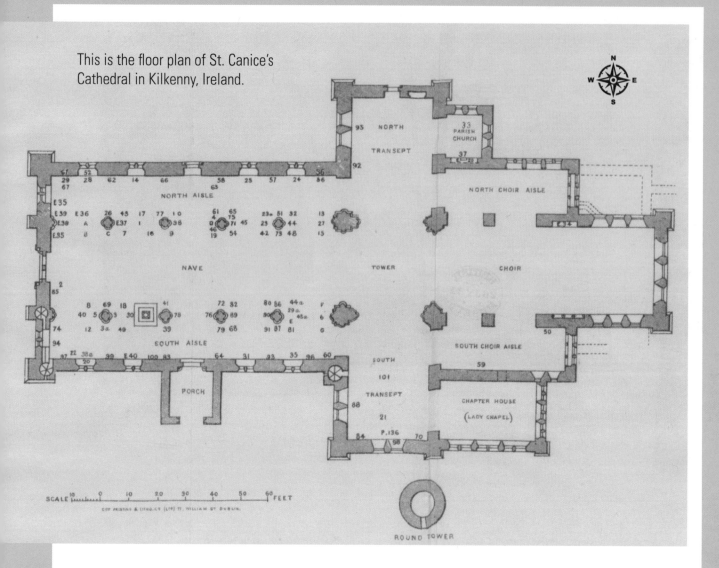

During the medieval period, cathedrals were built in many towns across Western Europe. Technically, a cathedral is a church that is the seat of a church official called a bishop. Because of their prestige in being associated with the bishop, cathedrals were much larger and fancier than other churches.

All cathedrals also followed the same basic floor plan. They have a cross shape, with the entrance facing west and the rounded part that houses the altar (called the apse) facing east. The nave, which is near the entrance, is where people are during the service. The transepts are what form the sides of the cross and face north and south. They divide the nave from the choir. The part called the choir is usually raised higher and is where the choir is located during services.

Because all cathedrals had this design, someone during the Middle Ages could be a newcomer to an area but still know exactly where to go in a cathedral for a service. The services themselves were the same way. They were all conducted in Latin and they all followed the same order, whether the cathedral was in England, Italy, France, or elsewhere. For that reason, not only would a newcomer know how the cathedral would be designed, but that person would also know what to expect during the service.

| ANALYZE | What is the section below the south choir aisle? |

| CONNECT | If the entrance faces west and is near the nave, where do you suppose the entrance on this floor plan would be? |

Maps

During the Middle Ages, knowledge of Greek philosophers like Aristotle was largely limited to the educated monks in monasteries. Some of these monks, in turn, were inspired to consider philosophy through a Christian lens.

One of the most noted Christian thinkers of the Middle Ages was Thomas Aquinas. He was born in 1225 in Italy. Thomas started out as a son of a wealthy family. His parents wanted him to become an archbishop, but Thomas wanted to be a simple monk. After soaking himself in the Church's teachings and even more of the Bible, Thomas started to preach. Up until now, the Church had separated everything from the physical world from anything to do with the spiritual world. Thomas threw out this ridiculous idea. When he looked around him, he saw everything in the physical world as signs pointing to the Creator. You might say that Thomas Aquinas was the first apologetics teacher!

Even though Thomas never considered himself a philosopher, he was extremely influential on the world of philosophy. Thomas criticized philosophers for completely missing the point of thinking and seeking wisdom. This gentle monk knew this truth: Wisdom is a gift from God, and like Proverbs 1:7 says, "The fear of the LORD is the beginning of knowledge." Thomas believed in worshipping and serving God, the Maker of his brain and his ability to understand, instead of worshipping himself.

Italian Renaissance painter Carlo Crivelli's *Saint Thomas Aquinas*, 1476, part of a church altarpiece

MEDIEVAL CATHEDRALS

Notre Dame (no-TRA Dawm) is one of the most famous cathedrals in Paris. It is considered a masterpiece of French Gothic architecture. Gothic architecture was developed in France and emphasized height and light. On April 15, 2019, a tragic fire destroyed most of the roof, along with the building's spire.

Europe

The Reims Cathedral in France is noted for its connection to French royalty. Frankish leader Clovis, whom we will learn about later, was baptized here in the late 400s (though not in the current building). The Reims Cathedral was also the site where French kings were crowned for centuries.

Stained glass in Spain's Cathedral of Santiago de Compostela

Organ in Norway's Nidaros Cathedral. As with many of the cathedrals featured here, kings were crowned at this location. Also, like many of the other cathedrals listed, the cathedral switched from being Catholic to being Protestant during the Reformation, which we will study in a later chapter.

The Winchester Cathedral is noted for its size and beauty. Like many of the cathedrals shown here, it was rebuilt, renovated, and added onto over a period of centuries.

York Minster nave. The York Minster is a cathedral, but the word minster has its own separate meaning. Of Anglo-Saxon origin, a minster is a church that is either connected to a monastery or functioned as a missionary training center. Not all minsters are cathedrals, and not all cathedrals are minsters.

06

START HERE

Disobedience. It will always lead to bad consequences — some more severe than others. In Genesis 16, we read the story of how Abraham and Sarah took their childlessness into their own hands. God had promised them a child, but they became impatient. Instead of trusting in God, they tried to take charge. Abraham had a son named Ishmael with Hagar. Ishmael's descendants became the Arab people, and in the 600s, a new religion sprang up among them. I hope you are ready to embark on a journey through the scorching sands of a desert. Let's discover the impact that the Islamic faith had on the medieval world. . . .

If you were with me in Volume 1 of this series, you will remember that we learned about how one of Abraham's sons, Ishmael, became the ancestor of the Bedouin (BED-o-in) nomads of the Arabian Peninsula. Now, we are going to learn about how a religion called Islam took root in the Arabian Peninsula and then rapidly spread throughout the Middle East.

Our story starts in the seventh century, in the thick dust of the Arabian Peninsula, where tents of the wandering Bedouins dotted the countryside. It was around the year 622, in the city of Mecca, that a man named Muhammad claimed the angel Gabriel visited him. Muhammad did not like how many of his fellow Bedouins lived; he was disturbed by their irresponsible behavior. As a young man, Muhammad had spent much time by himself praying to the Bedouin gods.

On this particular day, Muhammad had been praying in a cave, when he claimed to have received a vision about Allah, a false god. Muhammad ran home and told his family what he had been told; they believed him and called him a prophet. Soon, Muhammad was preaching to whomever would listen to him. He encouraged his fellow countrymen to follow the commands he claimed that he had received.

One of these commands said that people who had a lot of money should share it with those who did not have much. Of course, this was a popular idea with the poor people but not appreciated by the wealthy. Before long, there was even more division between the two classes, as the wealthy treated the lower class, who had converted to Islam, with contempt. As more and more people in Mecca converted to Islam, fewer and fewer of them went to the city to offer sacrifices to the other gods. This made the merchants who sold to the temple crowds extremely angry.

Muhammad was forced to run away to a town called Medina. As Muhammad lived in Medina, he taught everyone about the false god Allah and the Quran (kuh-RAWN), his false holy book. He became popular, in fact, not just as a prophet but also as a powerful ruler. Muhammad decided that he wanted to rule Mecca also, so he started raiding camel trains traveling past Medina, taking supplies to Mecca. Soon, armies from both cities were fighting each other. This went on for over seven years before Mecca

Illustration of Muhammad leaving Mecca, 1920

finally fell to Muhammad's ever-growing army of Muslims. At first, Muhammad did not force conversions and instead required people who did not convert to pay a tax. Eventually, his attitude changed, and people were forcibly converted.

By the time Muhammad died in 632, Islam had spread to all modern-day Saudi Arabia, except for the northernmost section, as well as its neighboring countries on the Arabian Peninsula. After the death of Muhammad, one of his original followers became the new leader. For a period of about 30 years after Muhammad's death, several of his original followers led the movement. These men were called caliphs, and their time in power was called a caliphate.

This specific caliphate is called the Rashidun Caliphate, and Medina was its capital. During this time, Islam spread outside of the Arabian Peninsula to neighboring areas. Within a matter of decades, the Muslims had added much of the rest of the Middle East to their territory, including lands in Western Asia and North Africa. This expansion furthered the message but also ensured that there were thousands of well-trained, experienced Arab Muslim soldiers ("Rightly Guided Caliphs," n.d.).

Because these men had been followers of Muhammad, it was important to them that they continued to follow his teachings. As a result, his religious teachings and practices were strictly enforced ("Rightly Guided Caliphs," n.d.). These followers of Muhammad ruled one at a time and replaced each other upon death. However, the last one was murdered in 656, and his death started a civil war

Illustration depicts Muhammad arriving in the Arabian city of Medina

CONNECT During the Medieval Age, the Islamic world contributed substantially to the sciences. From the 8th century to the 16th century, the affluence of the Islamic society almost guaranteed that there would be successful discoveries and advances made. We are going to look at the medical field of science during the Islamic Golden Age. We will also discover a modern engineering wonder that has its roots during this time.

The study and practice of medicine was an important part of the Islamic culture in the Middle Ages. Their practices were patterned after the ancient Greek and Roman scholars. The most influential medical encyclopedia produced during this time was written by Ibn Sina, one of the greatest thinkers and writers of Islam's Golden Age. This five-book set became extremely influential in the medicine of Europe until the 1700s (Hajar 2013). The Islamic doctors and medical specialists didn't just write about their medical practices, however — they also advanced in many areas of actual treatment, such as surgery. They invented a large variety of surgical instruments, including forceps, scalpels, pincers, and lancets, to name just a few. Many of their procedures have been improved upon but still are used in their basic form.

Today, in the Middle Eastern country of Dubai, standing in a prominent position in an enormous 3.5 million square foot mall is what appears to be a huge elephant statue. This statue is actually a clock that was made to the exact specifications of a design engineered during the Golden Age of Islam. This amazing device was designed by inventor Al-Jazari, who worked as the chief of engineering for the Artuklu Palace (in modern-day Turkey) during the medieval period.

Al-Jazari is famous for writing and illustrating a book titled *The Book of Knowledge of Ingenious Mechanical Devices,* which was widely embraced throughout Europe for several centuries. The design for his elephant clock is awe-inspiring in its complexity: "The internal mechanisms of the clock, driven by floats in water tanks hidden in the belly of the elephant, activate the various components into mechanical motion every half hour" (Black n.d.).

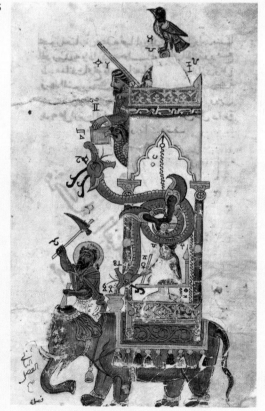

Illustration of Al-Jazari's elephant clock, 1315

that led to the Muslim religion being divided between Sunni and Shia Muslims. (To this day, the religion is still divided, with most Muslims being Sunni. The Shia, as a general rule, are centered in Iraq and Iran, though some also live in other Middle Eastern countries.)

The two sides were arguing about who should be the next caliph and could not agree on whom it should be. All the infighting led to the rise of another caliphate entirely — the Umayyad (ew-MY-id) caliphate. The Umayyads were a wealthy merchant family who only converted to Islam late in Muhammad's life. Nevertheless, they quickly became valued administrators for him and his successors. As the religion plunged into civil war in the dispute over who should rule, the Umayyads themselves emerged as the winners by 661.

Narration break:

Talk about what you read today.

Shia and Sunni Muslim children come together to watch a soccer game in Iraq, 2008.

The Umayyad Caliphate ruled from Damascus, and they oversaw an even more extensive expansion of the religion. Under the Umayyads, Islamic control stretched even farther west across North Africa, as well as farther into Central Asia, including the modern-day countries of Afghanistan and Pakistan. They also expanded into Europe, gaining control of most of what is today Spain and Portugal.

Interestingly enough, one of the barbarian tribes that had been such a problem for Rome was partially responsible for why Islam arrived in Europe. Even though Rome had fallen, many of the barbarian tribes still existed, including the Visigoths. The Visigoths' culture had actually been greatly influenced by the Romans, and they now considered themselves Christians and lived settled lives. Though they were originally from Eastern Europe, by the 500s, they were living in what is now Spain. Everything was going along uneventfully for them until the early 700s when there was a dispute over who would be king. Some of the Visigoths invited the Umayyads to come over and help them regain power over their kingdom because the Umayyads had reputations as excellent soldiers. This scheme was destined to end in disaster, though.

The Muslim soldiers who went to Spain were a group of people called Berbers. They lived across the Mediterranean in North Africa, where they still live today. By this point, the Berbers had only been converted to Islam for a matter of decades. When their general, Tariq ibn Ziyad, and his army arrived, they invaded and tried to take Spain for themselves. The Visigoths, who were divided by the dispute for the throne, were not able to ward off the attack, and within a few years, Spain was almost completely under Islamic control.

19th century depiction of the Muslim leader Tariq ibn Ziyad defeating the Visigoth king in Spain

Ruins of a
Muslim fortress
in modern-day
Spain

Though they continued the tradition of expansion, one thing that set the Umayyad
Caliphate apart from its predecessor was the fact that it was much more secular.
For the most part, the Umayyad Caliphate was not interested in strict adherence
to Muhammad's teachings or in leading the religion. The Umayyads, instead,
preferred to focus on developing the administration of their empire. This angered
more traditional Muslims, but it also transformed this caliphate into a government
that looked more like a traditional kingdom ("Umayyad Caliphate," n.d.). Before,
power had been held in the hands of Muhammad's closest followers, and power was
transferred between them. The Umayyads changed that and made it a hereditary
dynasty. They also cultivated wealth, which seemed counter to many of Muhammad's
early teachings, and expanded cultural activities like art.

Another policy the Umayyads enacted was Arabization ("Umayyad Caliphate," n.d.).
Muhammad and his initial followers were all Arabs from the Arabian Peninsula, who
spoke the Arabic language. As Muslim control expanded, however, not everyone they
ruled was an Arab or spoke Arabic. The people who lived in what is now Iran were
Persians who spoke the Persian language. The people of Afghanistan and Pakistan
comprised numerous tribes who spoke their own languages. Egyptians at this time
usually spoke Coptic, which used the Greek alphabet. In North Africa, the Berbers
were the dominant group, and they also spoke their own language. Arabization meant
that instead of everyone using their own local languages, Arabic became the standard
language used for government and trade. Arabic currency was also introduced, and
government officials tended to be Arabs. This is one reason why the Arabic language
is so strongly associated with Islam and Muslims even today, though many Muslims
are not Arabs.

Though the Umayyads greatly expanded, their progress was starting to slow down within 100 years. In the 700s, they suffered several defeats that prevented them from expanding their territory farther. Their expanse into Europe was halted by a famous battle in France in 732, which we will study in the next chapter, and the Byzantine Empire was eventually successful in checking the Umayyads' progress. Revolts and internal fighting broke out, and the Umayyads found themselves replaced with a new dynasty: the Abbasid Caliphate.

The Umayyads had mostly focused on the west as they expanded their rule in North Africa and Europe. The Abbasids, however, turned their attention to the east. They established their capital in Baghdad in modern-day Iraq (Esposito 2004, 78). They also emphasized their identity as a Muslim empire rather than an Arab one since so many of its people were not Arabs. Perhaps the biggest change is that the Abbasid Caliphate did not rule unchallenged (Esposito 2004, 78). Unlike the previous caliphates, who had ruled without serious internal challenges until the end of their dynasties, the Abbasids faced several rival Muslim caliphates. Despite their defeat elsewhere in the Muslim world, the Umayyads clung to power in Spain, ruling from the city of Cordoba for a few hundred years. (They were followed by the Almohad Caliphate, which controlled Spain and parts of North Africa.) The Fatimid Caliphate established itself in control of Egypt and other neighboring parts of North Africa.

Despite these challenges, the Abbasid Caliphate remained a powerful force. It still controlled a vast empire that stretched from the sands of North Africa to the mountains of Central Asia and from the southernmost point of the Arabian Peninsula to the Caucasus Mountains. They also continued the Umayyad tradition of supporting culture and science. Indeed, this period is often called the Islamic Golden Age because of the flourishing of science, mathematics, literature, medicine, and art that occurred.

NARRATION BREAK:

Discuss the caliphates.

Ruins of the Umayyad city of Medina Azahara in modern-day Spain

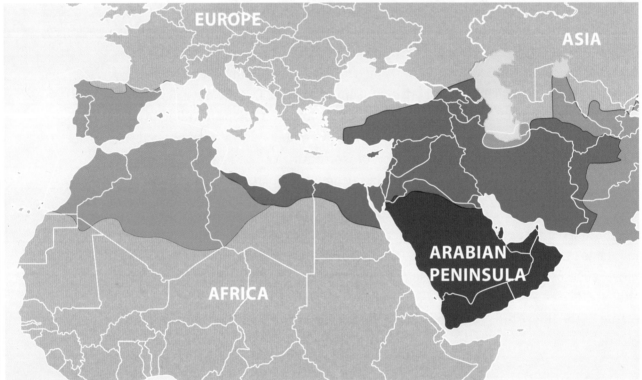

EUROPE

ASIA

AFRICA

ARABIAN PENINSULA

Age of Caliphs

- Prophet Mohammad, 622–632
- Rashidun Caliphate, 632–661
- Umayyad Caliphate, 661–750

This map shows how rapidly Islam spread through the Middle East, North Africa, and Europe during the 600s and 700s. As it shows, Islam was confined to the Arabian Peninsula when Muhammad died in 632. In the 30 years after Muhammad's death, Islam spread east, north, and west under the Rashidun Caliphate. The Umayyad Caliphate saw even more advances to the east and west. The Abbasid Caliphate is not depicted on this map, but it did not rule as much land as the Umayyad in the face of rebellions and other instability.

ANALYZE	Does the Islam empire shrink or grow over the years?
CONNECT	How long was it between the start of Mohammad's caliphate and the end of the Umayyad Caliphate? (Hint: Look at the map key.)

MAPS

When the Muslims invaded the Iberian Peninsula (where Spain and Portugal are located), their presence caused a major upset in the existing culture. Islamic culture at this time heavily borrowed from Arabic culture. Muslims were expected to speak Arabic and adopt Arabic culture even if they were not Arabs. In fact, the Muslims who invaded Spain were not Arabs — they were North African Berbers. Their culture was partially Berber and partially Arab. Their distinct culture mixed with the Christian and Jewish cultures that were already in Spain.

Among the distinct people groups who emerged from this new culture mixing was a group of Christians who remained unconverted to Islam yet adopted the Arabic culture of the Muslims, including their language (Burman 1994, 1). The Mozarab (mo-ZAR-ab), or Mozárabes as they are called in Spanish, lived under Muslim rule relatively peacefully for centuries (Burman 1994, 1). Interestingly, these people often lived in their own special sections, right inside large Muslim cities (Burman 1994, 19–20). They led prosperous lives and ruled their own communities with their own officials (Burman 1994, 19–20). They built and maintained their own churches and monasteries and even translated the Word of God into Arabic (Burman 1994, 14, 19–20).

Church History

Illustrated manuscript page from Leon Bible of 960. It was created in Spain during Muslim rule.

Mecca & Medina

All Muslims are supposed to go to Mecca on a pilgrimage at least once in their lifetime. This is called a hajj, and people who go on one are called hajji.

Saudi Arabia

Non-Muslims are forbidden to enter the city, as these road signs indicate. They can get in trouble for trying to sneak in. (Makkah is another spelling of Mecca.)

This photograph shows part of the city and part of the desert surrounding it. Mecca gets less than 5 inches of rain a year.

Medina is located about 300 miles north of Mecca. Muhammad lived most of his life in Mecca, but he is buried in Medina.

The city's economy is largely centered around the pilgrimages, including providing food, shelter, and other services. Millions visit the city every year to make the pilgrimage.

Medina is another pilgrimage city in Saudi Arabia. Like Mecca, non-Muslims are not allowed to enter it.

07

START HERE

God has always had the ability to orchestrate and use events to fulfill His plans. With His all-knowing wisdom and sovereignty, He has used mankind as instruments in those plans. One of my favorite examples of this in Bible times is the Persian king, Cyrus, whom God told, "I am the Lord; there is no other God. I have equipped you for battle, though you don't even know me, so all the world from east to west will know there is no other God" (Isaiah 45:5-6; NLT).

In this chapter, we will learn about how, throughout several centuries in the medieval period, the Muslim conquest was halted at the border of Frankish territory. One of these kings, Charlemagne, would become one of history's most famous and powerful rulers. As you hear his story, along with the Frankish kings before him, pay attention to the evidence of God's hand during this time in world history. You may want to ask yourself these two questions: How did God enable these kings to stop the spread of Islam into a huge portion of Europe, and although Charlemagne did not follow God's laws perfectly himself, how did God use him to protect His Word?

THE FRANKS AND CHARLEMAGNE

In our last chapter, we read about the Visigoths, one of the barbarian tribes. Like the Visigoths, many of the barbarian tribes that had been such a threat to Rome had now adopted Roman ways — they were no longer considered "barbarians." One of these tribes was the Franks, and they lived in what is now France, Belgium, and Germany. When the Western Roman Empire still existed, the Franks had actually joined forces with the Romans and some other barbarians to defeat Attila the Hun and his followers. You might remember reading about them in Volume 1 of this series. The barbarian tribes did not always like each other or Rome, but they disliked the Huns even more. At this time, the Franks had a strong leader who was able to unite all the tribes in the region. This Frankish leader's name was Merovech (mer-o-VEK). Unfortunately, after the crisis, they all went back to fighting among themselves.

In the year 481, Merovech's grandson, Clovis, inherited his tribe's throne. Clovis remembered how his grandfather had united the tribes of Gaul long enough to fight against the Huns. Through wars and diplomacy, he also succeeded in uniting the Franks, and he eventually became a Christian. The Franks, like the other formerly pagan Germanic barbarian tribes, became a Christian nation. The new Frankish Empire now ruled all of Gaul, which is what France was called then, with Clovis as their king. We actually get the word "France" from the word "Frank."

Clovis also decided that he needed to come up with strict laws that everyone had to follow. (His new set of laws reminds me somewhat of Hammurabi's Code, which you may remember if you studied Volume 1.) Up until now, all the tribes had followed their own laws, and Clovis knew if this continued, there would be too much division to keep his empire united. So, Clovis ordered his scribes to write down his new set of laws, which he called the Salic Laws. One of these laws would have a major impact on the laws of many future European countries — it prevented women from inheriting kingdoms. The Frankish Empire continued to grow strong, united under their national religion and following their universal law.

A couple of hundred years after Clovis' death, the Franks had lost some of their power. Infighting and confusion over who would rule had weakened their control. One of the contestants for the throne was a man named Charles Martel. The word "Martel" means "the Hammer." Charles

Illustration showing the Franks in battle

did not become king easily. Many people did not want him to be king. He was even thrown into prison by his stepmother to keep him from becoming king. Charles did not let this stop him, however. He escaped, gathered his army, and fought those who opposed him. By 718, he had won control of the Franks.

In the same year that Charles Martel became the leader of the Franks, the Muslims successfully conquered Spain after a war that had lasted seven years. As Islamic rule had spread throughout Spain, other Europeans watched nervously. Everyone knew the Muslim army was a powerful force with which to reckon. The surge of Islamic victories was something of a tidal wave, wiping away everything in its path. Their warriors believed that their false god, Allah, would not let them be defeated. However, they were about to meet someone who would do just that!

CONNECT

If you are an American, you are probably familiar with the fact that our president is not a king from a royal family. He or she did not become president simply because of being the eldest and the successor to the "throne." Our type of government is completely different than that. Are you at least 35 years old, born in the United States, and have lived here at least 14 years of your life? If you fit all these qualifications, then congratulations, you have a shot at becoming president of the United States of America!

But imagine with me that you are from a royal family and circumstances would have it that all heirs to the throne have either died or abdicated their rights to rule. You are the successor to the throne, but there's one small problem keeping you from the throne — you are female. For this reason, you are not allowed to rule, despite your family history. This is exactly what would have happened if you were a female in the Frankish or French royal family. This law of succession was rooted in the Salic law, which was written in the 6th century. Whenever the need arose, this law was put into action to make sure a female was not put on the throne. That's because most medieval people did not believe that it was a woman's place to rule.

There were other types of laws for succession throughout European kingdoms that did not follow Salic law. For instance, for many centuries, the Holy Roman Emperor was elected by a group of princes. In England, the eldest son, regardless of whether he was the eldest child, would become ruler. A woman could become the queen but only if she did not have close male relatives who were eligible for the throne. For instance, one of the English kings we will learn about later is Henry VIII. He had two daughters and a son. Even though the two daughters were older, the throne went to the son. It was only after the son's death that his sisters could be made queen.

These rules of succession change periodically, however. In 2013, the rules of succession changed right before Prince George of England was born to his royal mum and dad, Prince William and his wife, Kate, the Duchess of Cambridge. As of right now, little George is third in line to the throne, after his daddy and grandfather, followed by his younger sister, Princess Charlotte. The new rules state that there is no longer male dominance in the succession — in other words, it is the oldest child who is the first heir, whether they are male or female (BBC 2015).

Depiction of Muslim soldiers in France, 19th century painting by Julius Schnorr von Carolsfeld

17th century illustration of Charles Martel

Odo flees from the Muslims

The Muslims who had taken Spain thought they would sweep through Frankish territory the same way they had conquered Spain. At first, it appeared they would do exactly this because they pillaged and plundered the small villages and towns all along the border. For several years, they conducted raids in Frankish land and even gained control of some parts of what is now France, though they had also been defeated by a local duke named Odo in 721.

In 732, the Umayyad Caliphate seemed intent on invading the land for good. Odo called upon Charles Martel for help, though he and Charles did not always get along. The Muslim raiders met Charles Martel's army in between the cities of Poitiers and Tours, which are in modern-day France. The Muslims, expecting an easy victory, were stunned by the strength of the Frankish army. Charles Martel drove his army hard, forcing the Islamic raiders to run and flee. The Islamic tidal wave had been stopped, though they remained in control of much of Spain for centuries.

After his defeat of the Muslims in that famous battle, which is known as both the Battle of Tours and the Battle of Poitiers (poy-tee-AY), Charles continued to expand his kingdom in wars with neighboring areas. When he died, he divided his kingdom between his sons. His grandson — Charles I, a man known in history as Charlemagne — would expand the family's rule far beyond the mighty empire they already controlled.

NARRATION BREAK:

Talk about the Franks and Charles Martel.

Last time, we learned about Charles Martel. He had a son named Pepin the Short. And Pepin the Short had two sons, named Charles and Carloman. These two sons each inherited part of Pepin's kingdom after their father's death, but Carloman himself died a few years later. As a result, Charles inherited the entire kingdom. Charles was a great military leader who had his heart set on conquering the surrounding lands.

Charles was also concerned about the people of his empire. He worried that they were slowly returning to their old ways and that they were forgetting how to be Christians. Charles decided to hire hundreds of monks to copy the Scriptures and other classic Christian works to ensure their preservation. He also expanded education to teach more people how to read. He commanded that all children be baptized and brought to church. Charles looked around and decided that his kingdom also needed to be cleaned up and the road systems repaired.

All this renovating effort and conquering of the surrounding lands went on for 30 years until Charles was the ruler of a huge empire. He rebuilt old Roman roads and old Roman structures and built new buildings with the flair of old Roman architecture. Everywhere he went, Charles conquered "in the name of God." As part of this, he forced his new subjects to either be baptized or die. Of course, this is no way to win people over to Jesus. At this time, since religion was so closely joined with the government, ruling powers around the world often forced people they had

Charles Martel
(grandfather)

Pepin the Short
(son)

Depiction of Charlemagne

conquered to join their religion. It was seen as a way to unite kingdoms and ensure everyone was loyal, but that is not what should motivate people to convert or to want others to do so.

Charles also used religion to his advantage outside of his conquests. When Leo III became pope upon the death of Adrian I, some of Adrian's relatives strongly opposed the new leader of the Church because they thought one of them should be pope instead. They accused Leo III of stealing from the Church. Some of Adrian's supporters jumped Leo during a religious procession and tried to cut out his tongue and jab out his eyes (Graves 2010 "Leo"). Leo escaped, though he was badly hurt, and made his way to Charles (Graves 2010 "Leo"). Leo and Charles decided to help each other. Charles declared Leo innocent of the charges, and the men who had attacked Leo were banished (Graves 2010 "Leo"). In return, Leo agreed to a public demonstration of Charles' power and authority.

At the Christmas Day communion service in 800, Leo III crowned King Charles and declared him "Charles, the most pious Augustus, crowned by God . . . great and pacific emperor" (Graves 2010). Charles, the Frankish king, had become Charlemagne, emperor of much of modern-day Western Europe. Charlemagne simply is the English way of saying Charles the Great, which in French is Charles le Magne. Charlemagne had revived the hope for a renewed Western Roman Empire. He never had a set capital, but he spent much time ruling from both Rome and Aachen, a city

This illustration shows the pope crowning Charlemagne.

in what is now western Germany. By the time of his death in 814, he had expanded his reach into a small part of northern Spain, as well as into Central Europe.

Both the Church and Charlemagne benefited from his ties to the pope. The pope's crowning of Charlemagne was a way to legitimize the new emperor's control over Italy and Rome, but it also confirmed the pope's authority and indicated that the pope himself wielded much political power. If he could crown kings and emperors, could he not also revoke their power?

Meanwhile, Charlemagne's empire, the Carolingian Empire, flourished. Charlemagne placed administrators throughout the empire to ensure that things ran smoothly, and he also introduced standardized weights and measures, which improved trade. While Charlemagne was on the throne, his army was well-organized, and no attacking tribes were successful at breaking into his empire.

Charlemagne and his wife. The other women in the illustration could be two of his daughters or servants.

After his death, however, the empire was divided among his three grandsons. This was the Frankish custom. Instead of giving the entire empire to one heir, it was split. We know from studying history that when a kingdom or an empire is divided between more than one ruler, trouble usually follows because people get greedy and arrogant. Of course, this was the case with Charlemagne's empire. The squabbling continued for quite some time until it was decided in 843 to divide the land among Charlemagne's remaining grandsons, three brothers.

Eventually, some of the kingdoms that resulted from this division re-joined together and formed something called the Holy Roman Empire. This empire considered itself the true successor to Charlemagne's rule and wielded considerable power in Europe and with the Church. This is one of the most significant legacies of Charlemagne's rule (and the Holy Roman Empire that followed): kings and rulers were increasingly becoming intertwined with the Church. These rulers appeared to gain the authority for their rule from the Church, and the Church itself was increasingly involved in political matters.

Narration break:

Discuss Charlemagne and his empire.

Charlemagne's throne is preserved in Aachen, Germany.

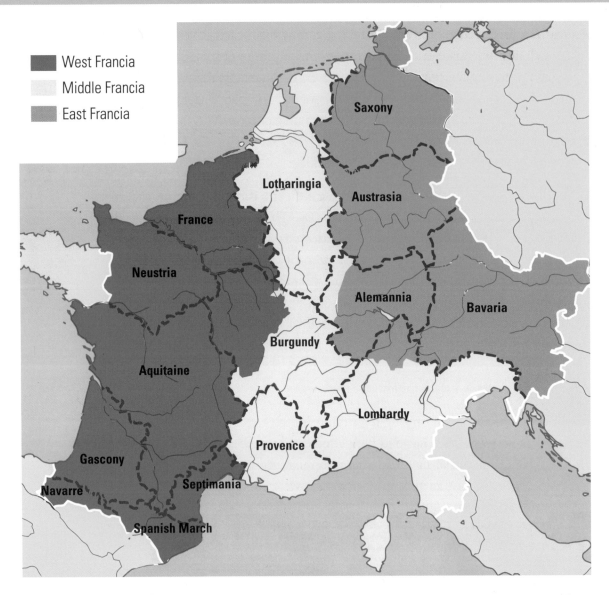

Legend:
- West Francia
- Middle Francia
- East Francia

Labels on map: Saxony, Lotharingia, Austrasia, France, Neustria, Alemannia, Bavaria, Burgundy, Aquitaine, Lombardy, Provence, Gascony, Septimania, Navarre, Spanish March

The map shows how Charlemagne's kingdom was divided among his grandsons. One of the brothers, Charles the Bald, received West Francia. That's the land in red. Another brother, Lothair, received Middle Francia, which is lavender. The other brother, Louis the German, received East Francia, the orange part of the map. The squabbling and fighting did not end once the land was divided, unfortunately.

Over time, West Francia became the Kingdom of France and, eventually, the country of France. Middle Francia and East Francia joined forces and became the Holy Roman Empire. The Holy Roman Empire was a dominant force in Europe for centuries, eventually coming under the control of the Hapsburg family. The Holy Roman Empire lasted for over 1,000 years, only ending in 1806. The modern countries of Germany, Austria, Switzerland, the Czech Republic, Belgium, and the Netherlands, as well as parts of several other surrounding nations, were all part of the Holy Roman Empire.

It's important to know about the Holy Roman Empire because of the important role it played in Europe throughout the Middle Ages. We will be learning a lot about this empire throughout the rest of this book, and it is helpful to know where it was located and its relation to other kingdoms at the time.

ANALYZE Does the amount of land given to each grandson look fairly equal?

CONNECT Which three countries have land shared between two different grandsons?

MAPS

Merovech's grandson Clovis united the Franks, just as his grandfather did, but he was also responsible for his people becoming Christian. His actions helped his people become a Christian nation and helped Christianity continue to spread throughout Europe. Clovis' biggest priority was always uniting the Franks. To that end, he married a princess of the neighboring tribe, the Burgundians. His new wife, Clotilda, was a Christian, and she wanted Clovis to become a Christian, too. Clovis did not want to become a Christian, however, and he refused to convert.

Legend says that one day, Clovis was fighting a battle against the Alemanni tribe. His army was doing very poorly and sustaining heavy casualties. Clovis looked up to the sky and told God that he would serve Him forever if He would give the Frankish army the victory. The legend goes on to say that the army's energy and strength were miraculously revived, and they went on to win the battle with renewed vigor. After the battle was over, Clovis returned home to speak to a priest about Christianity and be baptized. He was now an emperor of his new kingdom and a Christian.

After Clovis achieved his goal of uniting the Franks, he wanted them to stay united. He wanted to avoid a repeat of what had happened earlier in their history when their unity fell apart. He decided that having a common religion would help, so he decreed his empire would be a "Christian Empire." When he was baptized into the Church, he ordered over 3,000 of his men to be baptized, too. Of course, being baptized does not make you a Christian, but in Clovis' mind, it did.

Clovis' conversion and his insistence on his people converting were important, though. He was one of the first kings of the Germanic tribes to convert. Many of the other Germanic tribes who were not pagan had begun calling themselves Christians, but their beliefs do not reflect what the Bible teaches us about God and Jesus. The Christian Church was very alarmed at this development and relieved that Clovis and the Franks did not also follow these false teachings. The Franks actually became the most powerful Christian kingdom in Western Europe at this time, and they were a powerful force in medieval politics for many years.

Clovis' wife converts him to Christianity

AACHEN

Charlemagne did not have one set capital. In fact, it was not uncommon at all for medieval rulers to travel and have numerous capitals. His winter capital was Aachen, a town that dated back to Roman times. It's still in existence in modern-day Germany, near the borders with Belgium and the Netherlands.

Germany

Cityscape of Aachen's Old Town, which features many historic buildings.

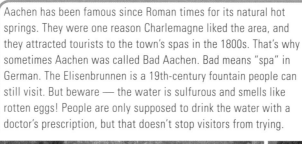

Aachen has been famous since Roman times for its natural hot springs. They were one reason Charlemagne liked the area, and they attracted tourists to the town's spas in the 1800s. That's why sometimes Aachen was called Bad Aachen. Bad means "spa" in German. The Elisenbrunnen is a 19th-century fountain people can still visit. But beware — the water is sulfurous and smells like rotten eggs! People are only supposed to drink the water with a doctor's prescription, but that doesn't stop visitors from trying.

Replicas of the Holy Roman Imperial regalia are still on display in Aachen's city hall. The actual regalia is now located in Vienna, but they resided for many years in Aachen because of its role in coronations. They include the crown, a Bible, and sword.

The Cathedral was built by Charlemagne and contains his burial place, though nobody knows the exact location he is buried within the building.

Inside is an octagon-shaped chapel built for Charlemagne. For centuries, Holy Roman Emperors were crowned here.

08

START HERE

In this chapter, we are going to travel through the Five Dynasties and Song dynasty period of Chinese history during the Middle Ages. The dynasties that rose and fell and the changes that they brought to the people of China during the time of the Five Dynasties tend to be somewhat confusing, so make sure that you take the time to discuss and take notes as you go. I truly hope you enjoy the beautiful scenery of the Chinese countryside and the rich colors of the culture as we travel through our story together.

Although God certainly has blessed the world with an abundantly rich array of talents and artistic ability, you will notice on our journey through this story that the Chinese culture of this time period was focused on power, prestige, and the worship of false gods and nature. I am reminded of Romans 1:25, which says, "They traded the truth about God for a lie. So they worshiped and served the things God created instead of the Creator himself, who is worthy of eternal praise! Amen" (NLT).

While kingdoms and empires rose and fell in the West, the civilizations of the rest of the world were also moving into the Middle Ages. Because it is impossible to learn about everything that happens simultaneously but in different places on earth, we have to do a little "continent-skipping." If you were to place your finger on your globe to mark the location in which the events of our last chapter took place, your finger would be pointing at Europe. If you were to turn the globe to the left a few inches, your finger would now be resting in Asia.

In this chapter, we will be taking a tour through the Chinese dynasties that ruled during the years between 907 and 1279. If you were with me in the first volume of this series, you might remember that we learned about the Tang dynasty, which led us up to the year 907. The Tang dynasty ruled China for several hundred successful years. In fact, this period of Chinese history was so prosperous and successful with inventions, arts, and culture that it is sometimes called China's Golden Age. It was during these years that a form of printing press was invented, which helped the Chinese book production to grow and flourish, and that the Chinese realized that gunpowder could be used in weapons. Chinese culture grew so much that it became a strong influence on the nations around it.

The time period after the Tang dynasty and before the next lasting dynasty is called the Five Dynasties period. This period, which was only 53 years in length, was a period of extreme political tumult in Chinese history. The first four of these dynasties were actually a series of rulers that were set up by force and rebellion but were quickly overthrown by the next insurgent ruler.

The whole series of turbulent events began when a rebel leader named Zhu Wen unseated the Tang ruler on the throne in the year 907 and established his own Hou Liang dynasty. Just a few years later, in 912, Zhu was murdered by his son, and his short-lived dynasty was overthrown by one of its generals, Li Cunxu (kun-SOO), who set himself up as the ruler of the next dynasty. This dynasty (the Hou Tang dynasty) lasted 13 years before it was toppled by a rebel general, Gaozu, who teamed up with the Khitan, a semi-nomadic people from Central Asia, to gain control of China. Gaozu established the Hou Jin dynasty, the next of the Five Dynasties, which lasted for ten years and ended when he failed to pay his tribute to the Khitan. As a result, he was

Cave painting from Mogao Cave shows Tang dynasty-style architecture

Thirteen Emperors Scroll. This noted scroll features 13 of China's emperors throughout history and dates back to the Tang dynasty.

kidnapped and carried away into captivity, ending his rule and, of course, his dynasty.

The next dynasty (the Hou Han dynasty) was established by one of Gaozu's former generals. This general established himself as emperor, took the throne, and pushed the Khitan back out of China. This dynasty lasted only four years before yet another rebel general usurped the throne and set up his own Hou Zhou dynasty. He helped China slowly progress toward a more stable government, but unfortunately, the emperor died, leaving the throne to an heir that was only a baby. Of course, you probably guessed what happened next — there was a rebel general, General Zhao Kuangyin, who seized the throne. He ended the Five Dynasties period and started his own Song dynasty, which lasted into the 13th century.

Although there was plenty of political upheaval during the 53 years of the Five Dynasties period, the art and culture continued to develop as it had in the Tang dynasty before it. This continued development of Chinese culture gives us a hint that the everyday life of the Chinese citizens must not have been too terribly affected by the continual changes of dynasties at the governmental level.

Chinese art and poetry also saw significant changes during these years. In the world of art, flower painting, which had previously been an exclusively Buddhist art form, became a part of the nonreligious painting styles and gained immense popularity. Also relatively new to Chinese culture was an interesting form of poetry called ci (Mote 2003, 21). This lyrical style of poetry had uneven lines and rhythms that were written specifically to accompany musical tunes (Mote 2003, 22). Ci poetry became very popular during this time in Chinese history (Mote 2003, 21).

NARRATION BREAK:

Talk about what you learned about ancient China.

CONNECT

In our last chapter, we learned that the Islamic scientific disciplines were much more advanced in their Golden Age than anything that was happening in Europe at the same time. Similarly, during this time period, the art of printing was much more advanced in China than in other places in the world. There is evidence that the Chinese had discovered the art of printing by the 2nd century. This is quite possibly true because China had discovered how to make paper and ink. The three basic ingredients needed for successful printing are paper, ink, and surfaces, which can be used to create relief carvings. In the early years of this primitive type of printing, the Chinese used marble pillars as their carving surfaces, but as the centuries passed, they learned how to use the wood blocking technique.

Wood block printing, which appeared first around the 6th century, was a more manageable type of printing. The first step was to write with ink on a piece of paper (Lechêne 2018). This paper was then applied face down to the surface of a smooth block of wood that had been coated with a rice paste to protect the ink (Lechêne 2018). Next, an engraver chiseled away all the non-inked areas, leaving only the reversed text standing out in relief (Lechêne 2018). This "stamp" was then brushed with ink (Lechêne 2018). Prints were made by pressing paper onto the block (Lechêne 2018). Think about how much work this would be and how long it would take to create one book! There are several surviving printed works created with this technique, from the 8th through 10th century. One of these is a collection of Chinese classics in 130 volumes that was begun in the year 932 (Lechêne 2018). Can you imagine how much time and effort this took?

The oldest known printed book in history is a Chinese copy of an Indian Buddhist text called *The Diamond Sutra*. It was discovered in 1900 and dates from the 800s.

It was in the year 960 that General Zhao Kuangyin — whom we learned about earlier in this chapter — started the Song dynasty. The general had gained control of the country when the previous emperor died and left an infant heir to rule. The Song dynasty period, as it was called, is usually divided into Bei (Northern) and Nan (Southern) Song periods. The Song dynasty ruled in South China only after the year 1127 (Department of Asian Art "Southern Song Dynasty," 2001).

General Zhao Kuangyin became the first emperor of the Bei Song dynasty, and because he was a master of diplomacy, he used his powers of persuasion (along with a bribe) to entice his would-be opponents to support him. China finally had a competent ruler who knew how to set up a steady administration. General Zhao established his rule in Northern China, then turned his eyes to expansion into the Ten Kingdoms in Southern China but died before he could act on his plan to expand.

After Zhao's death, the rulers who followed him ruled well, but over time their government weakened. You may remember a semi-nomadic tribe called the Khitan that I mentioned in the first part of this chapter. They were responsible for helping one of the rebel generals overthrow the existing dynasty in return for tribute. These Khitan and their kingdom (the Liao Kingdom) were overthrown by another tribe, called the Juchen. It was the Juchen who burst through the Northern Chinese border and conquered the Northern Song government in 1127. After establishing their own government, the Jin dynasty in the north, the Juchen tried to conquer the Song regions south of the Yangtze River but were unable to take ground. This was the beginning of the Nan (Southern) Song dynasty period.

Life during the Song dynasty was prosperous and economically and culturally successful. The use of paper money became more common, literature and the arts took enormous strides, and cities grew in population and wealth. Large cities flourished and grew (Mote 2003, 164–165). Schools, both state-funded and private, successfully trained students to do well in the Chinese civil service examinations. Commerce, philosophy, art, and poetry were embraced and highly regarded during this period of Chinese history. Art was so highly valued, in fact, that wealthy merchants took great honor in becoming a popular artist's sponsor or patron. Architecture and sculptures of this period also became more intricate and complex. The towering pagodas were hundreds of feet tall, with the tallest of them being 360 feet in height (Kuiper 2011, 278). The Song period's sculpture was mostly centered around representations of Buddha. He is the central figure of the false religion of Buddhism, which was a major religion in Chinese history. Buddhism incorrectly teaches that people can find relief from suffering and pain inside themselves. The Bible tells us, though, that pain and death exist because of sin and that the only way to overcome them is through Jesus.

It was in South China, in the year 1127, that the first emperor of the Nan Song dynasty established his rule. Lin'an, which is present-day Hangzhou, became the capital city of the new dynasty. Unlike the dynasties before them, the Nan Song dynasty did not fall because of revolt and rebellion from within; instead, it crumbled slowly because of outside pressure from the north. In the year 1211, the Mongols, led by Genghis Khan, attacked the Jin in North China and eventually toppled their rule. We'll learn more about the Mongols in another chapter. The Nan Song kept an uneasy eye on their new neighbors to the north, knowing instinctively that they would be the next target of attack. This attack came in 1250, when Genghis Khan's grandsons led their troops in a conflict that would last 29 years, ultimately ending in the fall of the Nan Song in 1279. China was now completely under the Mongol rule.

In a couple of chapters, we will learn the story of Genghis Khan and the Mongols and about the Yuan dynasty, which is what Mongol rule of China is called. One thing to remember as we study is that having a lot of change concerning who is in power causes political instability. It is difficult for people to live through this kind of turmoil, and it is hard on a country. However, God is ultimately in control. Despite everyone's scheming about who was going to be in charge next, God is the only one who decides who rules a country, and He is over everything that happens, regardless of who is on the thrones on earth. Even when bad rulers are on the throne of a country, God uses them as instruments to fulfill His plans.

NARRATION BREAK:

Discuss what you learned about the Song dynasty.

Song dynasty currency

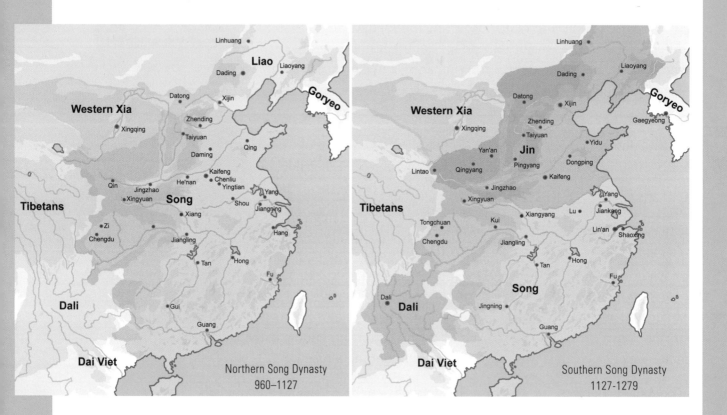

Northern Song Dynasty
960–1127

Southern Song Dynasty
1127-1279

The first map shows the expanse of the Northern Song Dynasty, which reigned over China from 960–1127. The other areas depicted on the map are the neighboring Western Xia and Liao empires.

The second map shows the extent of the Southern Song Dynasty, after a considerable amount of land was lost to invaders. On this map, the Jin is a reference to the Juchen, who had overthrown the Liao empire. The Dali kingdom, which is shown on the map, also sprang up at this time. Ultimately, they were all eventually conquered by the Mongols, whom we will study later.

The first Song capital was in Kaifeng. It was eventually moved to Lin'an (modern Hangzhou) during the Southern Song period.

| ANALYZE | Find the cities of Kaifeng and Lin'an on the second map. |
| CONNECT | How did the boundaries change on the two maps? |

MAPS

As Christianity spread and the Church grew, there were bound to be different opinions and interpretations of the Scriptures. You have probably noticed that people in the Early Church, just like the Church today, looked at issues from different angles and sometimes disagreed about various matters and theological differences. In some instances, groups of people who disagreed with each other would break away and start their own church.

In the Middle Ages, there were some Christians in Asia Minor and Syria who believed the teachings of a man named Nestorius. This man had been the bishop of Constantinople before he was condemned by the Church in 431 for teaching a view of the nature of Christ that was not agreed upon by other Christians (Appleyard 1850, 2).

By the end of the 5th century, the majority of the Nestorian Church, as they had begun to be called, had migrated to Persia, with several groups settling in China and India (Appleyard 1850, 3, 18). In the 6th century, the Nestorian Church survived a period of persecution, as well as disagreements within their group. By the time of the Arab conquest of Persia in 637, they were established enough to be recognized as a separate religious community by the ruling Caliphate and granted legal protection ("Nestorian" 2014). Under the protection of the Caliphate, the church prospered and became a prominent influence on the Arab culture for more than three hundred years ("Nestorian" 2014).

By the close of the 10th century, the church had grown and spread into Egypt, Central Asia, and even Eastern Siberia ("Nestorian" 2014). Indeed, during this time, the primary Christian church in Asia was the Nestorians. In 1551, a group of Nestorians were reunited with the Roman Church and were given the name Chaldeans. We will learn more about the Nestorian Christians and their influence on the world in a later chapter.

NESTORIUS.

KAIFENG

Kaifeng is no longer a capital of China, but it is still very proud of its history as one of the historic capitals of the country and as one of the important cities in the modern province of Henan.

China

All that is left of the imperial palace in Kaifeng is the Dragon Pavilion. The pavilion itself has been rebuilt numerous times due to it having been repeatedly destroyed.

Kaifeng's Imperial Street is a reproduction of a walkway the Chinese emperor would have used during the Song dynasty.

Kaifeng is on the bank of the Yellow River. A few hundred miles northwest of the city, the river forms the impressive Hukuo Waterfall. Kaifeng itself has been periodically destroyed by flood and rebuilt each time.

In addition to its history as an imperial capital, Kaifeng is also noted for having the oldest Jewish community in China. Here's a model of what their synagogue looked like. Jewish merchants settled in the city over 1,000 years ago. Though their synagogue and cultural traditions have long since died out, members of the community still preserve its memory. Kaifeng has long had a Muslim population, also descended from merchants long ago.

One of the city's most famous sites, the Iron Pagoda, is a relic of the Song Dynasty. The pagoda is not made of iron but is called that because the color looks like iron.

09

START HERE

Come with me as we continue our journey east, out of the massive country of China and into the smaller neighboring nations of Korea and Japan. In this chapter, we will find that both these countries' histories were greatly influenced by China. We will also discover how both Korea and Japan became their own unique cultural entities. Before you begin to study this chapter, make sure you have taken a few moments to see where we will be traveling; pause for a moment and study a map or a globe to locate both Korea and Japan. While you are looking, go ahead and compare the size of these two nations to the size of China. As we are studying this chapter, think about this question: How is it possible that a geographically tiny country can become a powerful nation? Throughout our study of history, you will discover that, many times, geographical size does not determine how powerful and influential a country becomes.

As we continue our journey, we will leave China. From there, it's a trip across the water to the Japanese archipelago. An archipelago (ar-kuh-PEL-a-go) is a stretch of water with a long line of islands. In this case, the islands make up the country of Japan. The four large islands, which make up the main part of the country, are surrounded by thousands of smaller islands. The Japanese Archipelago is so long that its northern end gets snow and below freezing temperatures in the winter while the southern end has mild, rainy winters, with the temperature staying in the 60s. As you can imagine, the plant and animal kingdoms are also extremely diverse because of this wide range of temperatures.

Ancient Japan was divided into many smaller tribes or clans. The Yamato clan became stronger and stronger, and within about 200 years, they had conquered the surrounding clans and had become the rulers of all Japan. Interestingly enough, this dynasty is still on the Japanese throne even now! Though other ruling families have been around a long time, the Japanese imperial family is the oldest to still currently sit on a throne. Becoming the rulers of all of Japan was difficult, but staying the rulers was even harder! They gained favor with their countrymen because they were excellent fighters.

The people of Japan worshiped many false gods and were given to many superstitions. Another way the Yamato clan came to power is by saying that they were descendants of these gods. They also told tales of how they had conquered evil gods to gain the favor of the good gods.

Once the Yamato were established, Japan became heavily influenced by Chinese culture through the two countries' neighbor, Korea. From about 57 to 668, Korean history is referred to as the Three Kingdom Period. It is called the Three Kingdom Period because there were three major kingdoms in Korea at that time. Before this time, Korea had been ruled by China, but the Koreans had rebelled and fought for their freedom. Even though they had won their independence, Korean culture was still heavily influenced by the Chinese. Most Koreans spoke and wrote in Chinese. Their religion had also been influenced by China, so many people observed the ways of Buddha.

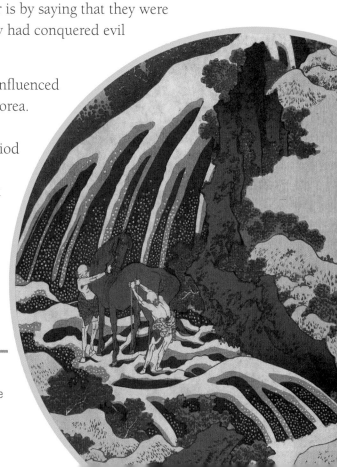

19th century woodblock print of a waterfall where the famous 12th century Japanese warrior Minamoto Yoshitsune is said to have washed his horse while in hiding.

Samurai armor. This set featured a mixture of pieces from different time periods, ranging from the 1500s-1800s.

Baekje (BIKE-shay), the Korean kingdom closest to the Sea of Japan, decided that they wanted to try to get Japan to be their friend. They had ulterior motives, though; they wanted help conquering the other two kingdoms of Korea. They sent presents to the Japanese emperor to try to impress him. The Japanese emperor was impressed with the gifts, especially a book written in Chinese. The Japanese wanted to know how to read this foreign language, so they requested that a tutor be sent to Japan.

The Korean teacher taught the emperor and his family how to read and write in Chinese and about Buddhism. Before long, many Japanese people were reading and writing in Chinese and following the false ways of Buddha. Chinese had become the language of the upper-class Japanese; only the common folk spoke Japanese. The Yamato emperors also borrowed ideas and methods of ruling from their neighbors in China. In this way, Korea and Japan were very much like China! They enjoyed the Chinese culture and ways of doing things so much that it was almost as though China had invaded and set up their rule. However, China still wanted to rule Korea and Japan completely.

China attacked Korea and wiped out the Baekje Kingdom in 660, and Japan, knowing they were probably next, sent in troops to help the Koreans. Japan didn't want to be Chinese, so after they helped the Korean kingdoms push the Chinese back, they became completely independent from China, including its culture. They no longer spoke the Chinese language, dressed in Chinese clothes, or used Chinese goods. They worked hard to become uniquely Japanese again. This was difficult because they had been doing everything the Chinese way for hundreds of years!

Japan is called the "Land of the Rising Sun," while China is called the "Land of the Setting Sun." Why do you think they are called this? Japan is to the east, where the sun rises, and China is to the west, where it sets. Both Japan and China thought of themselves as great nations, and both wanted to be the land of the sun.

NARRATION BREAK:

Discuss what you read today.

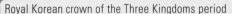

Portrait of Minamoto Yoritomo. In the 1100s, he established the shogun system that dominated Japanese society for centuries. The shoguns had substantial power in matters of peacekeeping, military power, and administration. Yoritomo's shogun system took power away from the emperors and allowed others to rule in their place but without overthrowing the imperial family.

Royal Korean crown of the Three Kingdoms period

The Japanese emperor was considered extremely important during this time and still is in Japan today. The emperor of Japan was not personally involved with running his country, however. He was more of a public figure, who lived in an elaborate palace and made public appearances. In reality, the power belonged to the daimyos (the lords).

You see, in many ways, Japan had a feudal system very similar to the one that existed in Europe in the Middle Ages. The king was at the top, with the daimyos (DIE-me-yo) (lords) and shoguns (generals) under him, and just like the European feudal system, the Japanese had knights. European knights fought for the lord of the castle or manor; Japanese knights, who were called samurai, fought for the daimyos, regents, and shoguns. The samurai developed as a group in the 1100s and quickly rose to prominence. As with Medieval Europe, the peasants were in the bottom of the class system in Japan, too.

As you might guess, the samurai had to go through a long training period, just like the European knights, whom we will learn more about in a later chapter. The samurai trained as soldiers, learning how to fight with and without weapons, but they were also expected to study poetry and other subjects that had nothing to do with fighting. These fierce warriors swore their allegiance to their lord and fought furiously to protect him and to conquer anyone that the lord wanted conquered. The samurai's clothing and armor were unique. Much like the knights in England, the samurai wore many layers of clothing, topped by rather elaborate armor, which was painted brightly in the colors of the lord's banner.

The samurai also had a strict code of conduct like the knights. This code, called bushido, dictated that the samurai behave with great honor and bravery. When they actually got down to the business of fighting, the samurai were fierce indeed! They could skillfully use two swords at once, and their skill with their other weapons drove fear deep into the hearts of their adversaries.

Life of a samurai was not altogether glamorous. Samurai were taught that there was nothing worse in the world than being shamed. So, if they were captured by their enemy (which they considered shameful), they were expected to kill themselves to save face. Because of the loyalty they were supposed to show to their leader, they

Japanese feudal system

Emperor: The emperor was a figurehead for the powerful shogun.

Shoguns and daimyos: A powerful military leader, the shogun ruled in the emperor's name. Daimyos were powerful lords who often led armies of samurai.

Samurai: Samurai warriors served the shogun and daimyos.

Peasants: Most Japanese were poor peasants who had no power.

Japanese helmets and swords that predate the time of the samurai

were also expected to kill themselves if he were killed. Their religion, Zen — a branch of Buddhism — ruled the samurai's lives with strict rules for life. Zen Buddhism falsely teaches people that they must look inside themselves for enlightenment; it also teaches that one needs to develop the discipline of the mind. This teaching became popular throughout Japan, but it is not biblical because it urges people to seek understanding outside of Scripture and God. At this time, Christianity had not yet reached Japan, and Japan's remoteness due to its island location isolated it from outside influences after the country decided it didn't want to follow Chinese customs anymore.

During this time, Japanese culture developed, and like the samurai way of life, it was heavily influenced by Zen Buddhism. Architecture and other arts became highly regulated forms. Buildings were designed to blend in with their natural environment and often had a distinct appearance, with the roof being a key focal point. Painting was a well-developed art form and a popular pastime for many people. The Japanese painting tradition, like many aspects of the culture, initially included a heavy Chinese

The traditional Japanese art of flower arrangement is called ikebana. Though arranging flowers is practiced in the West, ikebana is a complex art form, with several different styles, all involving their own specific rules.

Any type of tree can be used for bonsai—it is the techniques used to cultivate and care for it that makes it short, not the tree type itself.

influence. However, the country also developed its own unique style and traditions. Ink painting was a popular style. Music and theater also developed. One of the artistic traditions that Japan especially excelled in was ceramics. Japanese artisans created lovely ceramic pottery.

Many of the traditional art forms that developed during this time are still practiced in Japan today and have spread throughout the world. For instance, bonsai became a popular art form. This form of gardening focuses on small trees and their cultivation. Bonsai trees grow in pots and bowls like other plants but require special care. Another popular activity was the traditional tea ceremony. It took years of study to master the art of the ceremony. It involved serving green tea to guests, often with special ceramic dishes in small, specially designed tea rooms. Other traditional art forms that are still practiced in Japan included flower arranging and calligraphy.

NARRATION BREAK:

Talk about what you learned about Japan.

Utensils for the traditional Japanese tea ceremony include a kettle, containers to hold the green tea and water, and bamboo scoops. A special powdered green Japanese tea called matcha is always used for these ceremonies.

CONNECT

The study of language, called linguistics, is rather fascinating. In the ancient era of Japanese history, there was no written language to match their spoken one. It wasn't until the 700s that a form of writing called kanji was imported from China ("Kanji" 2017). Kanji does not have letters for spelling out words. Instead, like the Chinese writing system, it has characters that represent words ("Kanji" 2017). In this system, rather than spelling out the word "house," there would be a character that represented that word. Kanji was useful in writing the nouns, verbs, and adjectives of the Japanese language, but did not cover all the other types of words used in speaking ("Kanji" 2017).

To fill in the other parts of speech, the Japanese use kana, a writing system that they developed made up of two different syllabaries called katakana and hiragana. (A syllabary is a set of written characters that sometimes represents an alphabet. In Japanese, these writing systems allow people to spell words phonetically by showing sounds.)

Each of these syllabaries is used for a different purpose and is stylistically different from the other. Where katakana has an angular shape, hiragana is more like cursive ("Kana" 2016). Katakana is most often used to translate foreign words, as well as in children's books, billboards, emails, and text messages ("Kana" 2016). Hiragana is often used to make sure the word is in the correct tense, to show possession, or for other grammatical reasons ("Kana" 2016). If you were to read a typical passage of Japanese writing, you would find that it usually contains kanji, hiragana, and katakana ("Kana" 2016).

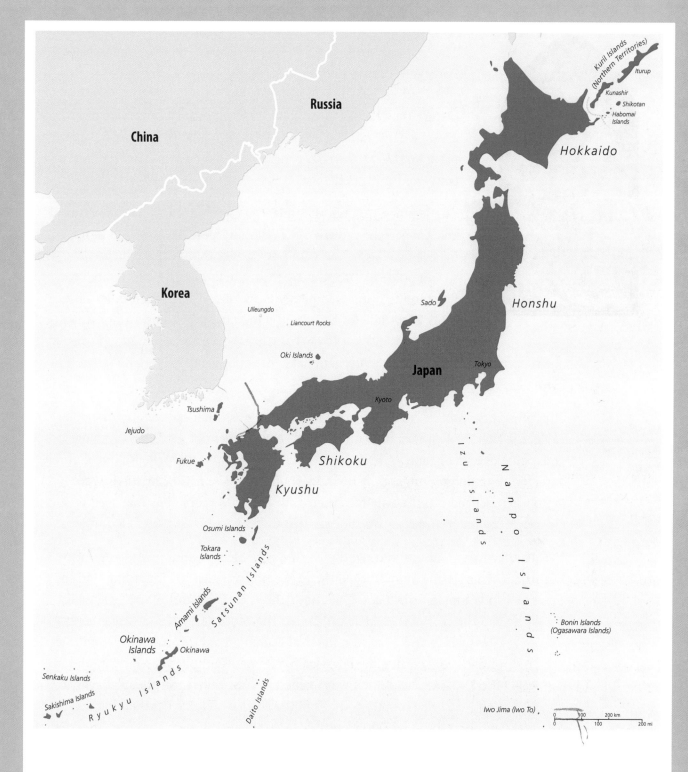

As this map shows, Japan and Korea are both close to China, as well as Russia. Japan consists of numerous islands. The northernmost island shown is Hokkaido (ho-KY-do). The island just below it is the largest — Honshu (hon-SHEW). That's where the modern capital of Tokyo (TO-kyo) is located, as well as the city of Kyoto (KEE-yo-to), which was the country's capital for much of its history. Close to Honshu to the south are the other two main islands, Shikoku (SHE-ko-kew) and Kyushu (KEE-yew-shew).

ANALYZE   Name four other island groups that are part of Japan.

CONNECT   Using the map scale at the bottom right, estimate how far Korea is from Kyushu.

CHURCH HISTORY

The title Kakure (also known as Kirishitan, which is taken from the Portuguese word, Cristáo, Christian) is directly related to the 16th- and 17th-century Japanese Christians — and what an interesting history they have! Christianity was first introduced to Japan in 1549, when Francis Xavier arrived with a large number of Christian missionaries. In the next century, up to a half million Japanese people converted to Christianity.

The Japanese ruler at the time, Oda Nobunaga, allowed and even encouraged the growth of Christianity because it helped him further his political agenda to gain power over Buddhism, which was a strong political force during this time in Japan. Christianity brought hope to the oppressed peasants and an all-important link to the European trade for the wealthy merchants. The next ruler, Toyotomi Hideyoshi, did not like what Christianity had brought to Japan, and he especially did not trust the international connections that this "new" religion had brought into his country.

In 1587, Hideyoshi demanded that all the foreign missionaries leave Japan, and a decade later, he followed up with a terrible enforcement of his demands. Nine missionaries and 17 native Christians lost their lives as martyrs. The Kakure Church was forced underground, and by the mid-1600s, there were no Christians who publicly practiced or acknowledged their faith. For 200 years, they managed to survive in secret, so much so that it was thought that there were no Christians left in Japan.

Kakure Kirishitans hid images of Jesus' mother in traditional Buddhist religious statues called kannons. The ones of Mary were called Maria Kannons. This mixing of Christianity with Eastern faiths was an unfortunate side effect of the isolation and persecution the hidden Christians of Japan lived in for centuries.

When they first went into hiding, the Kakure Kirishitan abandoned the use of Christian symbols and camouflaged their religious practices by including Buddhist and Shintoist practices. Over time, these symbols and practices actually became part of their religion, and as the centuries passed, the elements of Christianity and Eastern religions became mixed together. In the middle of the 19th century, the laws against Roman Catholics eased a bit, and in 1865, a Catholic church was opened in Nagasaki. Over the next year, 20,000 Kakure Christians stepped out of the shadows to profess their faith. Of this number, about 14,000 were able to establish a relationship with the Roman Catholic Church. However, it is interesting to note that there are still those who consider themselves to be "hidden" Christians; the mixture of pagan religious rituals and the secrecy once used to protect their ancestors have become a permanent and important part of their belief system (Kuhn 2015).

You have probably noticed the desire to protect ourselves is a major part of our human nature. The story of the Kakure Kirishitan is a sobering reminder that it is easy to want to camouflage our faith when we are faced with possible or impending persecution. Even if we are not facing physical persecution, we are each faced with this decision. It is important for you to understand that I am certainly not pointing a judgmental finger at these

Memorial in Nagasaki, Japan, to 26 Christian martyrs (both native believers and foreign missionaries) killed there in 1597. At the time, Nagasaki was well known for its Christian community. The martyrs' deaths touched off centuries of brutal persecutions of Christians.

people, but I do believe that we can learn a lesson from them. Because the Christian faith did not have much time to take root in their culture before facing persecution, the Kakure Kirishitan did not know or understand fully many of the deeper aspects of God's Word, and indeed, it is unclear whether they even had access to printed versions of the Bible (Cohen 2013, 23–24; Turnbull 1998, 21–22; Whelan 1996, 20–21). Let's take a closer look at how we can apply this lesson to our lives.

If you take a close look at what our current culture teaches about God, you will see many people who call themselves "Christians" yet do not actually follow what God's Word says (even though Bibles are readily available). Instead, they try to mix His Word with other teachings to make it more pleasant or easier to live out. There are even many church leaders who preach partial truths and do not mind picking and choosing verses to use in their "theology." Many of these leaders do not know the truth themselves and, therefore, cannot preach it, while others only want to make their congregations happy. It is easier than we think to hide than to trust.

We, my friend, all have to choose; we can either skim across the top of God's Word, only taking a few scant cupfuls, or we can dive in, drinking fully of the Living Word of God that will give us everything we need to stand firm. John 4:14 says, "But those who drink the water I give will never be thirsty again. It becomes a fresh, bubbling spring within them, giving them eternal life" (NLT). I can promise you this: The Word of God never fails.

There are going to be a million opportunities to camouflage your faith in order to fit in better with your peers or even escape persecution. We live in a world culture that is polar opposite of what God's Word tells us. I want to encourage you to read these Scriptures that pertain to this issue. Ephesians 6:10–20 speaks about the Armor of God. Ephesians 1:3–14 tells us about the amazing blessings that are ours through the sacrifice of Jesus Christ. Romans 8 tells us who we are in Christ Jesus. Galatians 5 teaches us about what we can do to remain free. And, finally, 2 Timothy 4 tells us to be prepared!

KYOTO

Kyoto was the capital of Japan for over 1,000 years before Tokyo became the capital in the 1800s.

Japan

The Imperial Palace complex at Kyoto is still standing.

The Nishiki Market is one of the most famous sites in Kyoto. This market is a popular place to buy traditional foods and ingredients. Japanese cuisine is well known across the world, and each area has its own specialty foods.

Kyoto still has many historic and old-style buildings because the city did not suffer the same heavy bombing that many other Japanese cities did during World War II.

Kyoto is also the home of numerous businesses. Perhaps the most famous is game manufacturer Nintendo. The company was started in the 1800s and only started making electronic games in the 1980s. It is still headquartered in Kyoto.

One of the most anticipated events every year in Japan is the blossoming of the cherry trees. Especially during that time, Japanese people enjoy spending time outside, admiring the flowers, and socializing with family and friends.

10

START HERE

You have probably noticed that throughout the study of history, there are varying degrees of history-changing (or history-making) people. Some of these history-changers are responsible for wonderful contributions to mankind while some are infamous because of their degree of terribleness. Still others brought wide-sweeping changes to entire cultures through conquest and raiding.

It is important for us to remember that although kings and rulers rise and fall, bringing blessing or disaster to their people, God is the ruler of all and will have the last say. Read what Psalm 22:27–28 says: "The whole earth will acknowledge the Lord and return to him. All the families of the nations will bow down before him. For royal power belongs to the Lord. He rules all the nations" (NLT).

In this chapter, we are going to become acquainted with a man who meets the criteria for being a history-changer. Genghis Khan became known in history as the Mongol leader who conquered a huge portion of the continent of Asia and even reached into Europe. His descendants also conquered and ruled vast areas, and the Mongol Empire greatly influenced the history of the world.

THE KHANS, GENGHIS AND KUBLAI

To the north of China, in a freezing-cold region with both mountains and plateaus, there lived a nomadic tribe of people called the Mongols. They lived in heavy felt tents and wandered the frozen land, eating animals that they killed when they stopped to sleep. The Mongol way of life and culture centered around fighting and strength training. Even from young ages, the boys were encouraged to develop battle skills and agility. They loved games involving horse-riding, archery, and wrestling. Mostly, the Mongols raided villages along the border. They robbed merchants and stole goods, but they did not usually venture deep into China. This all changed when a new leader named Genghis Khan (geen-gis KAWN) came along.

He was born in 1162 with the name Temüjin (ti-MOO-jen), the son of a tribal chieftain, though he experienced several years of poverty during his childhood after the death of his father. Temüjin quickly became a leader of his people and began working toward uniting the Mongols. The first step in Temüjin's plan was to conquer the other Mongol tribes so that he could be the one Mongol leader. After defeating other Mongol tribes, Temüjin would kill the leaders but incorporate the rest of the tribe into his own group. This brutal tactic ensured that there was no rival leader but that the people were loyal to him. Another way he gained loyalty was by promoting his most capable allies to positions of power rather than his own relatives. This broke with Mongol custom but guaranteed loyalty and competent rule. Soon, Temüjin was the leader of all his people. He then became known as Genghis Khan, which meant "universal ruler."

Next, Genghis Khan and his army of Mongols swept down from the north across the Chinese border, like a mighty wave of destruction. When they first attacked in 1209, they seized a kingdom in the northwest portion of the country. They burned and pillaged everything in their path, and within five years, Genghis and his army had conquered another kingdom in China, the Jins, and their capital of Zhongdu (modern-day Beijing).

Genghis then turned his attention toward the west. There rested the Khwarazmian (KAH-raz-mee-an) dynasty, a Muslim kingdom that had ruled Central Asia for about 150 years. Genghis and his army struck fear into the heart of everyone they came across. The Khwarazmian army didn't know how to handle these warriors. The Mongols so frightened people that many times the invaded

Depiction of Genghis Khan and his Mongol army

15th century depiction of the Mongol siege of Beijing

14th century illustration of Marco Polo's caravan to the East

people would lie down and give up without even a fight! Genghis Khan was an extremely battle-smart leader. With his well-trained, fast-moving, and completely ruthless army, he executed a series of amazing and outstanding campaigns.

The Mongols' empire spread, as did their terrible and fearful reputation. People were terrified of the Mongol army, with good reason. Genghis usually offered people the chance to surrender and pay him tribute, but if they resisted, the Mongols showed no mercy. It is estimated that millions of people were killed by the Mongol army. Genghis Khan was a brutal and violent man, but his reign was not all negative. He created a national mail delivery service and did not try to forcibly convert the people he conquered to his own pagan religion. The Mongols also gained a written alphabet for the first time under his rule.

Genghis Khan had made his terrible, sweeping rampage into China and Central Asia before his death in 1227, and his descendants enlarged the empire even more. They expanded into Eastern Europe, especially in what is now modern Russia, Poland, and Hungary. They also moved through the Middle East, conquering the Abbasid Caliphate and seizing their capital of Baghdad in 1258. Other rival Muslim caliphates ruled locally in places like Spain and Egypt, but general rule by a Muslim caliphate had ended for the time being. By 1260, the Mongol Empire had reached the end of its expansion.

The empire, which was the largest empire up to that time, stretched from the Yellow Sea in the east all the way to the Mediterranean Sea in the west. Once they stopped conquering, things calmed down, and the period became known as the Pax Mongolica, which means Mongolian peace. During this time, trade flourished. One of the most famous merchants to visit East Asia, including Mongolia, during this time was an Italian named Marco Polo. The stories of his travels fascinated people back in Europe.

Marco Polo knew and even worked for Genghis Khan's grandson, Kublai (KEW-bluh) Khan, who also expanded his control to all of China, making himself emperor. He and his army already occupied the modern-day city of Beijing, but he was not

This painting shows the Mongol Khan giving Marco Polo a letter of safe passage as he traveled back to Europe. This letter would serve as protection as Polo made his long journey.

satisfied with that. Kublai Khan pressed farther and farther south, conquering the Chinese cities and villages in his path. The Chinese fought back, using toxic gases to make deadly fogs, but the Mongols eventually overpowered them. After overcoming the Chinese, Kublai Khan set his gaze farther to the east. He sent a message to the Japanese emperor, demanding that Japan surrender and lay down their weapons. The Japanese adamantly refused to surrender without a fight and scoffed at Khan's demands. The Mongols were not used to this reaction to their threats.

The enraged Kublai Khan promptly commanded that a fleet of sturdy ships be built to attack the Japanese. The Mongols sailed for the Japanese islands, determined to beat them into submission. A strong wind commenced to blow, and soon the Mongol ships were being blown back toward China. The Mongols were stunned; they had marched through Korea and had easily conquered it, but this wind seemed almost supernatural! The superstitious Mongols decided to return to China, but many of their ships were sunk, drowning hundreds of soldiers.

Seven years later, the determined Mongols tried again to attack Japan. This time, they brought many more ships and thousands of more warriors. Again, they set sail for Japan. For the second time, strong winds and horrible storms — probably a hurricane — descended on the terrified men in their ships. This storm was even stronger than the first, and its strength was so incredible that many of the Mongol ships had no hope at all of survival. Thousands of Mongol warriors drowned, and their ships capsized. Once again, the Japanese were saved from the Mongols' invasion. Kublai Khan never did conquer Japan, but even so, he ruled the largest empire on earth for over 20 years.

Narration break:

Talk about Genghis Khan and the Mongols.

If you were with me in the first volume of this series, you will remember learning about how the Roman Empire swallowed up much of Europe and the Middle East, as well as parts of Asia and Africa. In fact, it was so far-reaching that its very size is what became part of its demise. In some ways, the Mongols were similar to the Romans. Like the Romans, the Mongols swept through much of the known world and conquered the peoples there, setting up their own government and rulers. Unlike the Romans, however, the Mongols were not savvy rulers, and the everyday administrative duties that governing takes were not their strong suit. Because of this, the occupying Mongols slowly but surely adopted the Chinese political and cultural models (Department of Asian Art "Yuan Dynasty," 2001).

This illustration of Kublai Khan hunting comes from a 15th century French edition of Marco Polo's popular book.

It was 1279 when the entirety of China finally fell to the Mongols, under the rule of Kublai Khan, grandson of Genghis Khan. For the first time, the Chinese people were not only Chinese, but they were also part of a much larger political entity, the Mongol empire. The Mongols were never completely embraced in China, and rebellions would eventually bring their dynasty to an end. This period in which the Mongols ruled China is called the Yuan dynasty period.

Wang Meng's *Wang Meng Writing Books under the Pine Trees* is a good example of the more personal artwork that developed and thrived during the Yuan dynasty. Meng's style was unique from earlier Chinese art and greatly emphasized the joy of solitary activities. He was more interested in capturing the atmosphere of solitude rather than creating a realistic depiction of a scene.

Let's explore how the Yuan dynasty period was different than the previous dynastic periods. We have learned that the previous dynasties, especially the Tang and Song dynasties, were productive and successful years for Chinese culture, art, poetry, architecture, sculpting, and literature. Printed books were much more common, thanks to a type of movable print printing press, and art was sponsored and encouraged at a government level. The artists of those periods were captivated by elements of nature and religion as their source of inspiration. Paintings of birds and sculptures of the Buddha were common, and the relationship between artisans and their wealthy sponsors was a valued one. This all changed when the Mongols took power.

The Mongols did not sponsor the arts like previous Chinese dynasties had. Because of this, the artisans and the literati, people who are interested and trained in literature and writing, became an ignored societal group. This shift in the Chinese culture moved the artists from a place of prominence and honor to a more hidden and less appreciated level in Chinese society. In turn, this caused the artists, who formerly found inspiration in trying to replicate nature around them, to turn inward for inspiration and expression. The artwork and style of this time were much more personally representative of the artists themselves. Also important to note were the changes in the pottery and ceramics industries of China during this time. In the porcelain world, an exquisite newcomer, blue-and-white ware, which was white porcelain with blue underglaze, made its appearance (Mote 2003, 513). This gorgeous porcelain ware is extremely popular among Western collectors even now (Mote 2003, 513).

Blue-and-white porcelain from the Ming period

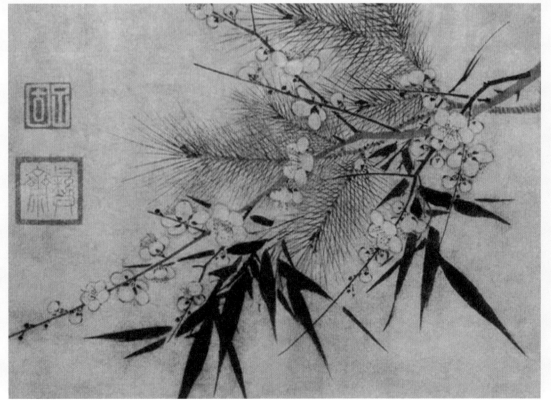

Zhao Mengjian's *Three Friends of Winter* is a good example of Song dynasty art. It focuses on 3 plants that are considered symbolic because they thrive during winter: pine, bamboo, and plum. Unlike during the Yuan dynasty, artwork created during earlier dynasties was dictated by strict rules. Painters were expected to follow conventions and imitate old masters rather than developing their own unique style.

CONNECT

Have you ever played the game "Marco Polo" in a swimming pool? Did you know it is named after a real person? Marco Polo was born in 1254 in Venice, Italy, the son of a merchant. His father was away when Marco was born, and he did not return until Marco was 15 years old. Marco Polo's father had spent many years working in Asia and had come home on a mission. The Mongol leader ruling China, Kublai Khan, had requested that a group of wise men come and tell him about Christianity. Marco was excited! Maybe his father, who had every intention of returning to China, would allow him to come with him.

Kublai ruled the Mongol Empire during the Pax Mongolica, the Mongol Peace. After all the years of turmoil and invasion, Kublai wanted things to be calm because that would help trade. He assigned his soldiers to guard the Silk Road because he wanted merchants and visitors to feel safe and welcome as they traveled. The Silk Road was hundreds of miles long, and it passed through mountains and deserts. Water was a precious commodity, only available at the widely scattered oases. Adventurous merchants and explorers who ventured this journey had to be sturdy, strong, and willing to be away from home for years at a time. It took at least three years to travel to the city of Beijing from Italy.

Early 20th century illustration of China during Marco Polo's time

Marco and his father set out on what would prove to be an extremely difficult journey. Marco became ill and had to rest for extended periods of time. It took Marco and his father 4 years for them to complete their journey. Marco stayed in China for a long time — nearly 20 years. Kublai Khan never did convert to Christianity, but he made Marco an official in his kingdom and gave him the job of settling disputes between Chinese officials. When Marco and his father finally returned home, their family members did not recognize them; they thought they had died long ago.

We know about the Polos' stay in China because Marco told all about it in his book, *The Travels of Marco Polo*, which he actually wrote when he was in jail! (Marco had become caught up in the political turmoil in Italy after his return.) Marco's book described, in great detail, the palace of Kublai Khan. His words would paint a picture of Asia for the people of Europe, so they could imagine the splendor of the Far East. Though some thought he was lying, others were inspired to travel and see for themselves. To this day, Marco Polo, his journeys, and his writings are still famous.

Eventually, Mongol rule began to collapse. Control fragmented between rival Mongol leaders, and the people they had conquered rebelled and overthrew them. China was no different. When the Mongols were driven out of China in 1368, a new dynasty was established by Zhu Yuanzhang, a native Chinese from humble beginnings. This new dynasty was called the Ming dynasty, and it would last well into the 17th century.

Although the Ming dynasty was a stable government, it is considered one of the most authoritarian dynasties in Chinese history (Lee and Chan 2016). That means that the ruler has all or most of the power and doesn't take others' feelings, opinions, or advice into consideration. This doesn't sound like a very good way to run a country, does it? There were some cultural changes for the better during the Ming dynasty, though. For example, the arts returned to a more honored place in society. Traditional drama, which had begun in the Song dynasty but had been outlawed by the Mongols, was restored in the Ming dynasty.

The Ming dynasty is marked by wars and struggles with the Mongols in the north and the Juchen in the northeast; both these neighbors tried to push their way into China with some success. The Ming were able to hold their boundaries at the Great Wall and spent much effort in fortification to maintain their safety. Eventually, bickering and discord within the governmental ranks had weakened the Ming from within, making them a target for invasion.

This invasion, which happened in 1644, actually came by invitation, when Ming military commanders asked for help from a neighboring tribe to the north to help fight off a rebel leader who was trying to usurp the throne. As we have seen before in history, this sort of invitation never ends well. Their neighbors, the Manchu tribe, had been pushing hard against China's northern border and were all too happy to help! When they were done smashing the rebellion, they stayed and established their own rule. This was the beginning of the Qing dynasty period.

NARRATION BREAK:

Discuss the Yuan dynasty.

RUSSIA

Golden Horde

KAZAKHSTAN

MONGOLIA

**Empire of the
Great Khan**
(Yuan Dynasty)

UKRAINE

MOLDOVA

UZBEKISTAN

KRYGYSTAN

TAJIKISTAN

Chaghadai Khanate

CHINA

GEORGIA

ARMENIA   AZERBAI

TURKMENISTAN

TURKEY

SYRIA

IRAN

AFGHANISTAN

Ilkhanate

IRAQ

JORDAN

PAKISTAN

NEPAL   BHUTAN

EGYPT

SAUDI
ARABIA

UNITED ARAB
EMIRATES

OMAN

BANGLADESH

MYANMAR
(BURMA)

INDIA

UDAN

DJIBOUT

YEMEN

LAOS

THAILAND

CAMBODIA

VIE

ETHIOPIA

→ Genghis Khan's invasions
→ Later Mongol invasions

MAPS

This map shows the Mongol Empire after it was divided following Kublai Khan's death. Nevertheless, it still depicts how vast the empire was, as well as invasion routes used by Genghis Khan and other Mongol leaders. The country boundaries on the map are modern and do not reflect the boundaries at the time.

ANALYZE	What do you notice about the expanse of the Mongol Empire during the time of Genghis Khan versus under later rulers? (Genghis Khan's invasions are marked with orange arrows while the others are shown with blue arrows.)
CONNECT	What are the names of the four divisions of the Mongol Empire?

We have learned that the Mongol Empire had a lasting influence on the world; now, I want to share with you how Christianity had a profound effect on this massive and influential empire. Back in the Church History section for Chapter 8, we learned about an Eastern church that history calls the Nestorian Church. This church, along with the Roman Catholic Church, was important to the culture of the mighty Mongol Empire during the 13th and 14th centuries (Shan 2011, 29). The Nestorian Church was absorbed into the Mongol Empire through military conquest as the Mongols invaded lands with longstanding Nestorian Christian populations, while the Roman Catholics were sent into the Mongol Empire as ambassadors and missionaries (Shan 2011, 29). The missionaries hoped that by converting the warlike Mongols, they could put an end to the brutal invasions threatening Christian populations throughout Asia and Europe (Shan 2011, 29).

Ultimately, the Mongol royal families became greatly influenced by this new religion, even if it did not transform their culture's emphasis on warfare and conquest. The Mongols were known for their openness to basically all religions, from Islam to Buddhism to Western Christianity to Nestorian Christianity (Shan 2011, 31). They also blended other religions with their own traditional shamanism (Shan 2011, 31), a belief system that encompassed everything in their lives and included worship of nature and ancestors. When Christianity came along, some of them mixed it into their stew of religion, but others took it seriously.

In the early 13th century, before the Catholic missionaries arrived in the Mongol Empire, Nestorian Christianity was popular and extremely influential in the royal families' lives. A number of conquered Nestorian Christian Turkic princesses married into the Mongol royal family (Shan 2011, 32). These women, who raised their children to be Christian, and a few Nestorian Christian men, serving in the high positions of the Mongol court, wielded great power in Mongol politics (Shan 2011, 32).

This painting shows Marco Polo and his brother passing a letter from the Khan to the pope, Gregory X.

There are numerous historical records from this time that show the Christian influence on Mongolian and Chinese cultures and politics. Interestingly, in most instances, these influences were due to upper-class women who influenced their families for generations (Shan 2011, 41). We have no way of knowing how pure these women's faith was, but we do know that their beliefs were passed down from generation to generation and, therefore, was preserved and spread.

MONGOLIA

Genghis Khan remains a highly respected figure in Mongolia. This statue of him stands east of the modern capital of Ulaanbaatar (ew-lan-BAH-ter). The country is modernizing, but traditional customs and ways of life remain popular.

Mongolia

Naadam (NAW-dum) is a yearly festival celebrated throughout Mongolia. It celebrates the traditional nomadic lifestyle, especially the sports of wrestling, horse racing, and archery. These archers are wearing traditional clothing.

The Gobi Desert covers an expansive part of Mongolia, as well as parts of China. Bactrian (two-humped) camels are native to Mongolia.

Horses have long been important to Mongolian culture. In fact, there are more horses than people in Mongolia. Most Mongolians first learn to ride as toddlers, and horses remain the most important animal owned by the nomads in the country. Mongolians also drink horse milk and eat horse meat.

About one-third of Mongolians are still nomadic. Here is a family in front of their ger, the traditional portable home they live in. Gers are often also called yurts outside of Mongolia. Genghis Khan and his warriors lived in gers. Even Mongolians who live in cities often still prefer living in a ger.

Ger interior

11

START HERE

As we have studied our way through our previous chapters, I hope you have noticed the variety of distinctive cultures that we have explored. I want to take a moment to make sure that you understand the difference between culture and religion. Although most of the time, cultures and religion are intertwined, they are not interchangeable. For example, if the people in a specific culture wear a certain style of clothing or shoes that have nothing to do with ungodly, sinful practices of a culture, God doesn't have an opinion about it. However, if the culture promotes or dictates sinful practices that influence clothing styles that go against what God says is good, this does matter to Him.

In this chapter, we are going to be traveling into India, an almost diamond-shaped country, which is bordered mostly by the Great Himalayan Mountains and the Indus River at the northern edges and two great bodies of water on the southern edges. As with any country, its location and topography played an important role in India's history. In this chapter, we will learn about two of the major dynasties that ruled India during the Middle Ages.

THE GUPTA & MUGHAL DYNASTIES OF INDIA

In this chapter, we are going to shift our gaze to South Asia, specifically to the country of India. India's natural northern border is made up of the Indus River, running along its northwestern edge (the land surrounding this river is now the country of Pakistan), and the Himalayan Mountain range and the Ganges (GANJ-eez) River, along the northeastern edge. These natural barriers protected India from many of the invasions that the rest of Europe and Asia were enduring throughout these centuries.

The land of India is vast, with a multitude of various terrains. The Himalayan Mountains and Ganges River in the north create a lush environment for an extensive variety of animals and plants. This habitat ends rather abruptly when you leave the Ganges River area and travel either south or west. This is the Thar Desert, and as you would expect a desert to be, it is hot and sandy.

In their ancient days, the people of this civilization first came to be farmers and merchants along the banks of the Indus River. They eventually became known as the Indus River Valley Civilization and had quite an impact on the world of art, architecture, and pottery before eventually collapsing. If you were with me for Volume 1, you might remember reading about this civilization.

During the ancient days, the people of India lived scattered here and there. The mountains, rivers, and deserts made it easy to have separate kingdoms and tribes all living independently from each other, each with their own kings. Although the people of India were separated geographically, most followed the false religions of Hinduism or Buddhism. We are not going to do an in-depth study on these religions; it is important to remember that they worship false gods and that their followers need to hear about Jesus, the same as everyone else.

Around the year 319, a king of a small kingdom near the Ganges River decided that he would like to unite all the kingdoms of the northern part of India. King Chandragupta (CHAWN-dru-GOOP-tuh) began to conquer little kingdoms near his. Chandragupta's son, Samudragupta (SAW-moo-dru-GOOP-tuh), and his grandson, Chandragupta II, both conquered more and more kingdoms until they ruled all northern India. We call this the Gupta Empire.

Illustrated scene from the *Mahabharata*, one of the classic poems of Indian literature.

Under the Gupta Empire, India flourished and prospered. Art, poetry, and literature made significant advances. Sculptors created amazing works of art from iron and copper, and scholars wrote books about mathematics and astronomy. Medical advances were also plentiful during the Gupta Empire. The lands under Gupta control were united, peaceful, and rich. They also felt safe, with their strong, well-trained army.

During the 400s, a people called the Hephthalites (HEP-thah-light) flooded over the northern border of India and attacked the Gupta Empire. It is not quite clear who these people were. Some have argued they were the same as the Huns of Central Asia who threatened Rome, but others say they are a different group entirely. Regardless of who the Hephthalites were, King Skandagupta (SKAWN-du-GOOP-tuh) united the armies of India to stop the attack. When they were able to withstand the Hephthalites, the people of India gave their king the credit for unifying their forces against the invaders.

Hephthalites were not just a threat to India. As this painting shows, they also represented a threat to what is now modern Iran. In this painting, Iranian leader Sukhra defeats the Hephthalites.

The invasion had weakened the Gupta Empire, however, and little by little, small sections of the kingdom broke away and became independent again. By about 500, the Hephthalites had overrun Gupta land, and the Gupta Empire was a shell of its former self. Within a few decades, Hephthalite rule had been overthrown in India, but the Gupta Empire and its Golden Age had come to an end.

In its wake, several regional kingdoms developed. For example, much of western India came under the control of the Rashtrakuta dynasty while much of northern India was ruled by the Gurjara-Pratihara dynasty. Part of eastern India was now controlled by the Pala dynasty, and the Chola dynasty was over much of the southern portion of the country. There were many other smaller kingdoms in the land, so India was fragmented between many local rulers. Next time, we'll learn about how that made the country vulnerable to invaders.

NARRATION BREAK:

Discuss the Gupta Empire.

Most of the regional kingdoms in India during this time were Hindu or Buddhist, but they were not able to work together to ward off other invaders. For centuries, India had successfully repelled most foreign invaders. This all changed in the 1200s. Much of the land north of India had become Muslim centuries earlier and had been ruled by the various Muslim caliphates. Muslims had led periodic raids into India for plunder, but these military actions were never intended as permanent invasions. That would change when the Abbasid Caliphate collapsed after being conquered by the Mongols.

The result was chaos. Another result was that mamluks, Muslim soldier slaves, started to gain power. The Abbasid Caliphate had relied heavily on these well-trained, effective soldiers, many of whom were Turkic people from Central Asia. After the demise of the Abbasid Caliphates, mamluks began to seize power for themselves. Mamluk dynasties came to power throughout the Middle East, including in Egypt. Their interest in India also increased, and the northern part of the country was invaded and came under mamluk control. This time period in Indian history is called the Delhi Sultanate since the mamluk rulers proclaimed themselves sultans (kings), and they eventually made the city of Delhi their capital. There had been Muslims living in India before this, but this development caused more Indians to be Muslim and ensured that Islamic cultural influences became a part of Indian culture.

The Delhi Sultanate brought changes to India, but it also may have protected India from the Mongols, who still tried to invade. The Mongols were fearsome, excellent soldiers, and their skill on horseback made them an especially effective military at this time when many other nations did not have good cavalries. The mamluks, however, were also skilled, experienced soldiers and excellent riders. Even though the Delhi Sultanate withstood the attempted Mongol invasion, they benefited from the Pax Mongolica once things settled down. As we learned in the last chapter, once the Mongols controlled the Silk Road, traders benefited from the safety. Trade along the Silk Road, as well as by sea, helped make the Indian kingdoms wealthy and powerful.

Bābur and his men fighting at Panipat in 1526. Though his opponents were on elephants and his own men were on much smaller horses, Bābur's forces had more advanced weapons.

This 16th century painting shows further Mughal advances through India under Akbar, Bābur's grandson. Here, the Mughals are defeating Hemu, a Hindu man who claimed the throne.

Though India withstood the Mongols when they were conquering much of Asia, India eventually fell under the control of a leader of Mongol heritage, though he considered himself a Turk. Bābur was a descendant of the Mongol conqueror Genghis Khan. He was also descended from another Central Asian conqueror named Timur, or Tamerlane. Like his ancestors, Bābur was a skilled military leader. Though Bābur was of Mongol descent, he considered himself a Turk because his people had long lived with Turkic peoples in what is now Uzbekistan. Their culture was heavily influenced by Persia, as well. His language of choice was Persian, and his religion was Islam.

Bābur started his conquests closer to home, moving through what is now Pakistan and Afghanistan first. He raided India several times, but he did not launch a full invasion until 1525. With his strong army of fast and furious warriors, Bābur attacked the Delhi Sultanate. The sultan of Delhi was not concerned, though. After all, his army outnumbered Bābur's army ten to one! The sultan also had war elephants, which were commonly used at this time, and his soldiers were armed with spears, bows, and swords.

Bābur may have been outnumbered, but his army was made up of well-trained veterans, many of them on horseback. He also had modern muskets and artillery, and his men on horseback had better maneuverability than the sultan's men who were riding elephants. The artillery especially caused the elephants to panic. In the end, Bābur and his army conquered the Delhi Sultanate, and he named himself the new sultan in 1526. The surrounding kingdoms quaked in fear because they knew they were next. Bābur expanded his domain to include much of northern India, but he died in 1530, so it was up to his descendants to manage the empire he had created. They were called the Mughal dynasty because Bābur was a descendant of Genghis Khan the Mongol.

Like the Delhi Sultanate, the Mughals did not control all of India, but they expanded farther south than their predecessors. They made a significant impact on the country and culture. Bābur's descendants reorganized the administration of the empire and proved themselves to be especially skilled in that regard. The Mughals themselves were Muslim, but the early Mughal rulers tried to integrate Muslims and Hindus together. Art and architecture also flourished during this time. The official language of the Mughal Empire was Persian, and much poetry of this time was written in that language. Persian was eventually replaced as the language of choice by Urdu, a form of Hindi (a native language of India) written in Persian script, and poetry in that language flourished, too.

NARRATION BREAK:

Discuss what you read today.

CONNECT

The Taj Mahal, one of the most beautiful structures in all of India, was built on the orders of a heartbroken husband for his beloved wife, who had passed away during childbirth in 1631. The husband, the Mughal emperor Shah Jahan, wanted an elaborate castle-like mausoleum with its own mosque and elaborately landscaped gardens and pools to commemorate her. This elaborate structure is surrounded by a 42-acre complex. It took 20,000 workers hired from India, Persia, Europe, and the Ottoman Empire a span of approximately 20 years to complete all the gates, buildings, gardens, and pools in this complex (History.com "Taj Mahal" 2011).

Widely considered a masterpiece of Mughal architecture (which combined Indian, Persian, and Islamic styles), the Taj Mahal is made of white marble, which reflects the changing colors of the sky (History.com "Taj Mahal" 2011). The building is designed with four facades, each almost identical to the others and each with an arch that is 108 feet at its highest point ("Taj Mahal" 2018). The ornate central dome is an impressive 240 feet ("Taj Mahal" 2018).

If you were to visit the Taj Mahal complex, you would undoubtedly notice two features repeated throughout the design of all the buildings and gates. These decorative features are quite intricate and add touches of color to the white marble of the Taj Mahal and the reddish sandstone of the mosque and gates. First, there is an inlay of beautiful, semiprecious stones arranged in intricate designs on many of the walls. These floral and geometric designs of stones add bright color to the white marble ("Taj Mahal" 2018). The second design feature you would see is the writing on the walls. This writing is designed to be visible and readable even for visitors at a distance on the ground ("Taj Mahal" 2018). There are many walls in the complex that have large sections of the Quran inscribed in calligraphy ("Taj Mahal" 2018).

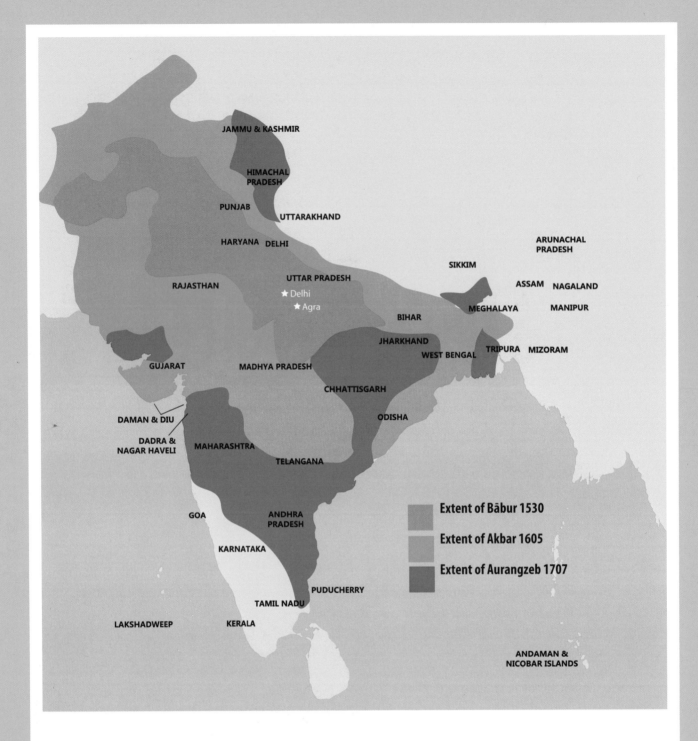

This map shows how the Mughal Empire expanded under Bābur's successors. At its peak, the Mughals ruled most of modern India, as well as Pakistan and parts of Afghanistan. Akbar was Bābur's grandson. Aurangzeb (AR-ung-zeb) was Akbar's great-grandson. Under him, the empire reached its height. His son, in turn, was the last ruler in the family. The Mughal Empire continued after his death, but it was weakened and ended in the 1800s.

ANALYZE | Based on the map, how much of India did the Mughals control by 1707? How does this compare with the amount of land the Mughals controlled in earlier periods?

CONNECT | How many years were between the extent of Bābur and the extent of Aurangzeb? (Hint: Look at the map key.)

In John 20:24–29, we read the story of the Apostle named Thomas. This man was one of the 12 disciples of Christ while He was here on earth in human flesh. In these verses, Thomas had missed the first time Jesus showed Himself to His disciples after His resurrection, and he doesn't take their word for it when they share the amazing news. Jesus, knowing the doubt in Thomas' heart, appears again to His disciples and instructs Thomas to touch the scars made from the crucifixion. Thomas then knows that this is Jesus and proclaims, "My Lord and my God!" (John 20:28). Thomas would continue to proclaim the name of Jesus for the rest of his life.

CHURCH HISTORY

After the Holy Spirit came and descended upon the Apostles in the upper room, they went out to spread the good news of the gospel to all who would listen. Thomas went to India to be a missionary for Christ. The good news was gladly embraced by many in India, and thousands were added to the Church and to the Kingdom of heaven. This spreading of the gospel was met with great hatred by the pagan priests who had formerly had great influence and control over the Indian culture. Thomas was eventually martyred for his faith in Christ, but the Thomas Christians of India lived on and continued to spread the good news of the gospel.

Even today, Thomas Christians number several million in the Indian state of Kerala (approximately 20% of the population in that area) (Zacharia 2016). The disciple who doubted had become one of the most faithful servants of Christ. This can be a lesson to each of us. Jesus knows and can handle our doubts. His grace is big enough to cover it all. We need never feel like we cannot come to Him with all of our concerns or fears. Psalm 62:8 says:

> Trust in Him at all times, you people;
> Pour out your heart before Him;
> God is a refuge for us.

Open air crosses are common in the Thomas Christian churches in India.

Agra

Taj Mahal as viewed from the city of Agra. Though Agra is no longer the capital of India, it remains a popular tourist destination due to its history as the Mughal capital.

India

Though the Taj Mahal remains the city's most popular site, Agra Fort was where the Mughal emperors lived for many decades. This photograph shows one of the balconies.

The royal tombs inside the Taj Mahal

India is well known for its unique, delicious cuisine. Each region has its own specialty, but meals are often served on a thali (a large platter holding smaller bowls of food). People help themselves and usually eat the food in a set order. The platter below includes traditional Northern Indian favorites like lentil dishes, curries, vegetables, buttermilk, and breads.

The Mughals enjoyed planting Persian-style gardens. This was one of many ways that the Mughal culture was heavily influenced by Persian culture. One of the most famous of these gardens is the Mehtab Bagh, which the Taj Mahal overlooks.

Agra actually features numerous Mughal-era tombs, including that of Akbar, Bābur's grandson.

12

START HERE

When you hear the word "Viking," you might imagine burly men with horned helmets and round shields who went raiding and pillaging wherever they felt like it, and you would be mostly right (minus the horned helmets!) — but there is much more to their story! In this section of our story, we will discover that the Vikings made an immense impact on the culture of Europe, an impact that is still felt today. As we work through this chapter and learn about these notoriously ruthless people, I want you to remember that God can reach any people group and save the lost. The call of the gospel can penetrate the darkest of cultural practices. This reminds me of one of my favorite verses, Psalm 43:3:

Oh, send out Your light and Your truth!
Let them lead me;
Let them bring me to Your holy hill
And to Your tabernacle.

THE VIKINGS AND THEIR ESCAPADES

We have spent several chapters looking at what was happening in Asia, including the famous conquerors like Genghis Khan. But there were other conquerors who also posed a threat to people during the Middle Ages. Europeans feared them just as much as people were afraid of Genghis Khan and his terrifying Mongols — they were from the kingdoms of Norway, Sweden, and Denmark and were North-men or Norsemen. Our name for these people comes from their own word for raiding adventures. When they were about to go out for one of their raids on one of their neighbors, they said they were "fara í viking" ("go[ing] on a Viking") (Online Etymology Dictionary n.d.). Soon, this name for their raids is what they themselves were commonly called.

The Vikings started venturing farther away from their lands in the north during the 700s because they were in search of better farmlands, which is how they spent their time when they were at home. These men were excellent boat and ship makers, and they made special ships called longships that were designed to ride through shallow water. These Viking ships are still admired worldwide for their uniqueness and versatility.

The Vikings had an enormous impact on the future of huge areas of Northern Europe. They were responsible for establishing trade routes, founding towns, and greatly influencing the cultures and trades of Britain, France, Poland, and even Ireland. So, whether by invasion or by settling, the Vikings left their mark all over Europe. Swedish Vikings ranged into Russia and Eastern Europe, while the Norwegian Vikings settled in the Orkney and Faroe Islands north of Scotland and invaded Ireland. The Vikings invaded countries all along the Mediterranean Sea coast, including Spain, Italy, and Sicily, but when they attacked Constantinople and the Byzantine Empire, they soon found they were no match for the well-trained armies there.

The Vikings could not conquer Charlemagne's empire, but in 911, the king of France gave the Vikings land in northern France to settle. He thought if he gave them their own land, maybe they would stop their looting and pillaging. Soon, those Vikings were calling themselves "Normans," which meant "Northmen." Their land the king gave them was called Normandy, and this part of France still has that name today.

King Alfred's ships battle the Vikings, 897. Alfred fought the Vikings on both land and water.

Leif Erikson

If you have read *America's Story Volume 1,* you might remember the story of a Norwegian Viking named Erik and his son, Leif. Erik, who was called "Erik the Red" because of his wild, bright red hair and wild, crazy temper, was forced to leave his home in Iceland (most of which, ironically, is very green!) and move to Greenland. Greenland is mostly covered in ice, except for a narrow strip along the coastline. It is his son Leif who is credited with being the first European to discover the continent of North America around the year 1000. Even though the account of this discovery was not widely believed until almost 500 years later, the tale of this new land was passed down through legends told around the Vikings' fires.

The Vikings also had a significant impact on England. Earlier in this book, we learned about Britain and how the pagan Anglo-Saxons from what is now Germany and Denmark had invaded and conquered much of the land after the Romans left. Over the years, the Anglo-Saxons had settled down, converted to Christianity, and now controlled and lived in almost all of England. When Vikings from Denmark arrived in Britain, the Anglo-Saxons were terrified! Viking raids of England started in the 790s, but they launched an invasion of England in 865 led by a family of brothers after their father had been killed while on a raid in England. Their names included Halfdan and Ivar the Boneless; apparently, they were extremely tall and thin. Word of how ruthless the Vikings were had spread far and wide, and accounts of the pillaging and plundering struck fear in the hearts of even the toughest, strongest people.

Carl Rasmussen's *Summer in the Greenland coast circa year 1000,* 19th century painting. This painting shows a Viking longship.

At this time in Britain, there was not a strong king on the throne ruling everyone. Britain had been divided into seven smaller Anglo-Saxon kingdoms. When the Vikings swept into Britain, they burned everything they came across. They were not Christians, and they had no respect for the Church, so they pillaged and plundered the monasteries. They stole the images, ornate fixtures, and precious metal and wood from the churches.

Once the Danish Vikings settled into their new home after conquering large sections of Britain, they invited relatives and friends back home in Scandinavia to settle near them. Swarms of Danish Vikings answered this invitation, and soon all central England was under Viking control. This area became known as the Danelaw because it was under a Danish legal system rather than an Anglo-Saxon one. The original Anglo-Saxon people still lived there, too, but the leaders were all Danish Vikings.

NARRATION BREAK:

Talk about what you learned about the Vikings.

Vikings have captured the imaginations of artists and storytellers for centuries. Sometimes, artistic depictions of people and events overshadow reality. For many people, Vikings have horned helmets, as in this depiction. However, that image of Viking comes from the 1800s and not from what Vikings actually wore.

Viking longship

19th century sketch of the *Domesday Book.* William the Conqueror ordered a survey of England in 1085-1086. He compiled lists of landowners and resources in the *Domesday Book,* which is the best record of life in early Norman England.

Now that they controlled so much of England, the Danish Viking leaders decided to go down into southern England. Why not try to rule all of Britain? They sent one of their mightiest commanders to invade Wessex, the southernmost kingdom in England, in 871. The people of Wessex tried to pay the Viking invaders off, but that plan did not work well. The citizens of Wessex concluded that they needed to have a strong leader who could stand against the Viking commander, Guthrum. They chose a brave nobleman named Alfred.

Statue of King Alfred in Winchester

Alfred hid from the invading Guthrum and his army to gather an army and enough supplies to defend Wessex. They met the Viking army and defeated them at the Battle of Edington in 878. Thus, the Viking run of victory through England ended. They returned north and left the Wessex citizens alone. Alfred became known as Alfred the Great. After Alfred's death, however, the English kept having to fight off the Vikings. Things went well for a while. Alfred's son, Edward, was a powerful ruler who re-conquered some of the areas north of Wessex and defeated the Vikings. However, the kings who followed were weak and unable to defend England.

In the year 1013, one of Alfred's descendants, Ethelred, was defeated by the Danish Viking king living in England. By 1016, England was ruled by a Danish king named Canute. After that, the Danish Vikings ruled England. The Danish Vikings and the English lived side by side, married each other, and accepted each other's traditions. Around this same time, many of the Danish Vikings began converting to Christianity. When Canute's sons died, Ethelred's son Edward the Confessor became king. Life went along until a ruler had to be chosen to follow King Edward the Confessor because he had no heir. Of course, there was a great argument about who should become the next ruler of England. Most people wanted a nobleman who was from Wessex, like Alfred the Great. One nobleman from Wessex, Harold, was a good leader, and it seemed that he was the most logical choice.

However, as is the case most of the time in situations like this, someone else thought that they could do a better job and that they were the true heir to the throne. Edward the Confessor had a distant cousin who believed he had been promised that he would be the next king of England. William was not an Englishman. In fact, William was actually a Viking. Do you remember how we learned earlier in this chapter about Normandy and the Normans? William was a Norman.

There are varying accounts of what happened next, but we do know that there was a huge battle, the Battle of Hastings, which became one of the most famous battles in the history of England.

CONNECT

One of the most important legacies the Normans left for England (and, by extension, America) were the thousands of French words that are now part of the English language. Remember, even though ordinary people still spoke English, the Normans ruled England for hundreds of years while speaking French. Technically, their French was not purely French. Due to their own Viking heritage, the Normans spoke a unique form of French that is often called Norman French (or Anglo-French) (Stockwell and Minkova 2001, 36). Still, their words had an important impact on English vocabulary, especially in relation to fields like art, government, and food (Gramley and Pätzold 2004, 29).

At the West Stow Anglo-Saxon Village in England, people can see what an English village would have looked like before the Norman invasion.

Why do you think that is?

Because the Normans were nobles who did not have to work in the fields, they had the free time to devote to art, far more than an English peasant of the time. Likewise, because the Normans ruled the country, they had more of a need for words about government than ordinary Englishmen and women. These differences in their daily lives does much to explain why certain English words are of Norman origin.

Perhaps the most noticeable difference between the words the Normans used and the English peasants used is in food. In English, the words for animals are often in English (pig, cow, sheep, deer), but the words for them as food are usually from French (pork, beef, veal, venison) (Liberman 2009, 153). This distinction is often seen as reflecting the difference in how the English-speaking peasants would have interacted with these animals (by tending to them as livestock) versus how the French-speaking nobles would have (by eating them in a fancy feast) (Orsi 2015, 49–50).

Bayeux Tapestry. A tapestry is an elaborate woven canvas, often hung on a wall like a painting. This particular tapestry famously depicts the Norman Conquest of England from the Norman point of view.

The Battle of Hastings ended with the death of Harold Godwinson and the invasion of the Normans. Another people group now moved into England, bringing with them their own customs and culture.

The English living in the land spoke an early form of English and mostly lived on farms or in small villages with large commons in the center. These commons were large, grassy areas where everyone kept their livestock. This is the way the English had lived for many years, but after the Normans invaded and William, who became known as William the Conqueror, was king, life changed in England.

The Normans spoke French and had their own distinct culture. In their eyes, since they now ruled the land, they owned it — all of it. William concluded that he had the right to take the land and divide it among his generals and lords. Do you remember learning about the feudal system in Chapter 2? This is what the Normans practiced. William the Conqueror and the Normans owned large areas of seized land (or in some cases, they only governed land owned by the king), and they had many, many people working for them. The farmers, merchants, and villagers not only worked for these lords, but they also paid heavy taxes to fund building projects that the king or the lord wanted completed. In return, they were under the protection of the lord they served. These people were called serfs, and they were at the mercy of the king and the temperament of the lord.

England was not the only country who had to deal with the Normans. In 1169, a dispute over who ruled Ireland led one person claiming the throne, Dermot, to ask the Normans for help. The Earl of Pembroke, a Norman who lived in England, saw this as a great opportunity to gain control in Ireland, so he agreed to help Dermot in exchange for his daughter's hand in marriage and the region of Leinster. This Earl of Pembroke, whose name was Richard de Claire, was also known as "Strongbow." He asked his Norman lord friends to come with him on an invasion of Ireland. The Norman nobles invaded Ireland, seizing land all over the country for themselves.

On the throne of England then was Henry II. He was also a Norman and one of William the Conqueror's descendants. He had received permission from the pope to invade Ireland years earlier, and Henry II decided to act on it in 1171. King Henry II had a large, strong army, so the Norman lords in Ireland laid down their arms and submitted to the king's demands. The Norman lords settled down to farm, lived off the fertile land, and extensively intermarried with the Irish. Ireland would remain under English control for approximately 800 years.

NARRATION BREAK:

Talk about what you read about the Normans.

This family tree shows Henry II's children. We will learn more about his sons Richard the Lionheart (3rd from the left) and John Lackland (far right) in a later chapter.

Silver Viking ingot. An ingot is a block of a metal that will be finished at a later time. Making metal into an ingot ensures the metal is easier to transport and store before it is processed further. These artifacts of Viking life have been discovered in several places across Europe where Vikings lived. This was discovered in England in what would have been the Danelaw area that the Vikings established and resided in. Another relic of Viking life in England is place names. Many towns and villages in eastern England have names with Viking origins. For instance, the city of York is of Viking origin, from the name Jorvik. Before the Vikings invaded, it was called the Latin name Eboracum (eb-o-RAY-kum).

As this map shows, the Vikings ranged far and wide in their travels and conquests. Their settlements branched out from their native Scandinavia to the British Isles, modern-day Russia, and France, as well as the distant island nations of Greenland and Iceland and even parts of Italy and North Africa. However, the Vikings conducted raids on many more locations.

ANALYZE   The map shows the areas the Vikings conquered. What parts of Europe were they most active in?

CONNECT   Which geographical areas did the Vikings mostly travel to — coastal or inland?

Thomas Becket did not want to take the job for which he was being nominated, but his friend, Henry II of England, insisted that he should become the archbishop of Canterbury. Even though Thomas did what Henry asked, he was certain it would not work out: "I am certain that if . . . it were to so happen the love and favor you now bear towards me would speedily turn into bitterest hatred" (Graves "Henry's Love for Becket Became Hatred" 2010). The two men had been friends for years, so Henry II thought nothing of what Thomas Becket said to him.

Thomas had been chancellor, and as such, he had lived a life of prestige, fancy clothing, and great wealth. He had worked hard to further King Henry's agendas, and his work had paid off because he had taken his job and position very seriously. Now as the Archbishop of Canterbury, Thomas lived a pure, devout, studious, and energetic life. The change in his lifestyle and focus was puzzling and alarming to the king, who had hoped that placing his friend in this position would allow him to make changes he thought needed to happen in the Church. But Thomas stood against some of the very issues that the king thought he could get Thomas to agree about.

Soon, the king's agenda and Thomas' zeal to do his job well began to clash, and before long, the two men were not talking. Their rift remained irreconcilable. One day, the king wished aloud that he could be rid of the obstinate archbishop. Four knights carried out his wish by killing Thomas in front of the Canterbury Cathedral's altar. He died bravely, saying, "I am ready to die for my Lord, that in my blood the Church may obtain liberty and peace. But in the name of Almighty God I forbid you to hurt my people, whether clerk or lay" (Graves "Henry's Love for Becket Became Hatred" 2010). To this day, people travel to pay their respects to St. Thomas Becket at Canterbury.

Depiction of Thomas Becket's murder in the Canterbury Cathedral. It is unknown whether Henry intended for his former friend to be murdered, but he did publicly repent for it.

NORMANDY

The French land given to the Vikings still retains its name of Normandy. This northwestern part of France is well known for its stunning scenery and lovely towns. This picture is of the harbor of the town of Honfleur.

France

William the Conqueror's castle still stands in his hometown of Falaise.

Agriculture still plays a significant role in the economy of modern Normandy. The area is well-known for the quality of its seafood, apples, and dairy products, all of which are part of the local cuisine. Normandy even has its own breed of cows, the Normande. These cows have a distinctive speckled appearance.

One of the most famous sites in all of France is just off the coast of Normandy. It is the medieval monastery town of Mont-Saint-Michel, which becomes an island during high tides. Here it is shown during low tide.

Many Americans are probably most familiar with Normandy because it was the site of the Allied invasion of Europe during WWII on June 6, 1944, D-Day. This photo shows an American soldier on the beaches after the attack.

William the Conqueror is also buried in Normandy. His tomb rests in the Abbey of Saint-Étienne, which he commissioned, in the town of Caen, approximately 30 miles north of his birthplace in Falaise.

13

START HERE

Can you imagine being required to
wear a metal suit weighing somewhere
between 60 and 70 pounds? Now, what if I
told you that you had to learn to walk around in
that suit or — even better — you had to learn to use a
sword while wearing this weighty outfit? In this chapter, we are going
to learn about the real life of the sometimes romanticized medieval knights and castles. Life was not easy
for many people during this time, but as we will learn in this chapter, some had a heavier burden to bear
(or, in some cases, wear) than others. If you have ever wanted to step back in time to spend some time in a
medieval castle, here is your chance!

Medieval Chivalry and Drafty Castles

In the feudal system, one of the most famous groups of people were the medieval knights. You might remember learning about the samurai when we studied Japan a few chapters ago. Just as the samurai fought for their daimyos, the knights of Europe fought for the lords to whom they had sworn allegiance.

Knights are famous for the heavy suits of armor they wore. Have you ever seen a knight's suit of armor? If you have, you know that it is all steel. The average suit weighed anywhere between 45 and 75 pounds! Even the horse wore armor to protect it during battle. Clank! Clank! The armor was often so heavy that riding a horse was the only way a knight could be mobile on a battlefield. On foot, they could barely move at all! This might sound like a bad idea, but at this time, being on a horse, even in all that heavy armor, was a big advantage to knights. That's because most ordinary soldiers were on foot, so the knights on horseback towered over them and could move much faster.

Besides being strong enough to wear all that armor, knights also had to be brave, willing to fight, and even willing to die. They went through a long training and testing period, and they had to follow a certain code — the code of chivalry (SHIV-ul-ree). The word "chivalry" and the idea for the code came from a group of lords in France during the 12th century. The French word for "horse" is *cheval*. These French lords followed a strict code of conduct, and soon all knights were expected to follow it also.

The code of chivalry was not an easy code to follow. First, the chivalrous knight had to be extremely brave. In fact, he had to be willing to do anything his lord asked him to do, even if it seemed foolhardy. Second, the chivalrous knight had to be honorable. This means that he not only had to be brave, but he also had to be polite and fair while he was doing his brave deeds. It was this honorable behavior that set knights apart from other warriors of the day. While other warriors were sometimes rather rude in their behavior, knights were expected to be polite and chivalrous.

Much of the literature from this time celebrates knights and their chivalry, but one thing to keep in mind about the code of chivalry that knights followed is that each kingdom had its own version. Another thing to remember is that the code of chivalry usually only extended to how knights treated nobles, noble families, and other knights. The peasants who lived on the land were usually not

Two knights jousting

16th century French engraving of a jousting tournament. Jousting was a popular sport with knights. It involved two men on horseback, armed with lances, charging each other. The goal was to knock the other person off his horse. As you can probably imagine, jousting was dangerous. In the tournament depicted here, the king of France was fatally wounded.

protected by this code, so knights and lords often treated them however they wanted. An example of this is how defeated armies were treated. Captured knights were often allowed to live in castles in some degree of comfort while their lord made arrangements to pay for their release. The defeated peasants who had been recruited into the same army, however, were usually killed after the battle rather than being taken captive.

Knights had to go through rigorous training, and many times, they had to work their way up to that privilege. If a boy wanted to be a knight, he had to start out as a page for another knight or even for a group of knights working for a lord of a manor. His job would be to clean up after the knights, including washing their laundry and shining their armor. When the page had grown a little, he might be made a squire. At this level, he was given the job of caring for the lord's horses, or he might be chosen to help the lord get his armor on. It was around this time that he would be introduced to weaponry. He would start trying to build muscles, so he could lift the heavy swords, wear armor, and learn the art of fencing.

Next, the knight-in-training would be allowed to ride the horses and learn to fight from there. This training included learning how to joust. The knight-in-training would be learning the code of chivalry during this time. By the time the young knight was 20 years old, he was expected to have learned everything he needed to know. Knights would then swear allegiance to their lord, and they usually lived in the lord's castle. This kept them close by so that they could quickly respond to their lord's commands, and it also meant that the knights had a place to stay and food to eat in return for their services.

NARRATION BREAK:

Discuss what you read about chivalry and knights.

11th century knights. Notice how in these images, knights' armor changed throughout the centuries. The style of armor also varied by country.

15th century German knight in armor

16th century German knight in armor

Castles were an important part of everyday life for the nobles and knights. The Normans were the ones who first really started to build castles in England. Have you ever wondered why the medieval lords and kings built castles? Castles became popular because they were effective at keeping invaders out. Castles were hard to attack, which meant they had to be taken by siege. They were often well-stocked with food and supplies, too, which meant it would have to be a long siege to force the people in the castle to surrender. Before that happened, it was likely an ally's army would show up to break the siege. Castles were also big enough for the residing lord and lady to live comfortably with their family and to house the small army of knights who protected the family, along with the servants and caretakers of the estate.

If you have ever seen a picture or a drawing of a castle, you know that these were very large structures. They were built out of stone usually, and many times had a moat of water around them, which made them look like they were on a small island right in the middle of a pond. Whenever a castle had a moat surrounding its base, there was also a drawbridge. This bridge was kept drawn up against the side of the castle to keep out any unwanted visitors and lowered across the moat to allow welcomed guests to pass over into the castle.

As time went on, many lords built huge castles for their families to live in. These castles had high walls, huge fireplaces, and towers, from which guards stood watch. You may think it would be fun to live in one of these castles, but unless you like to be cold and damp, a medieval castle would not be a comfortable home in modern eyes. They did not have the electricity that makes modern day homes warm, so they were drafty and miserable. Most also lacked running water, and the bathroom inside the castle was often a hole in the ground called a garderobe. The garderobe emptied into the moat or an empty pit. As you can probably imagine, castles were usually dirty and smelled really bad! However, by the standards of the day, castles were the nicest

Though it's called a castle, technically St. Mawes Castle in southern England is not one. Built in the 1500s, this artillery fort served as protection in the event of invasion. It still shares some similarities with the design of castles.

places to live, especially when compared with the homes that most other people had.

By the 1200s, the castles of Europe were quite fantastic! How were these massive structures built? Let's go through the steps of building a castle. Here is a fictional (not true) though realistic look at how a castle was built. In our story, the king of England has given a rich noble, Sir Charles, the job of being the ruler of a certain area in Wales. Sir Charles decides that this is a good political move. After visiting Wales, he tells his wife, Lady Elizabeth, that he is going to take the job, but she doesn't have to pack yet; it will take at least four years to build the castle and at least four months to build their temporary home on their new estate in Wales. Lady Elizabeth sighs with relief.

Sir Charles sets out to find the perfect location for the town and castle that he intends to build. The location is important because the castle needs to be easy to fortify and protect. The castle will be in one corner of the town, surrounded by a wall and a series of towers and bridges. The town, which will consist mostly of homes for the peasants who work the surrounding farmland and pay taxes to Sir Charles, will also be surrounded by the wall with watchtowers. That meant the peasants living in the village were not protected if the castle was attacked or if raiders came through.

This is a huge project! Sir Charles will need hundreds of tradesmen to construct the town and castle. Word goes out around the countryside, advertising for masons, carpenters, quarrymen to dig and shape rocks, blacksmiths to keep tools in working order, mortar makers, and strong men to dig clay and rocks for the building project.

After the locations for the town and castle are determined, the work begins at once. The first step in the building process is to make a temporary housing complex for the workers and knights (who are there to guard the project and land) and the temporary home for the noble family. Next, the diggers start digging a wide ditch all the way around the circumference of the town and castle. This is where the wall will be built.

Sir Charles and the architects set to work on designing the castle, while work on the wall starts. The diggers find a deposit of good, solid limestone and the digging commences. Quarrymen direct the workers to which stones should be brought to the building site, and soon, there are piles of stones and rock ready to start the wall. Masons start situating the stones while mortar makers mix and carry large slabs of mortar to slather between the rocks. It takes the men almost five years to finish the project. By this time, the town has grown to several hundred occupants. Sir Charles, Lady Elizabeth, and the children move into the castle, and life settles into a routine.

One of the routines of medieval castle life that might seem odd to us is that many nobles did not live in their castles year-round. They often had a few different castles they lived in, and they traveled between them. When they left, they usually took a large group of relatives and servants with them, often leaving the castle with a relatively small number of people to operate it. Kings also moved between castles frequently. In fact, one of the reasons castles were so big was because nobles knew they were expected to lodge, feed, and entertain the king and his large group of relatives and servants when he made his rounds through the kingdom.

NARRATION BREAK:

Talk about what you learned about castles.

CONNECT

Sometimes in history, a character who is hidden in the shadow of legend and mystery comes along, and we wonder who they truly are. Some historians argue that there is not enough historical evidence to prove this man even existed, but there are enough medieval records to the contrary to make me want to include his name in our story.

The story of King Arthur is told in the *Annales Cambriae* (The Annals of Wales), the *Historia Brittonum* (the rather legendary purported history of the British), the writings of a prominent church figure named Gildas, and the work of a Welshman named Geoffrey of Monmouth. Despite the appearance of the story of Arthur in all these literary sources, many modern historians doubt Arthur is real. Many believe the stories about Arthur stem from a difficult time in English history, one of invasion and instability, and that they grew as the tales captured people's imaginations (Wood 2011).

According to the bards and folklore, King Arthur was a British leader in the late 400s and early 500s. His many exploits as a leader are recorded in legends and medieval romances. Do you know what a legend is? A legend is a story with some basis in historical fact, but over the years, exactly what is true and what is not has become fuzzy and hard to determine. A medieval romance is a popular type of story from the Middle Ages. These stories celebrated chivalry and told adventure stories.

I think most of us have heard at least one version of the story of King Arthur, who had a legendary round table, knights, and a queen named Guinevere. It is believed that if he was, in fact, real, King Arthur was probably a British battle-chief rather than a king and that he won 12 battles against invading barbarians from the north when they broke through Hadrian's Wall. Hadrian's Wall was built starting in 122 by the Roman emperor Hadrian. The wall served as protection for the citizens of Southern Britain.

Regardless of whether the stories are true, King Arthur has emerged as one of the most famous characters in British history and literature and remains a popular figure even today. If you would like to read the legend of King Arthur, there are plenty of versions available!

A – Site of Water Gate

B – Eagle Tower

C – Queen's Tower

D – Well Tower

E – Lower Ward

F – Great Hall

G – Kitchens

H – Chamberlain Tower

I – King's Gate

J – Upper Ward

K – Black Tower

L – Granary Tower

M – North-East Tower

N – Cistern Tower

O – Queen's Gate

Green – Area built between 1283–92

Red – Area built between 1295–1323

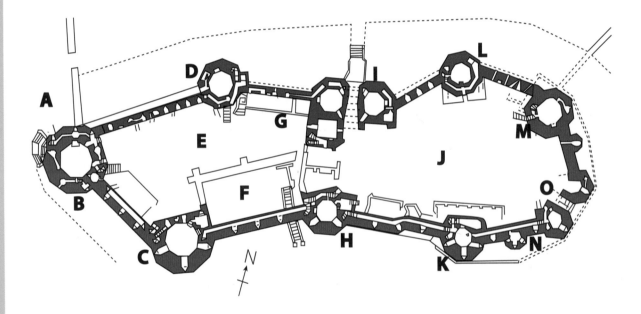

Caernarfon (KUH-nar-von) Castle was built between 1283–1323 in Wales by the English king Edward I. Edward had conquered Wales a few years before he started building the castle and intended Caernarfon as a base to solidify his control of the country. To this day, the heir to the British throne is known as the Prince of Wales. Since the early 20th century, the ceremony of bestowing this title takes place at Caernarfon.

Caernarfon is a good example of the layout of many castles in the British Isles at the time. Even though the exact design differed by location, most castles had many of the same rooms and features. Towers were important because they were lookout posts and allowed people to see any incoming invaders. Wards were open courtyards. The Great Hall is where important banquets and feasts would be held.

ANALYZE   Based on the blueprint, how does a castle differ from the building you live in?

CONNECT   How many towers does this castle blueprint have?

MAPS

The Knights Templar, also known as the "Poor Knights of Christ and of the Temple of Solomon," originally came into existence as "an order of fighting monks dedicated to protecting the Christians who visited the Holy Land" ("Knights Templar and Philip the Fair" 2010).

Although their original purpose was that of being a protecting force for the Christian pilgrims to Jerusalem, their work quickly involved a broader description. They bravely defended fortresses in the Mideast and gained great power, both politically and economically, because they were entrusted with the conveying of money to and from far-away lands. At their beginning, the Knights Templar were sworn to poverty, but because of their valor and work for rich bankers, they became exceedingly wealthy. The Knights Templar were greatly feared and envied by their enemies and widely respected for their ability and military might.

When the Christians lost the Second Crusade and Jerusalem was lost to the Islamic forces in 1187, the Templars seemed like good candidates for the blame. Soon, there were rumors flying fast and furious about them. These rumors included allegations of corruption and idol worship. Philip the Fair of France, who wanted to confiscate their wealth, endeavored to get the pope involved in his schemes. When the pope hesitated, Philip took things into his own hands by carrying out extremely cruel torture to force the Knights Templar to "confess" their wrongdoing. On March 22, 1312, the order of the Knights of the Templar was abolished, and sadly, the knights themselves were either imprisoned for life or burned at the stake for heresy. The rumors and allegations of corruption have since been debunked, and for the most part, the Knights Templar's reputation has been restored for history. However, their story reminds me of the Scripture that says, "Death and life are in the power of the tongue" (Proverbs 18:21).

This illustration shows the clothing that the Knights Templar wore during the 1100s.

MEDIEVAL CASTLES

One of the most famous castles in the world is England's Windsor Castle. Built by William the Conqueror, the castle is one of the royal family's residences. Here, British military members participate in a parade honoring Queen Elizabeth II's Diamond Jubilee (60th anniversary of being queen).

Europe

England's Alnwick Castle is noted for its Poison Garden. Though it's from modern times, the garden is inspired by the apothecary gardens kept in medieval times. Because all the plants are dangerous, visitors are not allowed to touch, smell, or taste anything in the garden.

This photo shows what Arundel looks like from inside its walls.

Arundel Castle in England was built shortly after the Norman Conquest by one of William the Conqueror's associates. Over the years, it has been heavily renovated and restored, especially after suffering damage in wars. In the early 1900s, it was remodeled to have modern conveniences, like electricity.

Many medieval castles had dark dungeons that were used as prisons. Here is the dungeon in Ireland's Blarney Castle.

Though castles were most popular during the Middle Ages, not all castles were built then. Neuschwanstein Castle was built in the 1800s in what is now southern Germany and is heavily inspired by the style of earlier German castles.

14

START HERE

At times, it is easy to feel like evil is winning. When we hear and see so much going wrong in the world around us, we may be tempted to think that the majority is bad. Before we read this chapter, I want to share a story about how God assured Elijah, one of His faithful servants, that there were those who were remaining faithful and not bowing down to the evil that has invaded this world. Please read the story in 1 Kings 19.

Since the beginning of the Islamic faith, Christians and Muslims have been at odds with each other. As we work our way through this chapter about the Crusades, it is important for us to remember that there are instances and events in history that show the humanness of all involved — no matter what religions they represent. These were extremely complicated historical events, so much so that we will only be learning a general overview of them. As you learn about the Crusades, it is important to remember that there were horrible decisions made on both sides. No one is right all the time, and when various religions feel that they have the right to force others to believe a certain way or be punished and even killed, terrible things happen.

Teachers: As with all other historical events, the Crusades are complex and have multiple causes. Neither side behaved well, and both sides were guilty of brutality and atrocities. Since we are approaching history from a Christian worldview, we are focusing more on the European Crusaders, who were not always a good witness for Christianity. Nevertheless, that does not mean that all Crusaders were bad or that they were the only aggressors in the conflict.

One of the most famous historical events of the Middle Ages is actually a series of events known as the Crusades. Earlier, we learned about how the Muslims spread from the Arabian Peninsula across North Africa and the Middle East and even into Europe, and how these areas were then ruled by a series of Islamic caliphates. The Muslims had also conquered and controlled the Jewish holy city of Jerusalem since 637. Jerusalem was sacred not only to the Jews but also to both Christians and Muslims.

In the 11th century, tensions eventually erupted as the ruling Abbasid Caliphate was losing land to the newly converted Muslim Seljuk Turks, who also began threatening the Byzantine Empire. By this time, the long-standing differences between western Christianity, centered in Rome, and eastern Christianity, centered in Constantinople, had caused the two churches to split in 1054. The one in Rome became the Roman Catholic Church, and the one in Constantinople became the Eastern Orthodox Church. Though the two churches had their disagreements with each other, the Byzantine Empire still asked their fellow Christians for help against the invading Muslims.

On top of this, there were also reports of difficulties for European travelers going to and from Jerusalem. During this time, Christians believed that everyone should make a pilgrimage to Jerusalem at least once. They thought they could show their desire to turn from sin by going on this ultimate pilgrimage. Although the Muslims had controlled Jerusalem and all the surrounding roads for many years, they had previously allowed the Christians to travel without much interference. The Seljuk Turks now controlled the city, however, and they started charging traveling taxes, and they harassed the Christian pilgrims constantly. They were also attacking Byzantine cities.

Sketch of Pope Urban II calling for a crusade

17th century Italian tapestry showing the Crusaders when they arrived outside Jerusalem

In 1095, Pope Urban II addressed these issues and the Byzantine request for help by preaching one of history's most influential sermons. He called for the European Christians to march on the Middle East and destroy the Muslims. Urban II saw this as an opportunity to bring the Eastern Orthodox Church back under the influence of the Catholic Church and a way to bring stability to Europe. If the various European kingdoms were united fighting the Muslims in foreign lands, then they would not be fighting each other at home.

Though these were his motives, it is doubtful that Pope Urban II thought he would get the response that followed. The astounded pope watched as the crowd began to scream and chant, "God wills it!" From every direction, men gathered together. Lords, ruffians, and serfs all swore to fight together to defeat the Muslims and free Jerusalem. There were all sorts of motivations for joining the Crusades. Some sincerely wanted to free Jerusalem while others sought adventure and still others were drawn by the promise of the riches they could loot.

Participants were also promised that they would get indulgences for helping to save the holy city of Jerusalem. An indulgence is a certificate that promises forgiveness for sins. In the medieval period, people often would pay money to build churches and do other things because they thought it was a form of penance (an outward sign of repentance) and would earn them forgiveness for their sins, but not everyone could afford to do that. For soldiers, mercenaries, and the poor, a Crusade seemed like the best way to be forgiven since they could receive indulgences for participating. Indulgences are not scriptural, however, and they would become a huge problem throughout the Middle Ages.

Regardless of their motives, these men sewed red crosses on their tunics and became Crusaders, soldiers of the cross. It was in 1099 when the first group of Crusaders finally marched toward Jerusalem. There, they recaptured the city. I am not going to go into the details of all that happened there that day. No words can express the horrors committed in the name of Christianity. Instead of trying to find a way to express God's love to the lost, those who claimed to follow Christ chose to kill them instead. This included all Jews and Muslims who were in the city when it fell. (The Eastern Orthodox Christians who lived there had already been forced to leave before the siege.) This is a very dark time in history, and one that is extremely hard to write about, but as we have learned, we cannot learn from history unless we learn about history. This was the first Crusade. After the Crusaders captured Jerusalem, they established four "states" in Palestine and Syria. For a while, everyone seemed to settle down a bit, as Crusader generals and nobles established a form of feudalism over the conquered lands and built Norman-style castles and estates.

Crusaders charge Muslim forces during the First Crusade

19th century sketch of a Crusader

NARRATION BREAK:

Discuss what you learned about the Crusades.

20th century Syrian painter Said Tahsine's depiction of Saladin and the defeated commander Guy de Lusignan after the battle of Hattin

Italian Renaissance artist Cristofano dell'Altissimo's painting of Saladin, 1500s. The artist lived centuries after Saladin died, so this painting is how he thought Saladin would look.

Christians held Jerusalem for 88 years, but then everything changed. A Muslim captain named Saladin, who was of Kurdish descent from what is now Iraq, had strategically worked his way up through the ranks of the Islamic army. At the time, there was a truce between the Muslims and the Christians, but raids on Muslim caravans caused another war to break out. In 1187, Saladin decisively defeated Christian forces in the Battle of Hattin. This battle took place in the hot Middle Eastern summer, and the Christian soldiers were overheated and very thirsty after not having access to water as they marched and camped. After this victory, Saladin then headed toward Jerusalem with his army. Saladin had dreamed and planned all his life for this venture. After a two-week-long siege, the city surrendered. Rather than slaughtering the residents like the Crusaders had done decades earlier, Saladin let people pay a ransom for their freedom. If they paid, they could leave. Those who could not pay became slaves. Saladin was now in control of Jerusalem and much of the surrounding area.

As you can probably imagine, European Christians were not happy when they found out about losing Jerusalem. It was rumored that the shock upon hearing the news about the Crusader defeats caused the pope of the time, Urban III, to die of a heart attack. Meanwhile, Saladin formed his own ruling Muslim dynasty called the Ayyubid (eye-YU-bid) dynasty, which rivaled the ruling Abbasid Caliphate and controlled what is now the modern countries of Egypt, Israel, Syria, Lebanon, and parts of Iraq.

The Second Crusade was an unsuccessful military expedition to the Holy Land, led by the French and Holy Roman rulers. The Third Crusade was largely devoted to trying to win back the land lost to Saladin. It pitted the famous English king, Richard

the Lionheart, whom we will learn more about in the next chapter, against Saladin. Richard defeated Saladin in battle, but he refused to lay siege to Jerusalem. The two men eventually reached a truce that gave the Christians some land along the coast in what is now Israel and Lebanon. The Muslims retained control of Jerusalem but agreed to allow pilgrimages.

Despite the truce, many were not happy with the terms. In 1198, a nobleman became Pope Innocent III. He called for another Crusade to free Jerusalem from Muslim control. A group of French nobles organized an army and arranged for the wealthy merchants of Venice, Italy, to buy supplies and build ships for their army of over 30,000 men. The Venetians also promised to provide ships for this Fourth Crusade in exchange for 84,000 silver coins. The Venetians were also promised half of what the Crusaders ended up winning, and that would have been a lot of money (Robinson 2006).

There was a problem, however — only about 10,000 Crusaders arrived in Venice on the appointed day, and they were well short of the 84,000 silver coins they owed. The Venetians were furious, and the Crusaders were now deeply in debt with seemingly no way to pay it off or use all the goods the Venetians had supplied. The Venetians then offered the Crusaders another option. The city of Zadar (located in what is now Croatia) was in rebellion against Venetian control. The merchants told the Crusaders that if they captured Zadar for them, the debt would be temporarily forgiven until the Crusade was over and it could be repaid. Many of the Crusaders were horrified by the suggestion that they should attack a city under Christian rule, so many deserted. Pope Innocent III also strongly condemned the offer, but the remaining Crusaders went through with it for the money.

Sketch shows Richard the Lionheart and Saladin fighting in battle in 1192. In reality, they never met in person.

CONNECT While the knights of the First Crusade readied themselves for battle with the Muslims, something else was happening. A monk called Peter the Hermit was gathering many of the common folk together. He claimed to have been the one who urged Pope Urban II to call for a crusade, though that claim was not true (McFall 2006). His calls to have a crusade also attracted some knights, as well as the peasants, which were the majority of his followers (Child, Kelly, and Whittock 1992, 16).

This Peter was a rather interesting person; he was well-known for his loathing of the bathtub and was quite a dirty, smelly man. He was also known to ride his donkey while wearing a dirty, brown monk's cloak. People jokingly commented that he and his donkey resembled each other (McFall 2006) with their brown coats and long faces. He gathered thousands of supporters, but the pope was concerned that they would not be good soldiers. He (as well as others) doubted that they had the discipline to follow orders and feared they would be impossible to command or control (McFall 2006).

Thousands of people followed Peter the Hermit, even though most of them never fought the Muslims. Instead, many of them turned into a rather wild, hungry mob. At one point, they even started a riot over shoes in Hungary (McFall 2006). They also stole a lot of goods along the way (McFall 2006). In fact, in addition to their problems with discipline and their inexperience, Peter had promised them that the Muslim Turks would run away after seeing them, which, of course, was untrue (Child, Kelly,

and Whittock 1992, 16). When they finally had a chance to fight, they performed poorly and were overrun by the Muslims — most of the survivors were sold into slavery (Child, Kelly, and Whittock 1992, 16). Peter was absent when his army was defeated, but he eventually made it to Jerusalem to join up with the actual participants in the First Crusade (McFall 2006). This strange occurrence became known as the People's Crusade, even though nothing Crusade-like ever came from it.

After capturing Zadar, the Crusaders were met by a Byzantine prince with a claim to the Byzantine throne. He had unsuccessfully tried before to convince the pope to sponsor a government overthrow. He promised that if he were Byzantine emperor, he would bring the Byzantine Empire and Eastern Orthodox Church back under Catholic control. Innocent III had turned him down, but the Crusaders agreed because he offered to pay them a lot of money in exchange for their help. The whole plan was rotten!

The Crusaders were successful in overthrowing the government and installing the prince as emperor in 1203. He became Byzantine Emperor Alexius V. However, within a matter of months, it became clear that their plan had not worked. Alexius V was unpopular with his people and unable to pay the Crusaders. He was overthrown and replaced by another emperor. Realizing they would never be paid, the Crusaders decided to take the city, sack it to steal its wealth, and install an emperor of their choosing. On April 12, 1204, Crusaders with red crosses emblazoned across the chests of their tunics sacked the city of Constantinople. Their behavior was disgraceful. They looted and destroyed the city's many churches and attacked the civilians. They ransacked the beautiful Hagia Sophia and stole many of its precious objects.

For 60 years after this sacking, Catholic Crusaders ruled the Byzantine Empire. Byzantine citizens who would not live under Crusader rule moved southeast to Nicaea. There they remained until the Byzantine Empire again took control of Constantinople in 1261. The shameful actions of the Crusaders on the Fourth Crusade caused political instability that considerably weakened the Byzantine Empire. Though it continued in existence for a couple of hundred years after retaking Constantinople, the Byzantine Empire was never as powerful as it had been.

Although the Crusaders' actions against the churches of Constantinople were not endorsed by the Catholic Church, they did serve to finalize the split between the Eastern Orthodox Church and the Roman Catholic Church. The churches had been officially divided since 1054, but these actions destroyed any hopes for a reconciliation. Other Crusades were periodically relaunched to take Jerusalem, but they never succeeded. The city remained under Muslim control.

NARRATION BREAK:

Talk about what you read today.

This miniature painting from the 1400s depicts the Crusaders sacking Constantinople a couple of hundred years earlier.

View of a Crusader
fortress in Israel

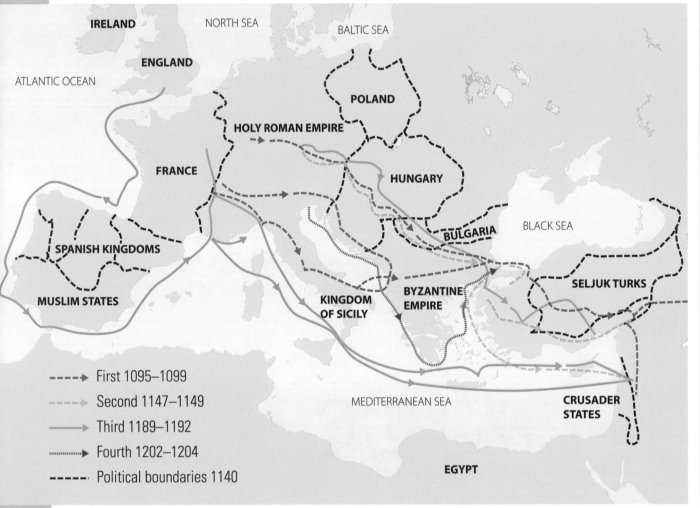

First 1095–1099
Second 1147–1149
Third 1189–1192
Fourth 1202–1204
Political boundaries 1140

Though there were several Crusades, the ones labeled as First, Second, Third, and Fourth are usually regarded as the most significant. The First Crusade is the one Pope Urban II called for. The Second Crusade was a response to the fall of the Christian Crusader kingdom called the County of Edessa. The Third Crusade was the one Richard the Lionheart led against Saladin. The Fourth Crusade was the excursion that led to the shameful sacking of Constantinople.

ANALYZE What do you notice about where the Crusades were launched? From which countries did these expeditions start?

CONNECT Did most of the Crusades travel by sea or by land?

The Schism (SKIS-m) of 1054, also called the East-West Schism, was the final separation between the Christian churches in the East and the Christian churches in the West. You will remember that the Church disagreed on many matters and that arguments and rifts had been occurring for hundreds of years. The disagreements were very much like any other that takes place. Mainly, the two churches argued because they based their theology on different views. The Western Church's theology was mostly based on Roman law, while the Eastern Church's theology was rooted in Greek philosophy.

As we have already learned, the two churches had many disagreements, on everything from the pope's authority to whether priests should be allowed to marry. Finally, in 1054, the Eastern Christian Churches, led by Michael Cerularius, their Patriarch of Constantinople, and the Western Church, led by Pope Leo IX, mutually excommunicated each other. Being excommunicated means that someone is not allowed to participate in the church's services and sacraments. This act of disownment stood for over 900 years, until 1965, when Pope Paul VI of the Western Church and Patriarch Athenagoras I of the Eastern Church mutually and simultaneously revoked the excommunication decrees ("Schism of 1054" 2017). The two churches, however, still have significant disagreements about doctrine and practices.

16th century French painter Cesare Nebbia's painting of the First Council of Nicaea in 325. This conference resolved conflict in the early Christian church. The disputes that erupted centuries later and caused a schism in the church were not able to be mended by such a council.

CRUSADER CASTLES

One of the legacies of the Crusades that are still visible in the Middle East are the Crusader Castles that were built by the Crusaders and still stand. One of the most famous is Krak des Chevaliers in Syria. The name literally means "Castle of the Knights" in French.

Inside Karak Castle in Jordan. Karak Castle was initially built by Crusaders before Islamic Mamluks (slave soldiers) took it over. It's well known for the many tunnels and passageways underneath the castle.

Crusader castles, like Kolossi Castle, were also built on the island of Cyprus. Richard the Lionheart captured Cyprus during the Third Crusade.

Arrow-slits in Belvoir Fortress in modern-day Israel. This Crusader castle reflects a common feature in castles. Arrow-slits on the tops of walls allowed defenders to shoot arrows at attackers.

Bodrum Castle in Turkey shows its Western influences with its stained glass that features heraldic symbols. During the Middle Ages, heraldry (the symbols used in coats of arms, family emblems) was very important. Even today, some families (especially those of noble birth) still have a coat of arms that represents its members.

15

START HERE

Perhaps no other name represents the Middle Ages more than that of King Richard the Lionheart. Most of us are familiar with the tales and legends centered around Robin Hood, Maid Marian, the cowardly Prince John, and, of course, the Merry Men of Sherwood Forest. Just typing these names brings to my mind the images of all the actors and actresses who have portrayed them in movies and plays I have seen in my lifetime. But what was the true story behind these now legendary figures? In this chapter, we will focus on the story of Richard the Lionheart — the king who stands out in history for being more interested in fighting in the Crusades than ruling his kingdom. We will learn also about Richard's younger brother, John, whom history would give the interesting name John Lackland.

LIONHEART, LACKLAND, & THE MAGNA CARTA

In our last chapter, we talked briefly about the English Crusader King Richard the Lionheart. He was the second son of Henry II of England and Eleanor of Aquitaine (AH-kwuh-tayn), France. You might remember reading about Henry II in Chapter 12. He was the English king of Norman descent who seized control of Ireland. After his parents separated, Richard lived with his mother in Aquitaine, where she schooled him in the arts of reading, writing, and languages. Richard was also trained for knighthood. Richard was a splendid knight in training. He made quite the handsome figure, with his broad shoulders, reddish-blond hair, and tall frame. In 1172, Richard became Duke of Aquitaine and swore his allegiance to the king of France. Richard and his father feuded over land for several years. In addition to England, the family controlled the western half of France. Despite his disagreements with his father, he became Henry II's heir at the age of 25 after his older brother died.

Four years later, news traveled from Jerusalem that Saladin had attacked and conquered the Holy City. Richard immediately made plans to become a Crusader and lead an army to retake Jerusalem. While Richard was still in the process of planning a crusade, his father died. The two had still been feuding, but days before his death, his father had confirmed Richard as his heir. Richard was now the king of England. Interestingly, Richard did not speak English and never learned it because his childhood was spent in France, and nobles in England didn't speak the language either because they spoke French! (This was a direct result of the Norman Conquest, which we studied a few chapters ago.)

To finance a crusade, Richard sold government offices in England to the highest bidder rather than appointing people who would do a good job. Becoming king of England had not changed Richard's mind — he was still intent upon reconquering Jerusalem. Being a Crusader was a lot more important to Richard than administering England as king. His actions placed England in a substantial amount of debt.

Richard then departed on his long-awaited crusade. The journey toward Jerusalem was tedious and had many snags. On his voyage across the Mediterranean Sea, Richard stopped at Sicily to rescue his sister, Joan, who was being held captive there. She had been married to the Sicilian king until he died, and now the new king would not allow her to leave.

Merry-Joseph Blondel's *Richard the Lionheart, King of England*, 1841

While he was in Sicily, Richard became betrothed to a princess from the Spanish kingdom of Navarre. This did not make a certain young lady in France very happy! You see, Richard had been betrothed to Princess Alice of France since they were both children. Alice's father, King Philip of France, didn't like the news of Richard's new betrothal, either.

After some difficulty with his ships and crews, Richard and his men finally arrived in the Holy Land. Here, they joined several other groups of Crusaders, led by a duke of Austria and the king of France. Neither of these men liked Richard, each for their own reason. The king of France took his men and went home because he was unwilling to listen to Richard. He was also mad about Richard not marrying his daughter. The Austrian duke refused to fly his banners lower than Richard's, out of respect for his political rank. So, Richard commanded his men to steal the banner and trample it in the mud. This insulted the Austrian duke so much that he swore his hatred of Richard, took his men, and went home. Richard was left with only his own army to attack the Muslims in Jerusalem and the mighty Saladin.

Several times during the Crusade, Richard was close enough to attack Jerusalem, but his knowledge of war tactics kept him from doing so. He knew that he and his men would suffer heavy casualties and would not be able to hold off the waves of Muslim armed forces that would surely attack from the south. Saladin himself admired Richard's intelligence, and the two men eventually reached a truce that allowed the Crusaders to keep some land, though Jerusalem remained under Muslim rule.

It was during this time that Richard received news saying that his younger brother, John, was trying to take over the English throne, and Richard decided that it was time for him to return home. His return trip was perilous. Richard was kidnapped by his sworn foe, the Austrian duke, as he passed through that area. Richard had been forced to take that route because he had to avoid the angry king of France, Philip II. Richard was locked away in a prison tower for so long that he was presumed dead.

Gustave Doré's engraving of Richard the Lionheart and his Crusaders praying before battle, 19th century

England was charged a steep ransom for Richard. Prince John and his loyal men fought and sabotaged attempts to pay it at every turn. Eventually, Richard did return to England and his throne. Some accounts of this story say the brothers, Richard and John, did not like each other, while other accounts state that Richard was actually quite fond of his little brother. At any rate, Richard pardoned his brother for his treasonous acts.

Richard did not stay in England very long. Soon, he was off to France to fight for lands that he claimed were rightfully his. It was here while he was fighting to conquer a little French castle that Richard the Lionheart was struck by an arrow. The wound became infected, as was common at the time, and proved to be the cause of his demise. King Richard died and left the English throne to his brother John in 1199.

NARRATION BREAK:

Discuss what you read about Richard the Lionheart.

King Richard pardons his brother John after his return.

John was a very different king than his brother had been. Richard himself was not a perfect king. He had not been very interested in ruling. He was especially uninterested in ruling England compared to his kingdoms in France, which is what he considered home. In the ten years that he was king, Richard actually spent only a few months in England. In his absence, the local nobles gained power because they were responsible for keeping things running in his place. The money raised for his participation in the Crusades and his ransom also put England into debt. Despite these flaws, he had been admired by many for his skill as a military leader and his courage on the battlefield.

John shared many of his brother's flaws but also lacked the qualities that had made Richard popular. More than once, he ran away from an enemy army. His cowardliness, especially when compared with his brother's courage, made him disliked. In addition, nobody took him very seriously. Even Richard had treated John like a child after he returned from captivity. John also did not look the part like his brother had. Instead, he was short, plump, and balding. He certainly did not make the same impression that Richard had! John was more interested in the daily routine of administering a government than Richard had been, but he was frequently cruel and made bad decisions.

A good example of how differently the brothers were perceived is in the nicknames they received. Though Richard was called "Lionheart," his brother John did not have such a glamorous name. He became known as John Lackland when his brother was king since Richard had inherited England. Remember, in the feudal system the king of a country owned all the kingdom's land. Even though the king gave his officers and nobles sections of land to govern, the king was considered the true landowner. This meant that, until he became king, John did not have any land. Even after Richard had died and John became king, he was still called John Lackland!

Illustration showing fashion in England in 1200: group of warriors, a hunter with a falcon, a jester, court ladies, and King John

That nickname ended up predicting something that happened while he was king. Because of his bad decisions, John lost the French territory that had been so dear to Richard in wars with the French king! All these battles with the French also cost a lot of money, so John greatly increased taxes. John also made nobles who did not participate in his wars pay extra money to support the war effort, anyway.

All this fighting with France and taxing of his people made John extremely unpopular! Though Richard's adventures had cost money, the nobles actually had more power when he was king since he was absent from the country. But since John stayed in England, the nobles still owed heavy taxes but also had their power substantially restricted. The noblemen became so angry that they gathered their own army, marched on London, and captured it. I suppose these men were tired of the king being above the law. They decided that the law should be the highest power in the land. The law should even be above the king. In 1215, the noblemen who had captured London met in a field called Runnymede. King John, knowing that he was extremely unpopular and far outnumbered, realized there was no way for him to recapture London. He dressed in his royal attire and went down to Runnymede to talk to the nobles.

The nobles had drawn up an agreement, which they demanded that he sign. This agreement included dozens of clauses that limited the king's power. This agreement also stated that the king could not throw the nobles or anyone else into jail unless they had received a trial. Of course, King John did not want to sign the agreement, but he knew that these nobles meant business. He later tried to claim the agreement was not valid, which caused another rebellion. John died shortly after that, and his son became King Henry III.

This agreement was called the "Great Charter" or the "Magna Carta." It was an extremely important event, not only for England but also for the whole world. The

King John accidentally lost some of his jewels and treasure in a waterway called The Wash. While he was escaping from his enemies, the waters rose suddenly and swept his baggage away.

CONNECT You might be wondering why the Magna Carta, a document signed hundreds of years ago in England, has any connection with America. Its assertion that the king was not above the law laid the groundwork for the legal system to recognize the rights of other citizens. This meant the king could not claim that he could do anything he wanted, regardless of the law. That idea is highly influential in both English and American history.

The Magna Carta also mandated that the nobles would advise the king as part of his Great Council. The tradition of Great Councils stretches back to the country's Anglo-Saxon days. Within 20 years, the Great Council was called Parliament. At this time, the members were not elected by the people — they were selected by the king — but they still provided an important balance against his power.

By 1300, the representatives had expanded to also include representatives from local sheriffs, religious figures, and town representatives. In the Middle Ages, Parliament was divided between the nobles and the religious representatives and the representatives for sheriffs and towns. This is why even today English Parliament is divided between the House of Lords and the House of Commons. Over the centuries, Parliament has changed, with members now being elected by the people. But it played an immensely important role in English history (there was much fighting between the kings and Parliament over who was really in charge) and in modern-day British politics. In fact, in England now, the Parliament, led by a prime minister, is the primary means of government. The royal family no longer actively rules the country.

The Magna Carta is important because it started the movement of the government of mankind, from the shadows of tyranny and dictatorship to a more fair and balanced government. No longer would rulers in England have absolute power. From then on, if the king wanted to make a major decision that affected the whole nation, he had to gain the approval of a group of other people. This was the beginning of the parliament system, and it was a start in bringing the feudal system to an end.

The English traditions from the Magna Carta and of parliamentary representation were also very influential on the American Founding Fathers. Though our Congress is not organized the same way, the founders of the American government ensured that there was a group of representatives of the people who provided a check and balance on the power of the president.

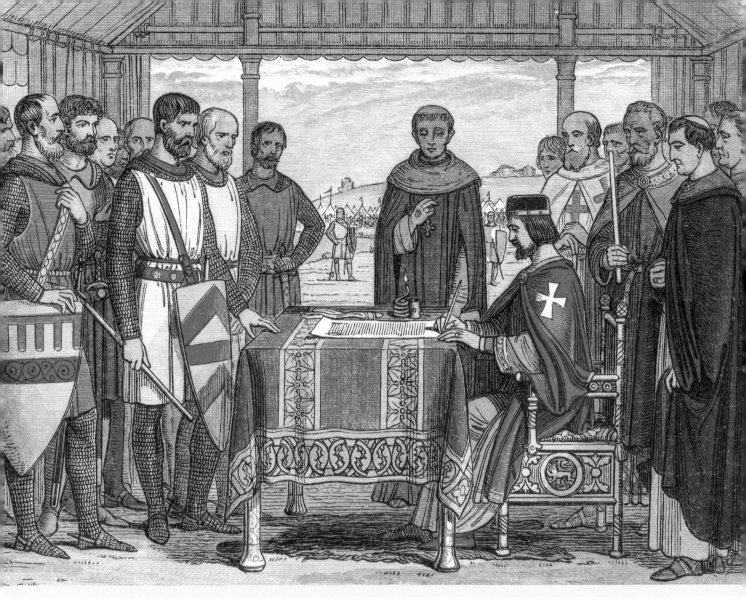

Magna Carta was revised many times over the years and has changed substantially from what it first looked like in 1215, but it helped establish the concept that everyone in England, including the king, was subject to the rule of law. This was a unique concept in the feudal system, which had given kings tremendous power. Before this agreement, power resided almost exclusively with rulers and the Church. The Magna Carta of 1215, however, provided other nobles some protection from the king. It was a document deeply rooted in resolving the nobles' dispute with King John, but it would have a powerful influence through the years on English law and even the founding of the United States! Within a matter of years, England also had an official Parliament (PAR-luh-ment), which included nobles and church and government officials to represent the people and to advise the king. This also further prevented the king from having too much power.

Illustration of King John signing the Magna Carta

NARRATION BREAK:

Talk about what you read about King John and the Magna Carta.

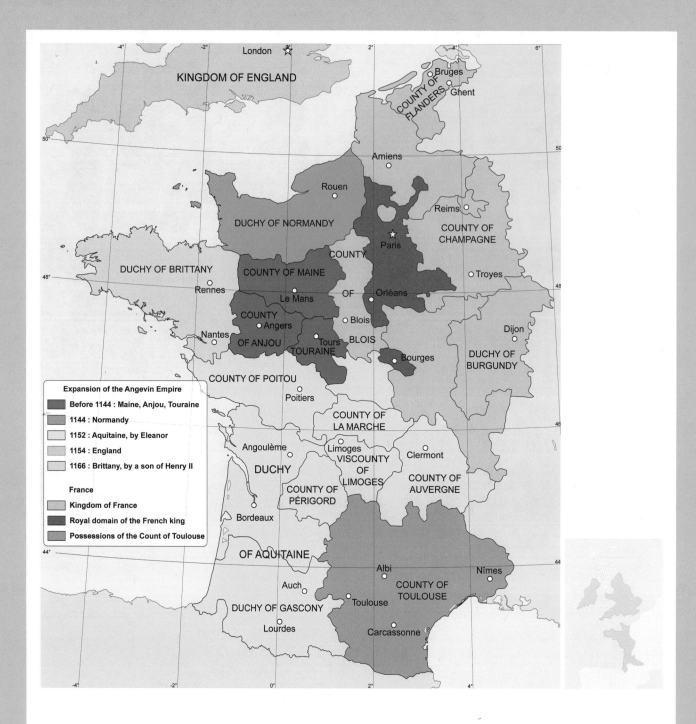

Today, we often think of England and France as very different countries, so it might have surprised you to learn in the chapter how closely they were connected during the Middle Ages after the Norman Conquest.

As this map shows, a substantial amount of land in modern-day France was under English control for a long time. This is called the Angevin Empire. Of course, the English kings who claimed this territory were of French descent themselves and often, as in the case of Richard the Lionheart, considered themselves more French than English. In Chapter 17, we'll learn about how these English claims were resolved, but it's important to understand the relationship between France and England during this period to understand the history of either country.

ANALYZE Based on the map, about how much of France was under the control of the English kings?

CONNECT In what areas was the expansion of the Angevin Empire before 1144?

Back in the Church History section of Chapter 12, we learned about a man named Thomas Becket, who was once a good friend to King Henry II. In a tragic turn of events, Thomas was murdered for standing up to the king. Henry had demanded that Thomas do something against his conscience and against the good of the Church, of which Thomas was the Archbishop of Canterbury. Henry II is the father of the King John in this chapter. King Henry II and his two sons, Richard the Lionheart and John Lackland, all believed that they had a right to impose taxes on the clergy and to promote their own courtiers as bishops (Vincent 2015).

When John came to the throne, he expected to be able to continue this crooked family tradition. Pope Innocent III refused this request and, instead, pressured the monks of Canterbury to elect Stephen Langton, who believed and taught that kings should be under the law (Vincent 2015). King John had a severe aversion to Langton because of these views and therefore refused to allow him to take office in England.

The pope responded to John's behavior by issuing an "interdict," which goes far beyond excommunication (banning an individual from participating in the church). This interdict halted the operations of the entire English Church for six years (Vincent 2015). King John retaliated with heavier taxes on the Church and the English barons (Vincent 2015). Eventually, Langton and some of the barons being accused of treason fled to France for safety from King John (Vincent 2015). These are some of the key events that led to the issuing of the Magna Carta.

This illustration shows monks being kicked out of their monastery during King John's troubles with the pope.

AQUITAINE

Aquitaine, the ancestral land of Richard the Lionheart's mother, is still a large region in modern France. It's located in the southwest portion of the country and is noted for its seaside location and varied geography. Other nearby parts of France include land that once belonged to Aquitaine. This photograph is of Rocamadour. Many medieval people made pilgrimages here, including Henry II of England. It was once looted by one of Henry's sons, also named Henry.

This photograph is of a small Aquitaine village, La Roque-Gageac, overlooking the Dordogne River.

The ancestral home of Eleanor of Aquitaine's family, the Palace of Poitiers, is actually no longer in Aquitaine. That's because the modern region of France that is called Aquitaine was only a small part of the region's territory during the Middle Ages.

The Pyrenees Mountains on the border between France and Spain soar far above the rest of Aquitaine's landscape.

Sign in Bayonne that is in three languages — French, Basque, and Gascon-Occitan. Occitan is a Romance language, like Spanish and French, which means it comes from Latin. Occitan has several dialects spoken across southern France. Gascon is the distinctive form spoken in parts of Aquitaine. Since it was the medieval language of the area, many believe Richard the Lionheart's native tongue was likely Occitan, though he also spoke French.

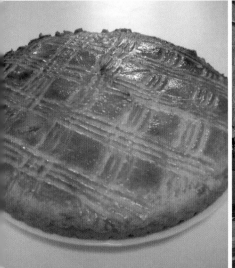

French cuisine is justifiably famous around the world. Aquitaine is well known for its rich dishes, including this traditional cake, called a Broyé du Poitou. Duck and goose dishes are also popular in the area.

Spanish Basque folk dancers. The Basque live in both southern France, including parts of Aquitaine, and neighboring parts of Spain. The Basque of Spain and France share a common culture and some Basque, especially in Spain, want a separate Basque nation.

16

START HERE

Plague! Just the sound of this word frightens me. We have come to a place in our journey through history that I must tell you the story of something that I wish we could quickly pass by on the other side of the street. However, this catastrophic event had such a long-lasting effect on the medieval world that we must pause for a chapter to give it at least a glance. The years filled with horror and anguish that the Black Death inflicted on all living creatures not only is one of the saddest and blackest events in all of history but also was responsible for a major shift in medieval European culture.

Before we journey through this chapter, I want to remind us of the truth concerning all events in history… both good and bad. God created the world and everything in it to be without sin. Sickness, including the plague, is one of the results of the sin brought into the world with the Fall. It is important to remember, however, that Satan will not have the final say. God and His people cannot be destroyed by Satan and his evil. Jesus says in John 16:33, "I have told you these things, so that in me you may have peace. In this world you will have trouble. But take heart! I have overcome the world" (NIV). Come along with me as we carefully walk through this dark section of our world's history.

THE BLACK DEATH'S HORRIBLE RAMPAGE

Teachers: Please pre-read this chapter and the notes for it in the Teacher Guide before the student reads. This chapter talks about the bubonic plague. It is an important but horrible event in history, and some students may find it difficult to read about.

I think we have all learned that life during the Middle Ages was quite different than what we are used to. We have discovered that many people were uneducated and could not read. We have also learned that the people who lived during this time always had to be aware and on guard against all types of enemies who might be ready to attack them. From the Vikings and Muslim raiders to the Mongols, wave after conquering wave of invaders poured over the borders, attacking the land, year after year. But nothing could have prepared the world for the invader that was about to strike. This was an enemy that no army on earth could stamp out with weapons and force. Kings and commoners alike would be conquered and slain by this dreaded disease.

Throughout the early decades of the 1300s, as traders arrived from the East with their beautiful wares to trade, they brought stories of the terrifying sickness sweeping across the Far East. This mysterious plague left a swath of destruction so devastating and so undiscriminating that terror tolled like the peals of a funeral bell in the hearts of all who heard. The Black Death hit China and other parts of Asia as early as the 1330s, and it left millions dead. The Black Death. The words hung in the air like a threatening, menacing cloud.

The invasion of this horrendous adversary arrived in Europe in the year 1347 on what should have been friendly merchant ships docked in the Sicilian port of Messina. These 12 ships had come from the Black Sea. As people from the town gathered to greet the sailors, they were met instead with the stench of death. Most of the sailors aboard the ships were either dead or gravely ill with strange boils and fevers. Also aboard these sea vessels were the carriers of a deadly plague. The townspeople of Messina sent the ships back out to sea in an effort to rid themselves of whatever evil must be lurking in the ships, but it was too late. The Black Death of Europe had arrived on the fleas that infested the ship rats.

16th century plague altarpiece from a German monastery. It depicts prayers to God for protection from the plague.

14th century Belgian miniature showing townspeople burying people who died from the Black Death

Let's take a few moments to stop and think through these horrible events in context. It is easy for us to read about historical happenings like this from a detached distance because, thankfully, most of us cannot even begin to fathom this kind of horrific disease. In our current world of clean running water, washing machines, strong disinfectant cleaners, sewer systems, and medicines, germs have a lot less friendly environment in which to grow, multiply, and spread. We must remember that, during the time that we are learning about, nobody knew about the existence of bacteria or viruses. In fact, there was no knowledge of the microscopic world at all.

In our modern times, scientists understand that this plague, the bubonic plague, also called the Black Death, was caused by a dangerous but easily treatable bacteria called *Yersinia pestis* (Centers for Disease Control and Prevention 2015). It was named after the 19th-century scientist (Alexandre Yersin) who discovered this germ (History.com 2010). This bacteria was transmitted by the bites of infected fleas and also through the air if an infected person breathed on someone else.

This may sound strange to you because, chances are, you have probably never experienced a fleabite. At the time of this pandemic, however, fleas were a real problem. Most people lived in an extremely unsanitary and just plain dirty environment. People often think that nobody bathed during the Middle Ages. That is not true, but modern people would be appalled by how dirty it was during this time — especially in cities. More and more people had been moving to cities, which were already severely overcrowded. People even threw garbage and dumped sewage in the streets because there was no system in place for removal. This sort of environment is very conducive for flea infestations. Furthermore, because fleas are the type of insects that like blood, where there are fleas, there are fleabites.

We now know that most sickness-causing bacteria and viruses can be transmitted through the air, through touch, or exposure to a sick person's saliva or blood. This is why we cover our mouths when we cough or sneeze, wash our hands with soap after using the restroom, use antibacterial salve on a cut before covering it with a bandage, and sanitize medical equipment with bacteria- and virus-killing cleaners. However, in the Middle Ages, people did not know that bacteria and viruses were what was spreading the disease. Instead, they superstitiously believed that if someone saw a person die of the plague, they, too, would become ill and die.

NARRATION BREAK:

Discuss what you read today.

Giuseppe Crespi's *Bernard Tolomei and the Plague in Siena*, 1735. This painting depicts a monk who tended to plague victims before dying of the disease himself.

Within a matter of years, the plague had quickly spread across Europe — through the Mediterranean kingdoms and on to Central Europe, England, and Scandinavia. As the plague spread and more people fell ill and died, fewer and fewer doctors would agree to treat patients. The doctors who did treat the ill did not have much success and most of the time would become infected also. These doctors often wore extremely odd-looking outfits that looked like a large bird costume. The beak of the costume was actually a primitive breathing mask filled with a strong-smelling substance, such as lavender and a mix of other aromatic herbs, to combat the foul smell of the plague. It was even believed that smelling herbs or burning incense would keep the sickness at bay because it changed the odor of the air. These doctors also carried a long pole to ward people off or to pick up the clothing and belongings of the plague victims to take the items to be burned.

You may be familiar with the little nursery song "Ring Around the Rosy." Many believe the origins of this seemingly innocent little ditty are actually connected to the Black Death of Europe. "The ring around the rosy" refers to the fever and rash caused by the plague. "Pockets full of posies" is talking about the herbs and flowers people wore on their persons in an effort to stave away the sickness, and "Ashes . . . we all fall down" refers to the way they burned people's clothes and possessions to prevent the spread of the disease. I've never liked that song, and when I learned about its possible origins, I finally knew why!

As the plague rolled across Europe, the stench of death was everywhere, lingering in every street, on every corner, in every house. If a person touched the clothes of a Black Death victim, they knew they would most likely be dead within four days.

This 17th century manuscript engraving shows the types of masks that people wore to protect themselves from the plague.

Close-up picture of a plague flea

There was so much death that, soon, people did not even bother to hold funerals for their loved ones. Instead, they buried the dead in mass graves and burned the clothing and belongings of the dead in an attempt to stop the spread of the disease. Houses were left empty as whole families died. Farms were left to decay, their crops rotting in the field. Animals roamed about the countryside, left by their dead owners to fend for themselves; many of them died of starvation or plague.

London was hit by the plague in the summer of 1348, and it is believed that anywhere from one-third to one-half of the city's population succumbed to it. The plague would ravage Europe for 50 years, in recurring epidemics every few years. Nobody knows the death toll exactly, but it was devastating. Some areas had fewer deaths, but others suffered a grim death toll of nearly three-fourths of the inhabitants. In its wake, the plague left millions of people dead across three continents; a staggering one-third of Europe lay in the grave.

As the tide slowly turned, and the plague proceeded to fade away, a new reality set in. Temporarily, wars and trade halted, though they eventually started back up. However, everything had changed. Before, the feudal system relied on large numbers of peasant laborers to farm the land of wealthy nobles. Now, there were no longer enough farm laborers to support this old system. This reduction in the number of laborers was devastating to the wealth of many of the landowners. Though they had once paid their serfs with housing and enough food to live on, they were now forced to pay wages for the same labors rendered. These changes were favorable for the laborers, allowing them to gain more materially than their class had for centuries. After the plague epidemics, peasants had more food and more money.

The 1600s saw repeated outbreaks of plague in numerous European countries. This illustration depicts the devastating 1656 plague in Naples, Italy.

CONNECT

I wish I could tell you that the plague simply disappeared at the end of the European Black Death period, but alas, I cannot. Over the next three centuries, the plague resurfaced, killing tens of thousands with every reoccurrence. The horrible disease brought London to its knees in the years 1664 through 1666, causing approximately 75,000–100,000 deaths. This was followed by a rampage through Cologne, Germany, and on the Rhine River from 1666–1670 and through the Netherlands from 1667–1669. Next, it hit the areas of North Africa, Turkey, Poland, Austria, Hungary, France, and Germany. Throughout 1675 through 1720, the plague took over 200,000 people's lives ("Plague" 2018).

The last plague pandemic happened at the end of the 19th century and the beginning of the 20th century, on the eve of major scientific breakthroughs that helped to get the disease under control ("Plague" 2018). The discovery of the microscopic world and its connection with the spread of plague made it possible to gain control over the horrific disease. Even to this day, there are cases of plague reported each year. Just as in the other cases of plague throughout history, the disease is still spread through the bacteria *Yersinia pestis*, which occurs naturally in the environment and is carried on wild rodents. Fleas are still the main way humans come in contact with the bacteria.

However, the few cases that are reported each year have a high percentage chance of recovery, thanks to the medications, including antibiotics, available now to treat it (Goldschmidt 2015).

Illustration of plague victims in Marseilles, France

After the plague in cities, there was a similar shortage of labor, and wages rose there, too. Peasants before had not really been able to move from the land they worked on as tenants for nobles. They lacked the resources to move or to pursue the long training period needed to learn a craft or trade through apprenticeship. The increase in wages, though, gave them more resources and an incentive to move from home and try their luck in a city. Because of these changes, in the years following the Black Death of Europe, there was a far-reaching societal upheaval like no other. It finally seemed possible to move up in social class. The dynamics of every class of people, from serfs to kings, had been sifted and sorted by the death of so much of the population.

Plague pit in London. Plague victims were often buried in mass graves (called plague pits in England). Plague pits were in use in England well into the 1600s.

Fear, blame, and prejudice were also present in many forms as the surviving population tried to make sense of the disastrous decades they had just lived through. For this reason, discrimination against Jews became widespread. Many Europeans were suspicious of why their Jewish neighbors did not seem to be as susceptible. Because they didn't understand how diseases worked, they did not realize that the Jews had better hygiene practices due to their religious customs and that they were also isolated from the disease since they often were required to live in separate parts of town called ghettos.

The Church itself had also been devastated. Many monks and priests had died in the epidemic because plague victims were often brought to them for medical care. There were now many openings in the Church, and requirements for joining were relaxed to fill all the vacancies. This meant that many of these new clergy members were not necessarily good at their job or knowledgeable about the Bible. Europe was a mess in every way, and it would take a while to regain a new sense of normalcy.

NARRATION BREAK:

Talk about what you learned about the plague.

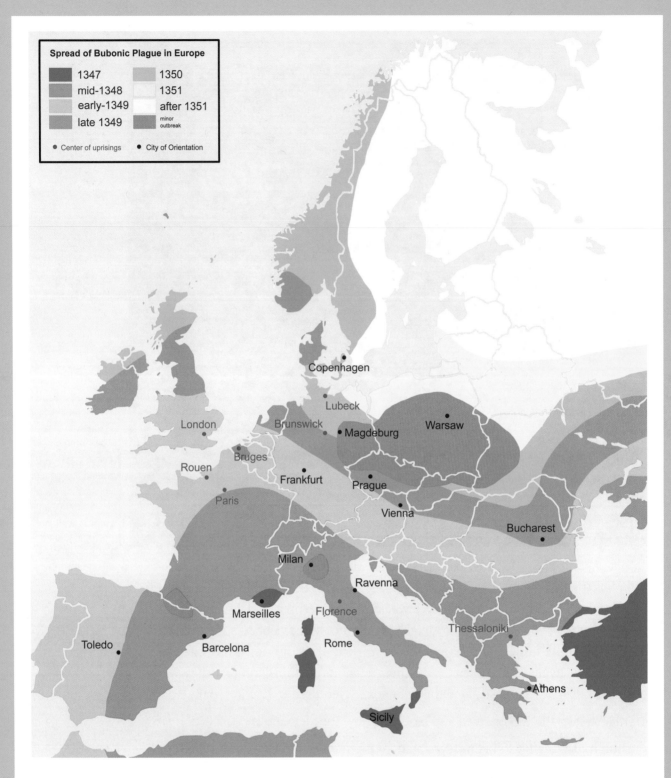

Spread of Bubonic Plague in Europe

- 1347
- mid-1348
- early-1349
- late 1349
- 1350
- 1351
- after 1351
- minor outbreak

● Center of uprisings ● City of Orientation

The Black Death spread across Europe over a period of several years. As the map shows, it started in 1347 in Sicily, but over the next few years, it expanded to terrorize most of Europe. It is important to remember, though, that the disease had been devastating Asia far earlier.

ANALYZE Do you see a general pattern in how the plague spread? If so, what is it?

CONNECT How many years did it take for the plague to spread from Sicily to Copenhagen? (Hint: Look at the map key.)

The disputes between the pope and national rulers reached its peak in the 1300s. As we have learned before, kings had considerable power during this time, but the pope did, as well. Conflict between the pope and kings was inevitable. Disagreements between the pope and the king of France even escalated into a physical altercation between Pope Boniface VIII and the supporters of Philip IV. In 1302, the pope had written several strongly stated bulls (letters), of which the most important was Unam Sanctam, which stated the pope was the supreme spiritual authority over all, including kings (Spielvogel 2012, 326).

In 1303, Philip IV rallied the French people against the pope, accusing him of a long list of crimes. French soldiers descended upon the pope's palace and arrested him there (Spielvogel 2012, 326). Local nobles freed him, but the shock of the experience proved too much for Pope Boniface VIII, and he died a short time later (Spielvogel 2012, 326).

In 1305, under pressure from Philip IV, the Roman Catholic papacy was moved to Avignon, France. Technically, Avignon was not under French control, but it was on the border with France (Spielvogel 2012, 326). The popes between 1305–1377 resided there instead of at Rome, as was the tradition. This time period is often called the "Babylonian Captivity" in the Catholic Church's history. The Avignon Papacy (ah-veen-YON PAY-puh-see) greatly led to the decline in papal prestige (Spielvogel 2012, 326–327). It was during this period that the popes and cardinals lived lavish and powerful lifestyles funded by taxes levied against the clergy. People also suspected the popes in Avignon were controlled by the French (Spielvogel 2012, 326–327). During the nearly 70 years in Avignon, the reputation and respect for the papacy tumbled to an extremely low level (Spielvogel 2012, 326–327).

Finally, in 1377, Pope Gregory XI moved the papacy back to Rome (Spielvogel 2012, 327). Soon afterward, he died, and the conflict continued as the Italians and French fought for the control of the Church's highest office. The Church ended up with two popes, one in Rome and another in Avignon. Across Europe, people were divided, with many choosing whom to follow based on how they felt about France. For France and her allies, the pope in Avignon was the pope. For other countries, like England and most of Italy, the pope was in Rome (Spielvogel 2012, 328). This division further undermined faith in the Church since each pope denounced the other. It got so confusing that, at one point, there ended up being three popes at the same time. In 1417, the other popes were removed from office, and only one pope remained in charge in Rome, but the damage to the Church's reputation had been done (Spielvogel 2012, 328).

The Pope's Palace in Anagni, where French soldiers arrested Pope Boniface VIII

Mt. Etna, on the eastern side of island, is one of Italy's most active volcanoes.

Sicily

Messina was where the plague arrived in Europe, but the city and Sicily, the island it is located on, both have a lengthy history. Over the centuries, Sicily has been controlled by the ancient Greeks, ancient Romans, Arabs, Normans, Italians, and more. The result is a culture that is a blend of all these influences.

Italy

One of the best examples of this effect on Sicily is the Cappella Palatina, the chapel the Norman rulers of Sicily used in the city of Palermo. It combines elements of Norman, Byzantine, and Arab styles. The Sicilian language is also a similar blend of influences. Though Sicilian is closely related to Italian, it also features words of Greek, French, Arabic, and other origins.

Sicilians have a well-earned reputation for being good cooks. Their pastries are especially famous. This is a tray of cannoli, a traditional pastry. Because many Sicilians emigrated to America during the 1800s and 1900s, Sicilian dishes are often enjoyed in the United States, as well.

Traditional Sicilian culture is still alive and well on the island. One of the many traditions is colorful, elaborate carts drawn by donkeys, mules, or horses.

Beaches of Messina, Sicily. The waterway is called the Strait of Messina, which separates Sicily from mainland Italy, visible in the distance. Because Sicily is an island, many Sicilians who live on the coast make their living fishing.

17

START HERE

In this chapter, we are going to learn about a period of time and a chain of events in English and French history that is still directly affecting those countries today. For quite some time, France had heavily influenced English culture. These countries have always reminded me of two siblings who have a hard time getting along. Their disagreements often turned into friction, and that friction turned into war. We will be journeying through an era of upheaval in their histories called the Hundred Years' War and the War of the Roses. Because the names of the individuals and families involved in this chain of events can be confusing, I encourage you to study the family tree in this chapter that shows who's who.

WARS AND ROSES OF 14TH-CENTURY ENGLAND

Have you noticed how England and France always seemed to be fighting each other? This went all the way back to when the Normans came over from France and conquered England. After that, English kings were of Norman descent and spoke French at their royal courts. Even the name of the ruling dynasty was French. They were called Plantagenets (plan-TAH-juh-net), after the last name of Henry II's father. They also still held considerable land in France. As a result, that land was subject to the French king. To the English kings, it would be preferable for that French land to be under English control completely, but France did not want to lose that land to England!

There was also a separate but related argument over whether the English king was heir to the French throne. This was because the kings of England at this time still married French noblewomen instead of English noblewomen. Their children were often related to royalty in both kingdoms. In 1328, when the French king died without any heirs, the English king, Edward III, believed he was heir because the French king was his mother's brother. The French, however, thought that would violate Salic Law and preferred that the throne pass to the French king's cousin on his father's side.

These disagreements led to a considerable amount of warfare between the two kingdoms in the Middle Ages. When the Black Death swept through Europe, the fighting stopped for a while. Many soldiers on both sides died, leaving the countries' armies weaker. When the plague outbreak was over, the war between them started up again. Altogether, England and France fought and quarreled for over a hundred years. These skirmishes and temporary times of peace, spanning 116 years, are called the Hundred Years' War.

Henry V, one of England's most famous kings, came to the English throne in 1413. He was the great-great-great-great grandson of King John, the king who was forced to sign the Magna Carta in 1215. Interestingly, Henry V was the first English king to prefer speaking English over French and promote its use in his royal court. Nevertheless, Henry V, who was a rather audacious man, demanded certain French land, some of which had never been in his family, as well as money and permission to marry the French king's daughter, Catherine. The French king, Charles VI, refused. The crown prince, also named Charles, sent

A drawing of Catherine of Valois. She was the daughter of King Charles VI of France, the wife of King Henry V of England, the mother of King Henry VI of England, and the grandmother of King Henry VII of England.

Medieval miniature depicting Battle of Agincourt, probably painted a few years after the battle

along an insulting reply, which included a mocking gift.

This response from the French royalty angered Henry V in the extreme! He gathered his army together to attack France. At first, it didn't go very well. The weather was miserable and rained constantly. Though he had seized a castle, he had lost a lot of men taking it, and many of the rest were sick. Finally, the English decided to return to their own country and try again the next year. When the French discovered the English army's plan, they sprang into action. They attacked the English at Agincourt in 1415. The Battle of Agincourt is one of the most famous in English history. Though his army was greatly outnumbered, Henry V expertly used his skilled archers against the French cavalry charges. Between the muddy conditions, the terrain, and the expertise of the archers, the English soundly defeated the French.

Henry V eventually married the French king's daughter, Catherine, in 1420, but he never did get to be the king of France because he died in 1422. King Charles VI also died around this time, which left both England and France without a ruler. Henry V and Catherine's one-year-old son, Henry VI, became the king of England, and some also considered him the rightful ruler of France.

Illustration of Henry V's marriage to the French princess Catherine of Valois

This marked the beginning of yet another disagreement. This time, there was civil unrest between those who wanted the French prince, Charles (remember the one who insulted Henry V?), to become king of France and those who instead wanted Henry VI, who was a baby, to be king. Those who wanted the infant English king to rule France followed a nobleman named the Duke of Burgundy. They were called Burgundians.

All this bickering about who should be the leader led to a civil war in France. The English, of course, sided with the Burgundians. Charles VII, whom the French called the Dauphin (DAW-fen, the title for the heir), knew he needed to keep control of his country's most important cities. With the help of an unusual young woman named Joan of Arc, the French rallied themselves enough to drive the English out. They gave the Burgundians a chance to swear their allegiance to France, and King Henry VI of England lost all claim to the throne of France.

This ended the Hundred Years' War. The biggest impact it had was in developing a sense of national identity in both England and France. Before the war, England had been heavily influenced by French culture through its nobility, and English kings held French titles and lands. After the war, these were lost. English became the language of choice in England, and the English became more interested in developing their own unique culture. Meanwhile, the French started to view themselves as a united nation rather than an assortment of local regions that happened to be ruled by the same king.

Narration break:

Discuss the Hundred Years' War.

15th century illustration showing English King Henry VI being crowned as King of France. The French did not accept this coronation as legitimate, and the Hundred Years' War ended his claim to the French throne.

FAMILY TREE OF ENGLISH KINGS

From William The Conqueror to Henry VII

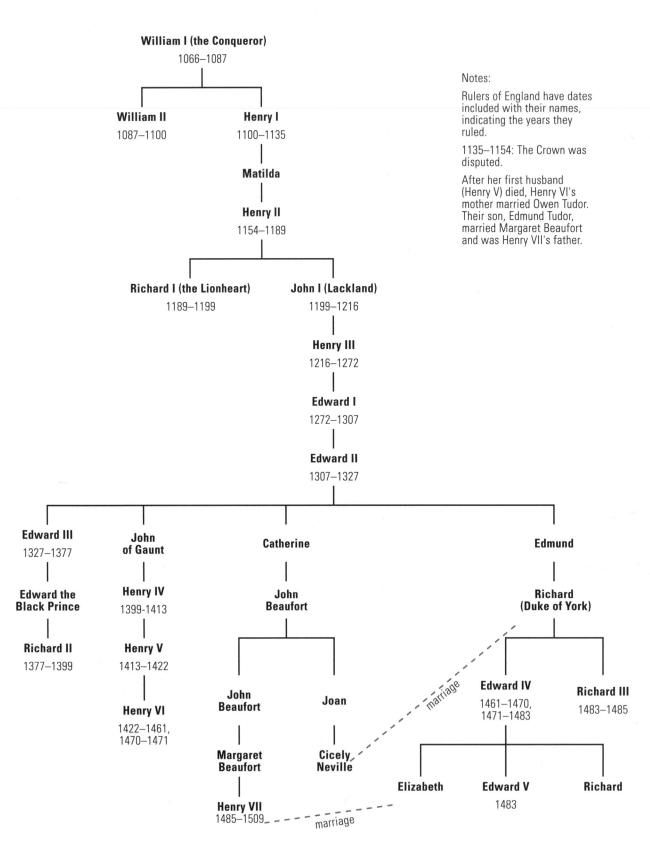

William I (the Conqueror)
1066–1087

William II
1087–1100

Henry I
1100–1135

Matilda

Henry II
1154–1189

Richard I (the Lionheart)
1189–1199

John I (Lackland)
1199–1216

Henry III
1216–1272

Edward I
1272–1307

Edward II
1307–1327

Edward III
1327–1377

John of Gaunt

Catherine

Edmund

Edward the Black Prince

Henry IV
1399-1413

John Beaufort

Richard (Duke of York)

Richard II
1377–1399

Henry V
1413–1422

John Beaufort

Joan

marriage

Edward IV
1461–1470,
1471–1483

Richard III
1483–1485

Henry VI
1422–1461,
1470–1471

Margaret Beaufort

Cicely Neville

Elizabeth

Edward V
1483

Richard

Henry VII
1485–1509

marriage

Notes:

Rulers of England have dates included with their names, indicating the years they ruled.

1135–1154: The Crown was disputed.

After her first husband (Henry V) died, Henry VI's mother married Owen Tudor. Their son, Edmund Tudor, married Margaret Beaufort and was Henry VII's father.

CONNECT In this chapter, we have taken a rather dizzying ride through several centuries of English history. We discussed several important members of the Plantagenet family and their roles in the conflict; however, there are a few more deserving of at least a glance. The Plantagenet family ruled England for hundreds of years. Henry II, whom we studied earlier, was the first Plantagenet king of England, and his sons, Richard the Lionheart and King John, were also Plantagenet kings.

John's son Henry III became king after his father's death and was also a Plantagenet. He seems to have had a hard time knowing the balance between making decisions as the ruler and trying to please the important people of his kingdom. His rule was marked by a number of major political and financial blunders (Morrill, Gilbert et al. 2018). Edward I, Henry's son, ruled from 1272–1307 and is known for successful administration and legal reform. He is sometimes called the "English Justinian" after the great Byzantine emperor, Justinian (Treharne 2018).

Edward II, son of Edward I, was not like his father at all. He made alliances with his father's enemies and aligned himself with untrustworthy parties ("Edward II" 2018). These alliances angered his wife, Isabella, who left him, formed an army, and in 1326, came back to drive out Edward II and his supporters ("Edward II" 2018). Four years after Edward II had been replaced by their 14-year-old son, Edward III, Isabella retired by joining an order of nuns ("Isabella of France" 2017). Edward III had grown up watching his father fighting with the barons for control of the land and his mother becoming increasingly politically prominent. Edward III worked to return England to the glory of the days of Edward I (Highfield and Tout 2018).

Edward III's grandson, Richard II, was the next Plantagenet king. He ruled from 1377 to 1399. Richard was a highly assertive and rather self-centered ruler who placed great value in his kingly office (Saul 2017). Richard II was eventually forced from office by his successor, his cousin Henry IV (Saul 2017). Henry's reign, from 1399 to 1413, was fraught with conflict and the inability to handle money well ("Henry IV" 2018). Henry IV's son, Henry V, whom we studied in this chapter, became king after his father.

King Henry VI of England was a deep thinker, and he liked to read the writings of both ancient and Christian philosophers. He preferred to spend hours quietly reading rather than ruling the government, which was handled by his ministers. Years went by, and as Henry VI grew older, his mind became weaker. He experienced spells of insanity more and more often. It became evident that he needed someone to help him rule, at least until he was stronger.

After much debate, Henry's officials concluded that England needed a substitute ruler, someone who could help when needed but would also be willing to step down when Henry was feeling better. The man for the job seemed to be a distant cousin, the Duke of York. (His grandfather and Henry VI's great-grandfather had both been sons of Edward III.) The Duke of York and Henry VI's wife did not get along, however. This disagreement quickly escalated into a civil war as the king and the duke and their supporters fought over the crown of England. This war became known as the

This early 20th century painting depicts a popular legend about the War of the Roses — that the families were required to pick their rose colors. That is unlikely to have happened, but the Yorks did have a white rose as their symbol while the other side (the Lancasters) were represented by a red rose.

War of the Roses because both parties involved had a rose on their coat of arms. The Duke of York had a white rose, and the king's rose was red.

The duke was killed in battle, and it seemed that Henry VI's reign would continue uninterrupted, but the duke's son stepped in to take his father's place against the king. The Duke of York's son was a strapping young man of 19 years. His name was Edward, and he was determined to be the king of England. Edward gathered his army and those loyal to his cause, and the War of the Roses continued as Edward's army attacked the royal forces. This time, the Yorks were victorious, and Edward had Henry VI removed from the throne and thrown into prison.

Edward took the throne and became Edward IV, but he had one small problem — he had secretly married the wrong woman. This woman, named Elizabeth Woodville, was not of noble birth, was older than Edward, and had been married before. Edward kept his marriage to Elizabeth a secret because he knew his family would not appreciate the fact that her first husband had died fighting for Henry VI! Only when his family tried to arrange a wedding for Edward with a foreign princess did he tell the truth about his marriage.

When the news of the king's marriage came out, Edward decided to move his wife and her family to the palace. He gave Elizabeth's brothers important positions in his government. The people of England did not like the fact that Edward had kept his marriage a secret or that he had given so many important government positions to his brothers-in-law. It was also shocking for the king to marry a woman who was not of noble or foreign birth. On top of all that, Henry VI's wife was not happy with her loss of position. She raised an army to march against Edward IV.

When Edward heard about her army, he ran away. King Henry VI was returned to his place on the throne. However, Edward was not gone for good! He was busy gathering

The Archbishop of Canterbury talks Edward V's mother into surrendering her children to the custody of her husband's brother, Richard III. It is not believed the archbishop was aware of Richard's murderous plans.

an army to help him get re-crowned. He marched back into England and captured King Henry VI again. No one knows for sure, but many believe that Edward arranged to have the elderly king murdered in prison. Once again, Edward was on the throne. He ruled for 12 years before he died and left the throne to his 12-year-old son, Edward V.

Edward V was too young to rule England on his own; therefore, his father's brother, Richard, offered to help him rule until he was old enough to do so on his own. Richard took over the throne and named himself King Richard III of England. Poor Edward V and his younger brother soon mysteriously disappeared. Rumor said that both youngsters were locked away to starve to death in the Tower of London. No one ever discovered the truth about their disappearance, but everyone has always believed that their Uncle Richard had them killed.

King Richard III was not destined to keep the throne, which he had so cruelly secured for himself. Another distant cousin, Henry Tudor, quickly laid claim to the English throne. In 1485, the two of them met with their armies at a battleground named Bosworth Field. Richard's army, nearly twice the size of Henry's, lost that day, and Richard was killed.

Henry Tudor became King Henry VII that day. His reign ended the War of the Roses, partially because he had defeated the previous king in battle but also partially because he was related to both the feuding houses. His father was Henry VI's half-brother, and his mother was related to Edward IV and Richard III's mother. To make things even more official, he married Edward IV's daughter (and his distant cousin), Elizabeth. These relationships can be very confusing to keep track of! The most important thing to remember is that the Plantagenets, who had ruled England for hundreds of years, had been replaced by the Tudors. The Tudor age of England had begun.

NARRATION BREAK:

Talk about what you read about the War of the Roses.

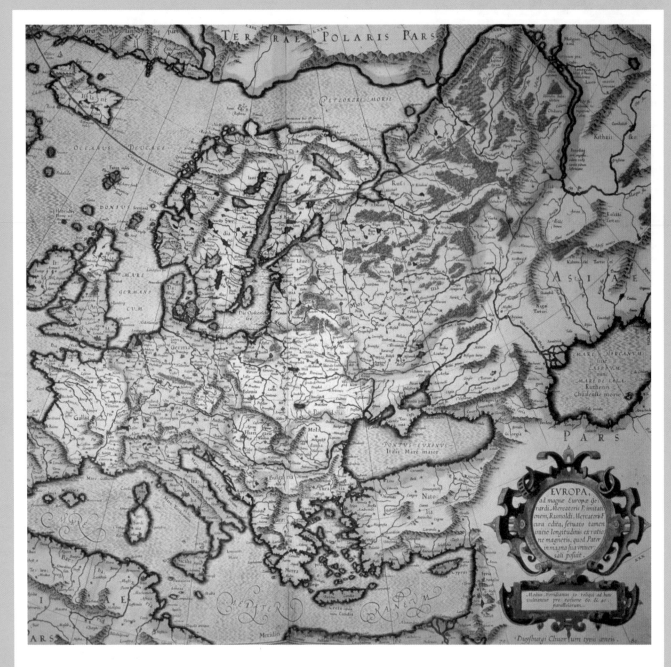

Europe in the 1400s looks more like the modern Europe we know today than it did during earlier time periods. However, there are still some significant differences. That's because a lot of history has happened between now and then — there have been wars, political negotiations, and government changes, among other events, that have shaped the modern boundaries.

Maps also look different as mapmaking techniques have changed over the years. Medieval maps such as the one above look different than a modern map due to changes in technology and changes in knowledge of geography, as well as updated boundary lines. This map is also in Latin since that was considered the language of the educated.

| ANALYZE | Based on previous maps you have studied, can you identify any of the countries on the map? Which ones? (Check your answers on a globe or atlas.) |
| CONNECT | Compare the look of this map to a modern one. What are the differences you notice? What are the similarities? |

MAPS

During the Hundred Years' War, the English attacked the French city of Orléans, one of the crucial cities in the area. The dauphin, which is what the French heir to the throne was called, knew he had to keep the city from falling into English hands, so they desperately fought to remain in control. It remained under siege for months. It was during this siege that the dauphin's men came to him with a young woman. Charles VII had received a message from Joan saying that she had seen a vision showing her how to save the city of Orléans. The dauphin had never met Joan before, and he wanted to test her. He gave his royal garments and crown to one of his officers and hid himself, dressed in plain clothes in the crowd. Joan came into the room, passed by the officer in the king's clothing, and walked straight through the crowd to kneel in front of the dauphin.

Joan proceeded to tell the dauphin about her vision. She believed that the saints had commanded her to gather the army and march on Orléans. After she secured that city, she was to take the dauphin on to the Reims Cathedral to have him crowned as king. At first, Charles VII was skeptical, but after having Joan questioned by the church officials, he decided to go with her conviction.

On they marched toward the city of Orléans, where the English and Burgundians had encamped. It was a fierce battle! Joan and her army were convinced they were fighting a holy war, with God helping. Finally, Joan and her soldiers forced the English and the Burgundians away from Orléans, thus becoming known as "Joan, the Maid of Orléans."

After Joan had escorted the dauphin to Reims and seen him crowned, she went on to fight battle after battle in her continued effort to free her beloved France from the grip of England. However, much to the dismay of her followers, Joan was captured. Charles VII did not try to get Joan back because he was in the middle of negotiating with the English. Instead, he let the English put her on trial for witchcraft. The English and Burgundians were convinced that Joan was a witch, and they were determined to find her guilty of crimes against the Church. She was found guilty and condemned to be put to death. Even after this verdict was handed down, Charles VII did nothing to help this young woman, who had been so instrumental to his crowning.

After being sentenced to death, Joan admitted to the charges. As a result, she was temporarily granted life in prison instead, but she quickly came to regret her decision to confess guilt. Her captors became convinced she would never change her beliefs about the rightful king of France or the visions and voices she received. In 1431, Joan was burned at the stake at the age of 19. In his old age, Charles VII felt guilty for abandoning Joan in her time of need. He had the Church re-examine the "evidence" against Joan, and 25 years after her death, Joan was pronounced not guilty. During her lifetime, she had been a national heroine in France, and she remains a popular historical figure there today.

Medieval French depiction of Joan of Arc

Loire Valley

Loire (luh-WAR) Valley scene. This part of France is often considered the dividing line between northern and southern France and is the location of many important cities and sites. Regarded as an iconic aspect of French culture, the Loire Valley was a favorite location for French nobles to build homes.

France

The Loire Valley city of Orléans was saved by Joan of Arc when she broke the English siege of the city. To this day, the city celebrates her memory. The second house, with the flowers in its windows, is a reproduction of the house she stayed in.

Another Loire Valley city, Tours, is where Joan had her armor made. Outside of Tours is also where the famous battle between Charles Martel and the Muslims occurred.

The Château de Chinon is where Joan of Arc met the French king and asked for soldiers to relieve the siege of Orléans.

The king's bedroom at Chambord

The Loire Valley is most famous for its many châteaux. The French word château (SHAH-toe) means a mansion or castle. The one pictured here, Chambord, is a château that for centuries belonged to the kings of France.

18

START HERE

Most of us are familiar with the story of Christopher Columbus and his quest for funding for his explorations. We may even know about how he went to the king and queen of Spain to ask for money to finance his journey but was initially refused because of a war they were fighting. Have you ever wondered about the rest of the story? In this chapter, we are going to go behind the scenes to learn more about Spain during this time. We will discover the backstory of both King Ferdinand and Queen Isabella, and we will take a more in-depth look at what type of rulers they were.

As we take this look, we will see how greed and hunger for power affected the decisions and actions of people in authority — even those who called themselves people of the Church. It is important for us to remember that, although evil can corrupt anything, even the Church, God will always have the last word. He sees the hearts of everyone and is the just and righteous Judge. Psalm 7:11 says, "God *is* a just judge, And God is angry *with the wicked* every day" (NKJV).

The Good & Bad of Ferdinand & Isabella

Before you begin reading this chapter, you may find it helpful to glance back at Chapter 6, which covered the Islamic conquest of Spain in the 700s. That was when Muslim troops from North Africa claimed most of Spain and Portugal for the Umayyad Caliphate. There would be a significant Muslim presence in Spain for more than 700 years.

By the 15th century, the inhabitants of the peninsula were from a long lineage of cultural and religious melding. To put the length of this time span into perspective, if you are an American, think about how long our country has been in existence as an independent nation. Let's start counting from the year the Declaration of Independence was written: 1776. At the time of the release of this book, the year is 2018. That is a mere 242 years, or not quite two and a half centuries. The time period we are studying in this chapter is nearly three times that length.

The three main peoples in this particular act of the grand history production are the Catholics, the Jews, and the Muslims. As we have been learning throughout this book, the Catholic Church had spread throughout Europe since the time of the Early Church. Most Spaniards were Catholic. If you were with me in the first volume of this series, you might remember the term that is used to describe the great dispersion of the Jewish people after the final Roman conquest of their lands. This was the Diaspora (DY-as-puh-rah). Since ancient times, the Jewish people had been scattered and settled in various places, including Spain. The Muslims who controlled Spain came to be known as Moors. They were a mixture of the native Berbers of North Africa and Arabs from other parts of the Middle East.

Muslim rule of Spain was not the seemingly simple case of a conquest, where invaders came, conquered, and replaced the existing government with their own. For the nearly 730 years that the Muslims held onto their control in Spain, there was an extensive cultural mixing between the Moors and the natives of the Iberian Peninsula. Christians and Jews were not considered equal citizens, but they could serve in the government and practice their religions without converting to Islam. There was also some intermarriage between the three groups.

Toward the end of this period, tension increased as restrictions on Muslims also increased, but much of the

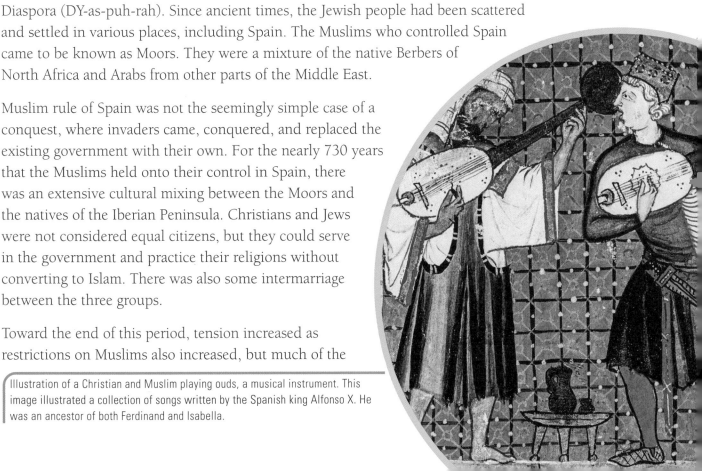

Illustration of a Christian and Muslim playing ouds, a musical instrument. This image illustrated a collection of songs written by the Spanish king Alfonso X. He was an ancestor of both Ferdinand and Isabella.

time period is regarded as a cultural golden age, where education and art, especially poetry and architecture, flourished. The results of the blending of culture during this time are still evident in modern Spanish culture. Even today, the Arabic influence can be found in the Spanish language, and Islamic architecture from this period can still be visited in Spain.

Throughout these centuries, there were periods of time, including during the Crusades that you learned about in Chapter 14, that conquests were led against the Muslims. These campaigns also occurred on a local level in Spain. The goal was to reclaim Spanish land from the Muslims. Many historians call these campaigns led by the various Christian states the Reconquista (ree-kon-KEE-stuh), which is Spanish for "reconquest."

The Battle of Puig in 1237 is one of many fought during the Reconquista. It's depicted here in a 15th century painting.

The Reconquista technically started in about 718, shortly after the country had come under Muslim control. At this time, the small northwestern Christian Iberian kingdom of Asturias stood up against the Islamic invaders. Following Asturias' lead, other small Christian kingdoms there, such as Navarre, Galicia, Leon, Aragon, Portugal, Castile, and the Spanish March, formed an alliance. These kingdoms came together in the name of the Reconquista, eventually limiting the Moors to the southern portion of Spain (Roberts 2017).

This remaining area of Muslim control, Granada, remained unconquered until January 2, 1492, when the very last Spanish Muslim stronghold finally fell. In the next section of our chapter, we will learn more about Ferdinand and Isabella, the king and queen who were responsible for this uniting of Christian Spain and the expulsion of Muslims and Jews from Spain. If you have heard the story of Christopher Columbus, you will no doubt recognize their names. The Reconquista is the war that Ferdinand and Isabella were engaged in when Columbus first approached them about funding his proposed voyage to search for a westerly route to the Indies. We'll learn more about Columbus and his journeys in the next volume of the series.

NARRATION BREAK:

Discuss what you read.

Before we can learn about Ferdinand and Isabella and their rule, we need to go back in time a little to learn about the ruler of Castile in the 1460s. He was King Enrique IV, and he had big plans to make his kingdom the most powerful in Spain. His plans included arranging a marriage between a rich nobleman and Enrique's own 13-year-old sister, Isabella. In return, the nobleman was to provide Enrique with enough soldiers to fight and conquer the other kingdoms. Isabella was horrified — the nobleman was much older than she, and the thought of the marriage made her want to hide. She prayed for deliverance from this terrible fate. On his way to the wedding, the nobleman became ill and died. Thus, Enrique's plan failed, and Isabella was free.

Four years later, Enrique again tried to use his sister to further his political gain. This time he promised her hand in marriage to the much older king of Portugal. Seventeen-year-old Isabella was again desperate to escape this fate. Secretly, she contracted a marriage with the Prince of Aragon, Ferdinand, asking him to consider marrying her. He agreed, and they married secretly while her brother was away.

Isabella's brother, Enrique IV

 Although little information has been found about the earliest Jews in Spain, it is believed that Jews may have lived in the country since the days of King Solomon, around 965–930 B.C. (Weiner n.d.). Jews follow the Old Testament laws but do not accept Jesus as the Messiah. In A.D. 409, the Visigoths conquered Spain, and in 587, their king, Reccared, converted to Roman Catholicism and made it the state religion. A few decades later, the Visigoths declared that only Catholics were welcome to live in Spain. Times were tough for the Sephardic (suh-FAR-dik) Jews. Sephardic is a term that comes from the Hebrew word for Spain: Sepharad (Weiner n.d.).

In 711, the Muslims came sweeping into Spain. Everyday life improved for the Jews under Muslim rule because they were able to live more peacefully with the people around them. Although they were protected under the Muslim law and could freely practice their religion, they were still singled out to pay a special tax. In 1098, the Christians reconquered Toledo, and by the mid-1200s, they were forcing more and more Jews to "convert" to Christianity. These new Jewish "converts" often continued practicing Judaism in secret.

When the Spanish Inquisition began, these converted Jews were tortured and killed for not being true converts. This makes me so very sad! We will learn about this period of Spanish history and about the grand inquisitor, Father Tomas de Torquemada (toe-MAS day tor-kuh-MAH-duh). This man convinced Ferdinand and Isabella to expel the Jews from Spain. These poor Jewish families, numbering around 300,000 people, were given only four months to convert, sell all their property and belongings and get out of Spain, or be executed (Frayer 2014).

In this Sephardi Diaspora (a diaspora means when people are dispersed from their homes and must live elsewhere), the Spanish Jews settled in large numbers in North Africa, Turkey, and Greece (Weiner n.d.). The Ottoman Empire was an especially popular destination. About a century later, others moved from Portugal to the Netherlands, where they could practice their religion openly (Weiner n.d.). Many also settled in other parts of Western Europe or moved to the New World (Weiner n.d.). There is more information about the Sephardic Jews in the Church History section of this chapter.

This painting depicts Ferdinand and Isabella meeting with an Arab ambassador.

Although their marriage enraged King Enrique, what could he do about it? His sister was already married, so he had to break off his plans with the king of Portugal. When King Enrique died six years later, Isabella became queen of Castile. Four years after she took the throne of Castile, Isabella watched her husband become King of Aragon. They ruled jointly, but their kingdoms technically remained separate. The decision to marry, though, was advantageous to them both. Isabella's Castile was a far larger kingdom than Aragon, and the arrangement ensured that all the land remained under Spanish control, not a foreign power.

Isabella and Ferdinand, often called the "Catholic King and Queen," declared Spain to be a Christian kingdom and made any other religion illegal. Once they had finally retaken Spain from the Muslims, they enforced tough restrictions against the Muslims who remained in Spain, as well as the kingdom's Jewish population. There were heavily political motives for this decision — banning other religions further centralized their control of the kingdom and was designed to ensure their subjects were united under one religion.

Of course, you and I know that you cannot force someone to believe something, and you most certainly cannot take away anyone's right to choose their religion. This type of rule is oppressive and is actually the polar opposite of how God interacts with us as humans. He is a God of justice, love, grace, mercy, and free will. Our free will is one of the main ways we are made in His image. He created us with the ability to choose and to live with the consequences, good or bad, that our choices bring. Ferdinand and Isabella took away their subjects' basic human right to choose. Not only did they take away that right to choose, but they also persecuted those who would not obey.

Even before Ferdinand and Isabella came to their thrones and united their kingdoms, the Spanish Jews had become the focus of persecution and pressure to convert to Christianity. Threatened with death, many Jewish people became "nominal converts" to the Christian faith. This means that they professed conversion to escape persecution and prejudice. They continued to practice their faith in secret. In 1469, Jewish converts who still secretly practiced their faith were denounced by the crown and declared to be a "danger to the existence of Christian Spain." The pope, intending to support the Church in its search for unity, eventually authorized Ferdinand and Isabella to name inquisitors to deal with this issue. These inquisitors were judges who held a vast amount of authority to question anyone who might be suspected of not being a true convert.

Thus began the rise of what history calls the Spanish Inquisition. This inquisition, which was a judicial institution established to root out people who disagreed with the Catholic Church, became a lethal weapon in the hands of power-hungry people. The first "grand inquisitor" of Spain would go down in history as a brutal and fanatical man. Dominican Tomas de Torquemada, who himself was descended from Jewish converts, used torture and terroristic tactics to cruelly "judge" his victims. He used public displays of his power in their sentencing, which sometimes ended with their death by fire, burned at the stake.

It was at his urging that Ferdinand and Isabella released an infamous proclamation in 1492. The Jews who had not yet converted to Christianity were given a choice. They could either convert or they could leave the country. Most chose to leave, so tens of thousands of Jews were expelled from the country. These Jewish people were forced to flee as refugees into other parts of Europe, as well as to Africa and Asia. Some who remained but refused to convert were tortured and murdered in the name of the Church during the Spanish Inquisition. This kind of power is appealing to many people, and unfortunately, we see instances throughout history where certain religions or people groups are targeted for persecution.

In later chapters in this volume, we are going to study two extremely important events in the history of the world — the Renaissance and the Reformation. For the most part, the cultural development of the Renaissance and the awakening and reforming of the Church during the Reformation bypassed Spain because the Spanish Inquisition made it difficult for other ideas and influences to reach the country.

Those found guilty by the Spanish Inquisition were sometimes forced to wear caps called corozas and tunics called sanbenitos before they were killed. This 19th century drawing by famed Spanish painter Francisco Goya shows someone forced to wear these garments.

NARRATION BREAK:

Discuss what you read about Ferdinand and Isabella and the Spanish Inquisition.

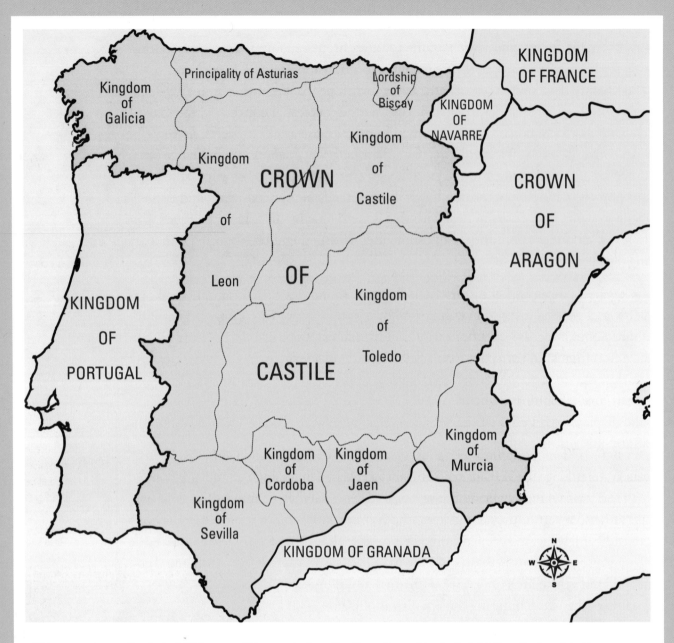

This map shows Spain in 1400, some 50 years before Ferdinand's and Isabella's births. During this time, Castile was ruled by Isabella's grandfather, Enrique III of Castile, and Aragon was ruled by Ferdinand's great-great uncle Martin.

The map is still a useful guide to understanding how much of Spain had been reclaimed from Muslim rule and how the country remained divided among various rulers. In addition to the kingdoms of Castile and Aragon, there was also Navarre, which finally joined with Aragon and Castile in the early 1500s, shortly before Ferdinand's death.

In 1400, the only remaining Muslim kingdom in the Iberian Peninsula, which is what Spain and Portugal are often called, was Granada. It would remain independent and Muslim until 1492.

The Kingdom of Portugal remained independent of Spain. We'll learn more about Portugal in a later chapter.

| ANALYZE | How many kingdoms are in the Crown of Castile (including the Lordship of Biscay and the Principality of Asturias)? |

| CONNECT | What are the kingdoms north of the Crown of Aragon? |

MAPS

In our chapter, we have learned about the cruel institution called the Spanish Inquisition. This terrible event is what led to the expulsion of the Sephardic Jews from their homes in Spain. Because Spain controlled colonies in the New World, the groups of Jews that settled there after leaving Spain were under the threat of the Inquisition even in their new settlements there. The tribunals (courts of justice, part of the Inquisition) were especially harsh in Mexico and Peru (Ryan 2017).

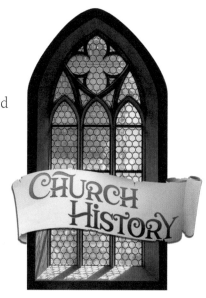

CHURCH History

Unfortunately, the Spanish Inquisition did not come to an end at the close of Ferdinand and Isabella's reign. It continued for centuries afterward, targeting Jewish converts suspected of still practicing Judaism, former Muslims, and those who disagreed with the Catholic Church ("Auto-da-fé" 2014). The public act of sentencing the "guilty" party during the Inquisition was a ceremony called auto-da-fé (aw-toe-duh-FAY, Portuguese for "act of faith") ("Auto-da-fé" 2014). These horrible events ended with the sentence being passed. These sentences included life imprisonment or the death penalty. The first auto-da-fé took place in 1481 in Seville, Spain, and the last was nearly 400 years later in the year 1850 in Mexico ("Auto-da-fé" 2014). In 2000, Pope John Paul II issued an apology for the abuses and deaths of the Inquisition. They also found in Spain that only around 1% of those accused and tried were executed (D'Emilio 2004).

Francisco Goya's *Scene from an Inquisition*, 1810s. This Goya painting shows an Inquisition trial in progress.

SPANISH ALCAZARS

Like most European countries, Spain has medieval castles. Many of them are a unique type of castle called an alcazar (al-KAW-zer). These castles were built by Christian kings and nobles but had noticeable Moorish features. This is the Alcazar of Segovia.

Spain

The Alcazar of Cordoba. This alcazar is noted for its lush gardens and was one of Ferdinand and Isabella's homes.

The Alcazar of Seville is famous for its Islamic-style architecture, despite being built by Christians after the area was reclaimed by Spain. This style is called Mudéjar (moo-DUH-har) and features arches and intricate designs.

The interior of the Alcazar of Seville. The word alcazar is of Arabic origin and means "the castle" or "the palace."

The armory in the Alcazar of Segovia features medieval armor and weapons.

The Alcazar of Segovia was a favorite home for the kings and queens of Castile. This is the throne room. In later years, the alcazar was used as a prison and military artillery school.

19

START HERE

As we have studied history together, we have watched the rise and fall of empires both great and small. If you were with me in the first volume of this series, you may remember the Babylonian King Nebuchadnezzar's dream statue (Daniel 2). This statue was gigantic, and each part of its body was created from a distinct type of metal representing the various empires and kingdoms that would rise and fall in history. Each and every empire mentioned there has fulfilled the prophecy. We should stand in amazement at the awesomeness of our God, the Alpha and the Omega. In the beginning, God. In the end, God. And every single moment of time in between, all safely in the hands of God.

In this chapter, we are going to be following the story of the rise and spread of one of the mightiest of all world empires. The Ottoman Empire, rising from a geographically tiny location and seemingly unimportant group of tribes, would eventually spread out to cover a large area. This empire would have a significant impact on its neighbors and for the languishing Byzantine Empire in particular.

THE MIGHTY OTTOMAN EMPIRE

The Ottoman Empire started out as many other empires had — small and seemingly unimportant. Their original territory near the northwest corner of Anatolia (an-uh-TOE-lee-uh), now called Turkey, is so minute that it is barely noticeable on a political map of that time. It was from this tiny Anatolian province that a band of Turkish tribes began their expansion. These Muslim Ottoman Turks made it their lives' mission to fight against the Christian Byzantine Empire and spread their Islamic faith (Yapp and Shaw 2017).

This empire was named for its founder, Osman I, who was a descendant of a nomadic tribe that had moved into this area from Mongolia several hundred years before. You might remember reading about the Mughal leader Bābur when we studied India. His family had lived among the Turks of Central Asia, and he had absorbed many aspects of their culture, which itself was heavily influenced by Persian culture. Bābur was not raised by the exact same group that Osman was, but these Turks shared a common ancestry and many aspects of their culture. Like the people Bābur knew, educated Ottoman Turks also valued Persian (as well as Arabic) culture.

Turks had formed the Islamic Seljuk dynasty in Iran and Mesopotamia and had led decisive attacks against the Byzantines, occupying large areas of their land. You might remember that one of the factors that led to the Crusades was the Seljuk Turks seizing Jerusalem and threatening the Byzantine Empire. A couple of hundred years later, the Mongols had subdued the Seljuks and the Muslim Abbasid Caliphate based in Baghdad. In the instability that ensued, Osman I expanded his territory by leading attacks against the Christian Byzantine Empire (Yapp and Shaw 2010). Osman I conquered the city of Bursa, which is situated in northwest Turkey, and made it the new capital of his empire.

Following Osman's death in 1326, his son, Orhan, ruled in his place. Under Orhan, the Ottoman Turks continued to expand, as more and more ghazis, warriors for the Islamic faith, came to join the fight against the ever-weakening Byzantine state. The empire continued to gobble up neighboring major cities, establishing their Islamic rule and religion everywhere they conquered. Orhan saw the opportunity to place himself in a highly strategic position when the Byzantine empire fell into a civil war between the rightful heir to the throne, John V Palaeologus (pay-lee-UHL-oh-gus), and a chief minister, John VI

Miniature portrait of Osman I, the founder of the Ottoman Turkish dynasty

Cantacuzenus (KAN-tah-kew-zeen-us), who wanted to usurp the throne. In return for helping Cantacuzenus, Orhan was given his daughter, Theodora, as his wife. Orhan also gained favor by laying siege to the important city Thrace, of which he gained control in 1345.

The Ottomans made an important conquest in 1362 when they conquered Adrianople, which is modern-day Edirne, Turkey. This was their first conquest on the Balkan Peninsula, which includes modern-day Greece. It would take the mighty Ottomans more than a century, but one by one, each of the important cities and regions fell under their control. The more the Ottoman raiders conquered, the stronger they became, and the richer they grew. Every conquest brought loot that filled their coffers more; the richer their coffers grew, the more dangerous the Ottomans became. Their ability to entice warriors to join their forces was impressive. The more warriors they recruited, the stronger their army became.

Generation after generation of Ottoman emperors expanded the empire farther; soon, they controlled all the lands around the city of Constantinople. The geography of this location also helped the Ottomans hold their conquests. The Balkan Mountains had very few passes, and with their death grip on the main invasion road, the Ottomans' authority in the area remained unchallenged.

In 1402, Emperor Bayezid, the grandson of Orhan, was defeated by Mongol raiders in Turkey. Bayezid, who had successfully extended the empire from the Euphrates River in the east to the Danube River in the west, was captured and died soon afterward. The Ottoman Empire was split among his sons. Of course, after his death, Bayezid's sons fought for control of the empire. Finally, his son Mehmed I won and reunited the kingdom. His reign was short-lived, however; he died eight years later in 1421. It was Mehmed I's grandson Mehmed II who would accomplish the long sought-after aspiration, the conquest of the great walled city of Constantinople. In the next section of this chapter, we learn the story of how this particularly persistent leader finally brought the last of the Byzantine empire to its knees.

NARRATION BREAK: Don't

Discuss what you learned about the Ottoman Turks.

Ottoman sultans

CONNECT The Janissary (JAN-ih-sar-ee) Corps was formed by the Ottomans in the late 1300s. The Janissaries were originally Christians from the Balkans who had been taken from their families as children and trained to become soldiers as adults ("Janissary" 2014). We will study about the devshirme, the draft of these young boys, even more in depth in Chapter 20, but for now, we will look at what these boys' role was in the Janissary. When these boys were removed from their homes, mostly by force, they were indoctrinated and "converted" to the Muslim faith ("Janissary" 2014).

This special elite force of Ottoman soldiers was first formed to be the sultan's bodyguards, the guards to Christian ambassadors, and the peacetime police of Constantinople ("Janissaries" 2011). From these roles, they moved up to guarding fortified places throughout the empire ("Janissaries" 2011). They are thought of as one of the most important parts of the regular army of the sultans. For several hundred years, the Janissaries did their jobs and fought where they were stationed. In June 1826, they revolted against Sultan Mahmud II, who responded by ordering cannons to be fired into the barracks, killing many inside ("Janissary" 2014).

16th century manuscript illustration depicting Ottoman soldiers

Remember back with me to when we learned about the mighty Byzantine Empire. This empire had risen, strong and mighty, after Emperor Constantine had moved the capital city of the Roman Empire to Constantinople. Even after the Western Roman Empire fell, the Byzantine Empire remained. The Byzantine Empire had been attacked many times throughout the centuries. They had withstood the attacks of the Muslims from the south, the Mongols from the east, and the Russians from the north. Throughout all these invasions, the great city of Constantinople had remained unconquered, though as we did learn earlier in this book, rogue Crusader knights had seized control of the city for a period of time during the Fourth Crusade.

However, the Ottoman Turks wanted to expand their empire, which lay along the Byzantine border. They were determined to expand their borders and spread Islam. Through the years, the Ottoman Turks attacked cities all along the edges of the Byzantine Empire, conquering and pillaging. Soon, the Byzantine Empire was smaller than the Ottoman Empire.

After a while, all that was left of the once-great Byzantine Empire was the great, walled city of Constantinople. The city's walls kept the Turks at bay, and the people inside began to believe that their city could not be captured. According to Byzantine legend, Constantinople would remain unconquered "until the moon went black." Of course, when anyone has this attitude, you know what is going to happen next!

Fausto Zonaro's painting of Mehmed II and the Ottomans entering Constantinople

Mehmed II had made it his life's mission to capture the city of Constantinople. His first step was to pretend to be friendly with the European envoys that visited his court. While he was keeping up this facade, he not only built his army up with thousands of men, but he also built massively huge cannons. By this time, the Ottomans had captured all the land surrounding Constantinople. It was only a matter of time before the city itself was attacked. That came in April 1453. Across the plain came monstrously huge cannons, which shot cannon balls so massive that it took many oxen to carry them.

The siege of Constantinople had raged for nearly two months when one fateful evening, the moon became mysteriously dark. The citizens of Constantinople were terrified. This surely must be a sign from God that theirs was an impending doom. Both sides believed that this event, which in reality was a lunar eclipse, signaled the end of the war. The citizens of Constantinople gathered at Hagia Sophia for the last Christian service. Outside the city walls, Mehmed called for his men to give all their remaining energy to break through the wall.

One week later, on May 29, 1453, the city of Constantinople fell to the Muslim Ottoman Turks. The conquering enemy swarmed into the city like angry ants, pillaging and destroying churches. Mehmed declared himself sultan (king) and had his throne placed in the center of the beautiful cathedral, the Hagia Sophia, while his men worked around him to change the once-holy building into a shrine and place of worship to their false god, Allah.

The fall of Constantinople marked a very important date: the true end of the Roman Empire from the ancient times. The Eastern Roman Empire had morphed into the Byzantine Empire and lasted for centuries, but it was finally gone. This loss was a devastating blow to Christians in Europe, despite their longstanding split over religion. Some in Europe called for Crusades to win back Constantinople, but no expeditions were organized. Although the effects of the Roman culture are still evident today, the fall of Constantinople was truly the first time since before the time of Christ that not one shred of the Roman world's influence remained in the form of an empire. This also meant that there was a new major empire for other kingdoms to deal with — the Ottoman Empire.

This impressive empire lasted until 1922. The Ottoman Empire is responsible for more than just conquering and plundering the lands around them to expand their empire; they also formed a powerful Islamic empire. It had been a couple of hundred years since the Muslim caliphates had been ended by the Mongol invasions. Isolated Muslim dynasties still ruled in places like Egypt, but the idea of a true caliphate that ruled a large expanse of the Muslim world had long been a thing of the past. The Ottomans, however, saw themselves as a new caliphate and acted like one. They emerged as a major world power and remained one until the 20th century.

The Ottomans also continued the Muslim caliphate tradition of being a center of culture by creating schools to encourage the advancement of the sciences and math. Scholars were invited to study there, and many textbooks were written by Ottoman scholars, teaching everything from rhetoric and literature to advanced algebra and astronomy logarithms. There are still well-preserved copies of these textbooks on display in Turkish libraries.

The Ottomans were also responsible for huge accomplishments in astronomy because of their well-organized astronomical institutions, including an observatory and "time keeping houses" (Ayduz n.d.). Their interest in the keeping of time was closely related to their desire to have certain times set apart for their ritual Muslim prayers (Ayduz n.d.). Because of this, almost every town had its own timekeeping house near the mosque, which is where Muslims worship (Ayduz n.d.). Interestingly, it is in the earlier centuries of their reign that the Ottomans made the most technological advances.

Seizing Constantinople did not end the Ottomans' quest to expand their empire, though it was certainly one of their most important and significant conquests. Through the centuries, they continued to expand throughout Asia, the Middle East, Africa, and Europe. We will learn more about their activities in Europe in the next chapter.

NARRATION BREAK:

Talk about what you read today.

This painting depicts Ottoman astronomers at work in Constantinople.

THE OTTOMAN EMPIRE IN 1683
- Ottoman Beylik, 1300
- Acquisitions, 1300 – 1359
- Acquisitions, 1359 – 1451
- Acquisitions, 1451 – 1481 (Mehmed II)
- Acquisitions, 1512 – 1520 (Selim I)
- Acquisitions, 1520 – 1566 (Suleiman the Magnificent)
- Acquisitions, 1566 – 1683

This map shows the Ottoman Empire at its peak, as well as how it progressively reached that point. Though Constantinople did not fall until 1453, the Ottoman Empire had expanded to include the surrounding territory well before then. After the conquest of Constantinople, the Ottoman Empire continued to expand.

ANALYZE What do you notice about how the Ottoman boundaries changed over the years? Did they shrink or grow?

CONNECT Compare this map to the map of the Muslim caliphates on page 70. What is similar? What is different?

After the Ottoman conquest of the lands that were formerly under Byzantine rule, the Muslim sultans had a problem on their hands: what to do with all the "People of the Book," as they called the Jews and Christians (Meyendorff 2018). Muslims called Jews and Christians "People of the Book" because of their connection to the Bible. They solved their problem by organizing and establishing separate religious communities called "millets." This system did not give the Jews or Christians autonomy, though, and the millets were arranged with many class differentiations. The Christian millet was called the Rūm millet ("Roman nation") (Meyendorff 2018). Although the Muslim Ottomans showed some tolerance, these two religious groups were not considered equal with the Muslim millet.

Christians were allowed to conduct their own religious ceremonies and take care of their own civil law. However, they had to remain loyal to the Ottoman Empire. The Christian millet was also not afforded the privileges of the ruling Muslim millet. For example, they were not allowed to bear arms or join the military service (Smith, Haldon et al. 2018). Also, as we learned earlier, they were required to deliver to the Ottoman authorities a number of their sons to be trained to be used in the Janissary or as government officials. If a Christian found himself against a Muslim in a court of law, the Muslim's word was taken over the Christian's (Smith, Haldon et al. 2018). Christian men could not marry Muslim women, and if a Christian converted to Islam and then went back to their original Christian faith, the sentence was death (Smith, Haldon et al. 2018). The Christians of the Ottoman Empire lived during difficult times, but it is important for us to remember that no matter how bad things are, God is still always with us.

This illustration from the 1700s shows Mehmed II with Gennadios Scholarios, a Byzantine monk he appointed as head of the Orthodox Church. Mehmed wanted someone over the Church to calm the uncertain political situation in Constantinople after he had conquered the city.

Peter Mundy was a British merchant who traveled extensively in the early 1600s. These illustrations of his are of a shepherd and Greek priest in the Ottoman Empire.

Ottoman Constantinople

Constantinople has been a leading city of the world for centuries. During its history, it has been the capital of the Eastern Roman Empire, the Byzantine Empire, and the Ottoman Empire. It is now known as Istanbul and remains an important city in modern Turkey.

Turkey

The Imperial Council met in a special location at Topkapı Palace. The Grand Vizier ran this council for the sultan and usually handled the day-to-day running of the government.

Interior of the Topkapı Palace. The design and decoration of the palace combines Islamic, Ottoman, and European influences.

The Bosporus is a waterway that divides Europe from Asia. Modern-day Istanbul stretches out on both sides of the Bosporus.

In the 1800s, the sultans moved to a new palace in Constantinople — Dolmabahçe Palace. As with Topkapı, the architecture blended traditional Islamic architectural features with European ones.

A few years after conquering Constantinople, Mehmed II built a palace, Topkapı Palace. It served as the home of Ottoman sultans for centuries.

20

START HERE

The Ottoman conquest changed the lives of thousands of people. Among the conquered peoples were those who lived on the Balkan Peninsula. The Christians here, once under the rule of the Byzantine Christian empire, were seriously affected by the Ottomans' Islamic rule. As we work through this chapter together, I implore you to think about the following two things: there is sacrifice that is sometimes required of us to remain faithful to Christ and also how the historical events covered in this chapter are both different from and similar to the historical time period in which we live. To be a Christian sometimes requires us to face hardships that others do not have to face. Why do we face them with confidence? Before beginning this chapter, I want to share one of my favorite Scriptures with you. I want you to think about what it says as you read this chapter:

So God has given both his promise and his oath. These two things are unchangeable because it is impossible for God to lie. Therefore, we who have fled to him for refuge can have great confidence as we hold to the hope that lies before us. This hope is a strong and trustworthy anchor for our souls (Hebrews 6:18–19; NLT).

Vlad Tepes, Ivan the Terrible, & More

Let's start our chapter with a short geography lesson. In the southeast of Europe, there is the large Balkan Peninsula. This region includes modern countries like Greece, Albania, Macedonia, Bulgaria, Romania, Serbia, Bosnia, and Croatia. In our last chapter, we studied an overview of the Ottoman Empire. We watched as they expanded their domain until they controlled a vast area. One of their conquests was the Balkan Peninsula. For many centuries, this area had been controlled by the Byzantine Empire. That's one reason why, to this day, most Christians in the Balkans are Eastern Orthodox. Over the years, as the Ottoman Turks had conquered parts of the Byzantine Empire, much of the Balkans also fell under their control. The Ottoman conquest was made easier by the division and unrest and fighting between the Balkan states.

As the Ottomans marched through the Balkans, systematically conquering state after state, most of the old aristocracies were removed from power and replaced with an Islamic government and ruler. As each state was conquered, the land was placed under the control of the sultan, the Ottoman leader. In an adaptation of Byzantine administration, the system decreed that since the sultan was their false god's (Allah) representative on earth, all land belonged to him. However, portions of it were placed under the control of military leaders to administer.

In the Balkan states of Bosnia and Albania, the Ottoman conquerors allowed many of the nobles to remain because they converted to Islam, and because of their conversion, they were allowed to keep their land. Under the Ottoman rule, there were great benefits, both financial and political, for converting to Islam. Most other nobles refused to convert and lost their land. Although the Balkan Christians were not outright persecuted into converting to Islam, they dealt with higher taxes and reduced rights.

One of these taxes levied was the devshirme (dev-SHEER-may). This "tax of sons" was imposed on Christian families in the Balkans. Though it was called a tax, it was not paid with money. Instead, it involved Ottoman soldiers taking male children from their families and sending them far away to Constantinople. There, they were converted to Islam, educated in one of the Empire's finest schools, and introduced to Turkish culture. Once they had graduated, these young men became trusted officials and officers in

16th century illustration showing the devshirme in action

the Ottoman government and military. Not all boys were taken nor were they taken every year, but it resulted in thousands of young men being taken from their families and homes by force. Though some families were pleased with the opportunities that the system gave their children and encouraged recruiters to take them, others were horrified and resisted by hiding their children or bribing officers not to take them (Morrison n.d.; Hain 2012).

During this time of Ottoman domination of the Balkans, there was another unusual historical figure. Sometimes in history, someone who was real and rather terrifying became the inspiration for a story or legend. I promise that I will not make this scary or gruesome, but I do want to tell you about a man named Vlad Tepes (teh-PESH), Vlad III. Vlad lived in the 1400s in what is now Romania. Vlad and his two brothers were the sons of Vlad II Dracul. Their father was part of the Order of the Dragon, a group of men who stood in defense of Christian Europe against the Ottoman Empire.

A good example of how stories capture the public imagination and how people view history is Bran Castle in Romania. People call it Dracula's castle because it matches the one described in the 19th century novel. It is the model for the one in the book but is not actually Vlad Tepes' castle.

At the time, Vlad II was ruling the Romanian region of Wallachia. As Ottoman influence in the area grew, Vlad II pledged loyalty to the Ottoman sultan, Murad II. The sultan wanted to ensure that Vlad II would remain loyal in his new allegiance, so he took Vlad III and his younger brother Radu for collateral in 1442. Vlad III spent several years living as a hostage in Turkey. Little is known about his time there, but after his father and older brother were murdered several years later, Vlad III embarked on a lifelong campaign of revenge against the Ottomans. He was incredibly cruel in his tactics and is believed to be the inspiration for Irish novelist Bram Stoker's novel *Dracula*. (The name Dracula means "Son of Dracul.")

Painting of Vlad Tepes (Vlad III)

Interestingly enough, Radu, Vlad III's little brother who was also forced to live as an Ottoman hostage, remained in Turkey as an adult and seems to have embraced Ottoman culture. He was close friends with Mehmed II, the Ottoman leader who seized Constantinople. In fact, Radu was part of an Ottoman military force sent after his older brother. Vlad III was eventually killed in battle, but he had considerable military success against the Ottoman Empire during his lifetime.

The Ottoman Empire retained influence in the Balkans for centuries and remained a threat to Europe well into the 1600s, but the Ottoman Empire eventually began losing its grip and sinking into an irreversible decline. As other neighboring kingdoms like Russia and Austria grew in power and the Balkans began resisting Ottoman rule, the Ottoman Empire lost its extensive holdings in southeast Europe. We'll study more about that and its consequences in the next volume of this series.

NARRATION BREAK:

Discuss what you learned about the Balkans.

19th century painting depicts Vlad III meeting with Ottoman officials

One of the Balkans' neighbors is Russia. We have not studied Russian history yet, but the country had been settled first by the Slavs and then by the Vikings. This new mingled people spread out over a vast area of Russia. When the Vikings had first come, it was a Viking warrior named Rurik who first settled there in the 800s, and the Slavs called him and his people the "Rus." This is how we get the word "Russian." As generations passed, the descendants of the Slavs and the Vikings grew into tribes, which scattered all over the land. Just like many of the other places we have studied, Russia was divided up into clans and tribes, which were not united under one king.

Through the years, the Rus leaders grew stronger, but they were unable to conquer many of their enemies because they were not united. By this time, the Mongols had conquered much of Russia, just as they had large portions of Asia. Mongol control of the area was relatively loose. Though they had to pay taxes and tribute, the Russians maintained their own culture (including their Russian language and Orthodox Christian religion), and most of their local nobles retained their positions.

Finally, after a couple of centuries of Mongol rule, one Russian prince was strong enough to unite the regions into one nation. Ivan was a prince of Moscow, and he was tired of how the nobles were always fighting among themselves. Ivan believed that all this division made them weaker and more susceptible to enemy invasion. He was right, too. Ivan was a descendant of the mighty Viking Rurik and was determined to be the one to shake off the control of the Mongols and unite his people. After he had formed a large-enough army to get rid of the Mongols, he set out to conquer the other regions of Russia. Ivan became known as Ivan the Great because he united Russia.

Ivan the Great's Bell Tower. This cathedral tower is within the Kremlin in Moscow.

The capital was the old town of Moscow, and Ivan had an important government center developed right in the center of the city. This government center is called the Kremlin, and it is still used today. It dates from long before Ivan's rule, but he had it enlarged and renovated. You might have seen pictures of the great onion-domed cathedral. Ivan the Great worked hard to advance education and culture in Russia. By the end of Ivan's reign, Moscow had become one of the leading centers of the Eastern Orthodox Church because Constantinople and the Hagia Sophia had fallen to the Ottomans. Ivan the Great died in 1505.

Ivan's grandson, Ivan IV, was not like his grandfather. This Ivan became known as Ivan the Terrible, and he became the first tsar (ZAR, emperor) of Russia. In Russian, "Ivan the Terrible" meant "Ivan the Fearsome." Ivan was a difficult leader. He was deeply suspicious that the country's nobles were plotting against him. Even Ivan's advisers were under constant

scrutiny. Many of them lost their lives because of Ivan's paranoia. Ivan's secret police were known for being corrupt, greedy, and brutal. In their tsar's name, they evicted nobles from their homes and executed others. After his beloved wife died, Ivan the Terrible went rather insane. His hair fell out, and he became even more worried that someone was trying to take his throne. During an argument with his son, who was a grown man and heir to the throne, Ivan hit him on the head and killed him. For the rest of his life, Ivan wore black and refused to be comforted.

Following Ivan IV's death in 1584, his son Fyodor I came to the throne. Fyodor was weak, both physically and mentally; therefore, he was unable to rule effectively. His brother-in-law Boris Godunov was more than happy to take control of running Russia. Godunov, who had learned the ways of the court and government by working for Ivan the Terrible, was responsible for the major achievements during Fyodor I's reign. When Fyodor died in 1598, he did not leave an heir, thus bringing an end to the Rurik dynasty.

Boris Godunov was selected to become the new ruler. Some, however, did not think he was the rightful ruler, which led to wild rumors that Fyodor's deceased brother Dmitry was alive and should be tsar instead. When a powerful aristocratic family named the Romanovs opposed him, Boris banished them and took extensive measures to protect himself against anyone who would want to usurp his throne. These measures, coupled with his inability to help his people's suffering during a famine in the years 1601–1603, quickly lost Boris popularity and support.

Part of uniting all of Russia involved subduing independent lands. This 19th century painting depicts the fall of Novgorod, one of the wealthiest and most powerful Russian cities of the time. Ivan the Great conquered it to ensure it was not a rival to Moscow.

19th century Russian artist Alexander Litovchenko's painting of Ivan the Terrible showing his wealth to an ambassador from England

CONNECT In our chapter, we learned about a Russian ruler called Ivan the Terrible and his son, Fyodor I, who was a weak ruler. After the death of Fyodor I, his brother-in-law, who had been helping him rule before his death, took the throne. Boris Godunov was a better ruler than Fyodor, but it was during his reign that something very strange happened. I mentioned that there were wild rumors flying around about Fyodor's deceased brother Dmitry being alive. This is the story of the False Dmitrys and the Time of Troubles.

There are three False Dmitrys in this story, the first of which came to challenge Boris Godunov's right to the throne. Many historians have concluded that this pretender was actually a monk named Grigory who believed that he was the rightful heir to the throne. His claim to being Prince Dmitry was rewarded with a threat of banishment ("False Dmitry" 1998). He fled to Lithuania where he began gathering support from some key Lithuanian and Polish noblemen in 1603 for his campaign for the throne ("False Dmitry" 1998). In the fall of 1604, he invaded Russia but was defeated. Although his campaign ended in defeat, he gained supporters who believed that he was the rightful heir to the throne. When Boris Godunov died in the spring of 1605, his infant son was mysteriously murdered. The first False Dmitry then became the new tsar.

His success as a leader was short lived. His favoritism toward the Polish who had helped him win the throne angered his Russian followers. Even his wife, Marina Mniszek, was the daughter of a Polish nobleman. In 1606, one of the Russian noblemen, Vasily Shuysky, turned against him and led a coup against the first False Dmitry. Vasily Shuysky murdered the pretender and took his place as the tsar.

In 1607, rumors began to fly about that Dmitry had survived the coup. Another pretender appeared to claim to be the tsar. Interestingly, even though he did not look anything like the first False Dmitry, the

When Boris suddenly died in 1605, the country was thrown into chaos. Boris' son was assassinated, and Russia entered the Time of Troubles, a 15-year period marked by a series of revolts, governmental takeovers, and coups. Finally, in 1613, Michael Romanov was elected as the new tsar. He was distantly related to the Rurik dynasty (his grandfather had been Fyodor's mother's brother) and was accepted as the legitimate ruler. This was the beginning of the Romanov dynasty, which would rule Russia for more than 300 years.

NARRATION BREAK:

Talk about what you learned about Russia.

second False Dmitry gathered a large following, including the Poles and Lithuanians who had supported the first False Dmitry ("False Dmitry" 1998). After gaining control in southern Russia, False Dmitry 2 marched on Moscow. In 1608, he established his own court and government administration in the village of Tushino.

When the wife of False Dmitry 1, Marina Mniszek, claimed that False Dmitry 2 truly was her husband back from the grave, he had as much power as Shuysky ("False Dmitry" 1998). However, with the help of Swedish troops, Shuysky was able to defend his throne. False Dmitry 2 was fatally wounded in December of 1610. Finally, in March 1611, the last False Dmitry, a man historians have identified as a deacon called Sidorka, gained support of certain key people. His campaign was cut short when he was betrayed and executed in Moscow in May 1612 ("False Dmitry" 1998). Thus ends the strange tale of the three False Dmitrys. The False Dmitry stories show us how very chaotic Russia was during the Time of Troubles.

Mikhail Nesterov's *Tsarevich Dimitry,* 1899. This painting depicts the real prince.

False Dmitry I

False Dmitry II

The Balkans and Eastern Europe are important parts of the world that will play a significant role in medieval and modern history. Many Americans are not as familiar with this part of Europe as they are with the Western part. This map shows the modern boundaries, which are very different from what this area looked like during the time period we are studying. It's helpful to familiarize yourself with the countries on the map by locating places you already know to orient yourself.

ANALYZE   Did you recognize the name of any of the countries featured on the map? Why were you already familiar with them?

CONNECT   How many countries are in the Balkans region?

Christianity in Russia began when the country was still called Rus. In an area called Kievan Rus, the leader Vladimir I accepted the Orthodox Christian faith. This conversion came about as part of a pact with Byzantine Emperor Basil II. In exchange for marrying Basil's sister, Vladimir converted ("Kievan Rus" 2016). Following his conversion, his people were also required to convert (McGurkin 2014, 401). This was not the first introduction of Christianity to the area, but it helped lead to its wide acceptance.

In the 9th century, even before Vladimir's conversion, the Bible was translated into Old Church Slavonic, "the first Slavic literary language," because of the work of missionaries Saints Cyril and Methodius ("Old Church Slavonic Language" 2018). (Slavic is a language family. Many Eastern European languages, like Russian, are Slavic.) Although Cyril (sih-RIL) and Methodius' work in Moravia in central Europe only lasted a while, their disciples created a new script for Slavic, based on capital Greek letters ("Old Church Slavonic Language" 2018). This alphabet is called Cyrillic, named after St. Cyril, and is still used by many Eastern European languages today. The Cyrillic alphabets used in modern Russian, Bulgarian, and Serbian are modified from the original. The Russian Cyrillic alphabet has even been adapted for use by non-Slavic languages ("Cyrillic Alphabet" 2015).

Boris and Gleb. They were the sons of Vladimir I and were martyred in 1015. They have long been popular religious figures in Russian culture.

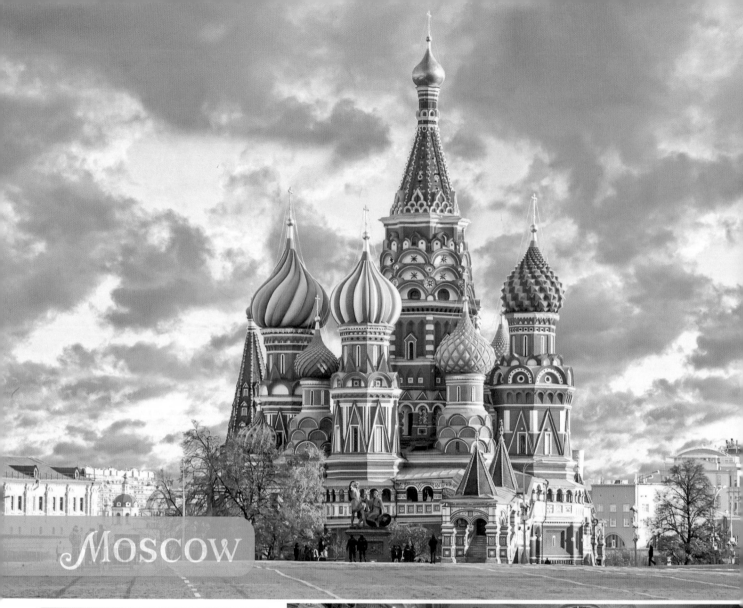

Moscow

Moscow was the capital of Russia from the time of the tsars to the 1700s, when the government relocated to St. Petersburg. In 1918, Moscow was again made the capital. One of the most famous sites in Moscow is the stunning St. Basil's Cathedral.

Russia

The Bolshoi Theatre is one of the most famous in all the world. It is the home of internationally acclaimed opera and ballet troupes.

The Kremlin is in Red Square. Like all of Russia, Moscow is noted for its harsh winters. The Russians are used to the bitter cold. In recent years, during the winter, Red Square has hosted a skating rink.

The Kremlin has been used by tsarist, communist, and the current Russian government as their headquarters.

Outside of Moscow is Kolomenskoye, a summer retreat used by Moscow nobles, as well as the tsars. The Church of the Ascension, the tall building in this picture, was built to celebrate the birth of Ivan the Terrible.

21

START HERE

Have you ever decided to clean out your closet — or perhaps your parents told you that it needed to be done and you begrudgingly agreed? Either way, cleaning out a closet can actually turn into an adventurous walk down memory lane! I recently did this and discovered a box of old keepsakes that I placed there a number of years ago. Over time, other objects were piled on top of it until I had mostly forgotten about its existence. When I removed all the other containers and boxes that had piled up on top, I remembered I had placed it there for safekeeping. Rediscovering the memorabilia stored inside was amazing! There were tiny booties worn by my now 24-year-old son, pictures of my children riding around on my husband's back, and even a bit of lace from my wedding veil. I was instantly transported back in time, and after sorting through the contents of that one box, my youngest daughter and I spent several hours looking at picture albums and reading old cards and letters that we have saved through the two-and-a-half decades of our family's existence. In this chapter, we are going to learn about the beginnings of a monumental event and era in history called the Renaissance, which means reawakening. In many ways, this waking up happened because of the rediscovery of something old and precious.

THE DAWN OF THE RENAISSANCE

In this chapter, we are going to learn about a period of history called the Renaissance, a time of grand cultural, social, and economic awakening. This period of growth, reawakening, and change is generally placed as occurring during the 1300s through about 1600, so it is important for us to remember that all these changes did not happen overnight or even in one century.

Throughout the Renaissance, many events opened the door and facilitated this change — far too many to learn about in one chapter. Therefore, we will focus on a few of the major contributing factors in this chapter, followed by a look at some of the major Renaissance artists in our next chapter. The beginning of the Renaissance, which started in Italy, is historically considered the end of the Middle Ages.

A couple chapters ago, we learned about how the Ottoman Turks fought long and hard against the crumbling Byzantine Empire. Their focus was on the high-walled city of Constantinople. This city had stood against invaders from every direction for centuries, but the city eventually fell to the Ottomans, who destroyed the Christian statues and symbols of the Eastern Orthodox Church. They even turned the beautiful Eastern Orthodox cathedral, the Hagia Sophia, into a mosque for the Muslim faith.

The fall of the great city of Constantinople would be instrumental in the development of the Renaissance, a change that would affect every single aspect of life in Europe, including the way people thought and believed. You see, Constantinople had been the center of the Eastern Orthodox religion for an extremely long time. For many centuries, this city was the safe-keeper of a large variety of classical writings from the time of the Greeks, beautiful manuscripts containing the Holy Scriptures and many other types of ancient writings and scrolls. These treasures were stored in Constantinople and cared for by the Eastern Orthodox Church.

When the Ottomans attacked and conquered Constantinople, many of these scholars and monks ran for their lives, taking many of these treasures with them. Although the ancient authors had been all but forgotten for hundreds of years by Western Europe and most of the world, these Byzantine scholars risked their lives to save the scrolls and manuscripts for future generations. As they fled to the west, these scholars searched for a place

Giovanni di Paolo's *Paradise*, 1400s. Unlike most of the famous Renaissance painters, di Paolo was based in the Italian city of Siena and not Florence. Siena is approximately 50 miles south of Florence.

Michelangelo's *The Creation of Adam*, circa 1511. This painting on the ceiling of the Sistine Chapel is one of the most famous in the world.

to re-establish their places of study. Most eventually settled in Italy, and new interest in learning and ancient writings began to develop there. These writings were not only biblical manuscripts but also writings from ancient Greek philosophers, which sparked interest in philosophy.

We have also learned about the horrible Black Death that destroyed more than one-third of the European population and how social classes and the economy changed dramatically in the aftermath. That social change marked the beginning of the end for the feudal system that had been in place since the fall of the Western Roman Empire. This restructuring and shifting of classes, both social and economic, also triggered interest in culture. That's because for many centuries during the Middle Ages, folks thought mostly about staying alive, keeping food on the table for their families, and making it through their lives without dying of the plague or some other type of mysterious illness. Survival was their focus. Now, with better wages and higher quality of lives, many people began lifting their heads from the daily grind long enough to take notice of the new artwork, philosophy, and literature that was appearing.

The result of these very different societal changes was a rebirth (renaissance) of interest in ancient art, philosophy, rhetoric, and writing. The Renaissance scholars were like the ancient writers in that they stressed practical human actions and individualism, but these new scholars also focused on the original intent and language of the scriptural text. This shift and restructuring, along with this new focus on learning and creativity, led many people to change the way they looked at life. Many started thinking differently about what was important. They began learning about philosophy and studying the classical literary works. This new way of thinking, where people were becoming interested in bettering themselves, was called humanism.

In our time, when we hear the word "humanist," we think of someone who worships human thinking, completely excluding God from the picture, but during the Renaissance, a humanist was someone who emphasized personal, human involvement with their life, including their relationship with God. Many Renaissance humanists believed God was interested in speaking to the individual humans He had created. This was very different from how the medieval Church operated, and it helped lead to the Protestant Reformation, which we will study in-depth in a few chapters.

NARRATION BREAK:

Talk about what you read today.

As we learned in the last section, the Renaissance started in Italy because this is where most of the scholars found refuge after the fall of Constantinople. At this time in history, Italy was not a united country, ruled by one central government. Instead, it was divided into city-states. These city-states were regions that were ruled by a major city. Some of them were ruled by elected officials, but many of them were governed by wealthy, influential families. One thing these city-states had in common was that they liked to fuss with each other. If they weren't dealing with a foreign intruder, they were bickering and warring among themselves. With all this fussing and fighting, stronger city-states eventually took over the smaller ones.

Let's learn about the five most historically important city-states. Florence was a large, influential city-state in central Italy that was governed by the Medici (MED-uh-chee), an extremely rich family of bankers. We will learn more about this family in a few moments because they were not only influential in their own city-state, but they were also an extremely important factor in the Renaissance. In fact, the Renaissance started in Florence, and the city was famous for the amazing artwork created there.

Next, we have Milan, a city-state ruled by other rich families — the Visconti and then the Sforza families. Milan was famous for their intricate metalworking, especially the armor. The next city-state, Venice, became powerful through trade with the Middle East and controlled the seas around the northeastern coast of Italy. You might remember how the shameful Crusaders that sacked Constantinople had financing and ships provided by Venetian merchants. That's because merchants from this city were well known for being wealthy due to all the trade by sea that the city was involved in,

The Pazzi Chapel in Florence, Italy, is a famous religious building. It was designed by Filippo Brunelleschi, one of the leading Italian Renaissance architects and engineers.

Portrait of Pope Alexander VI, painted by the Italian Renaissance painter Cristofano dell'Altissimo

and the Crusaders contracted with them specifically for this reason. Venetians were also famous for their beautiful glassware. Naples was a city-state that ruled much of Southern Italy at the time of the Renaissance. The final city-state, Rome (or the Papal States), was ruled by the pope, who also ruled the Catholic Church. Rome was also known for its gorgeous artwork.

Let's take a few moments to learn about two of the most powerful and prominent families who had vast influence in the Renaissance world. First, we will look at the Borgia (BOR-juh) family. The Borja (the Spanish version of their name) family originated in Valencia, Spain, but settled in Italy. The house of the Borgia was influential in the Church and politics, producing two popes, Pope Calixtus III and Pope Alexander VI.

This Alexander VI, whose real name was Rodrigo de Borgia, had 11 children, whom he famously used to further his political agendas. The Borgia family is known for being powerful yet corrupt and violent, willing to do almost anything to gain power. Interestingly, Alexander VI contributed to the development of the Protestant Reformation, which we will learn about in a coming chapter, because he was such a bad and corrupt pope who neglected the Church.

Michelangelo's Moses sculpture, early 1500s

The other powerful and influential family that I would like to tell you about is the Medici family. The Medici are perhaps the most famous of all Italian Renaissance families. Giovanni de Medici was a leader of the Florence merchants, and he started the Medici Bank, which would grow to be the largest bank in Europe. They established branches throughout Europe and were famously known as "God's bankers" because they were the bankers for the pope. Their bank would also become a world leader in a new style and technique of accounting.

They eventually ruled the city-state of Florence and later the Tuscany region from the 1400s to the 1700s. Like the Borgia family, the Medici produced several popes. Popes Leo X, Clement VII, Pius IV, and Leon XI were all from the Medici family. There were also several marriages between members of the Medici house and royal families of Europe. Perhaps the most famous marriage to a European royal family was between Catherine de' Medici and King Henry II of France. She became queen of France and was a great supporter of the arts and is responsible for bringing ballet to the French court. The Medici family was famous for its patronage of the arts. That means that they helped support artists. They found great honor in sponsoring artists, and a significant amount of the art and architecture that was produced in Florence during the early Renaissance period was due to Medici help and patronage.

Cristofano dell'Altissimo's *Portrait of Giovanni di Bicci de' Medici*, 16th century. Giovanni founded the Medici family bank in the late 1300s.

Raphael's *The School of Athens* depicts famous ancient Greek philosophers. Interest in ancient Greece and Rome increased during the Italian Renaissance.

Some of the most famous artists of the Renaissance were close friends of the Medici family. They supported and financed such artists as Michelangelo, Raphael, Donatello, and Leonardo da Vinci. They financed the work of the painter Masaccio and Brunelleschi, the Italian architect who rebuilt the Basilica of San Lorenzo. The Medici family also sponsored and encouraged the sciences. At one time, Galileo Galilei (gah-luh-LAY-oh gah-luh-LAY-ee) was a close family friend and tutored the Medici children in mathematics and science.

The Renaissance may have started in Italy, but it did not stay in Italy. Renaissance ideas, art, and philosophy spread to other European countries. This is called the Northern Renaissance. France was first to become privy to the new arts and sculptures of the Italian Renaissance when they invaded Italy in the late 1400s. King Francis I of France invited Italian artists to move to France. They greatly influenced French architecture, and soon, airy and spacious chateaus surrounded by beautiful landscaping replaced dark medieval castles. The Renaissance also spread to the Dutch and the Germans. In fact, German inventor Johannes Gutenberg (yo-HAHN-us GOOT-en-berg) made one of the most significant contributions to the Renaissance with his invention of the printing press. This revolutionized the world of book-making and helped bring the Bible into the hands of ordinary people.

NARRATION BREAK:

Talk about Renaissance Italy and the Northern Renaissance.

Donatello's sculpture of John the Apostle

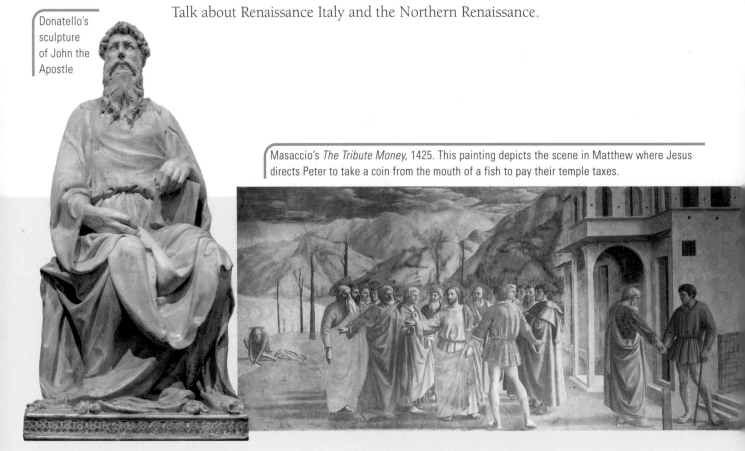

Masaccio's *The Tribute Money,* 1425. This painting depicts the scene in Matthew where Jesus directs Peter to take a coin from the mouth of a fish to pay their temple taxes.

CONNECT

We have learned that the Church had a strong influence on the culture of the Middle Ages. Certain aspects of that influence were helpful and necessary, while others were motivated by the want of power. Interestingly, one of the major areas of their control lay in the study of science. The Church prescribed to the thoughts and philosophy of ancient Greek philosopher Aristotle, especially his teachings about the universe. This man and his contemporaries taught theories that sound ridiculous to us now but were considered highly scientific at that time. One of these theories was about a geocentric universe. Geo means earth, so this means "earth at the center." To Aristotle, it simply made sense that the earth was an unmoving sphere in the middle of the universe. You noticed I said sphere: Aristotle believed that the earth was, indeed, round.

At the time of the Renaissance, many areas of life were progressing. One of these areas was astronomy. There were several prominent astronomers who made giant strides toward extremely important discoveries. In this section, we are going to learn a little about Galileo Galilei, an Italian scientist, natural philosopher, and mathematician. Galileo contributed to science with his discoveries about motion and astronomy and development of the scientific method (Van Helden 2018). One of his biggest contributions was in the field of astronomy. In 1609, he began working on developing a telescope. He studied the moon and drew the phases (Van Helden 2018). He discovered that the moon is rough and textured instead of smooth, as was believed before (Van Helden 2018). He also made significant discoveries about Venus, Saturn, and Jupiter, including Jupiter's four largest moons (Van Helden 2018).

When he discovered that the telescope shows far more stars than the naked eye could see, he wrote and published a short book about it. Galileo was not popular with the Church because he did not support Aristotle's geocentric model of the universe. Instead, he was a stanch supporter of astronomer Nicolaus Copernicus' heliocentric (sun in the middle) model (Van Helden 2018). At the time, the Catholic Church regarded the heliocentric view as heretical. So ardently did the Church oppose the Copernican theory of the universe that Galileo was reprimanded numerous times for writing about it in his books. In the year 1633, he was tried by the Inquisition and was condemned to life imprisonment (Van Helden 2018).

This painting of *The Last Supper* is a copy of the more famous version painted by da Vinci. This one was painted by an artist named Giampietrino about 25 years later.

This map shows what Italy looked like in the late 1400s. As you can see, it was divided into numerous city-states. Italy itself was not united for another few hundred years, and not all the territory shown as belonging to the Italian city-states ended up as part of modern Italy.

If you are looking for the major city-states we discussed in the chapter, you will find them all on the map. Can you see them? Venice is on the top right in northeast Italy. Milan is to the left, more in the northwest part of Italy. Florence, where the Renaissance started, is farther south than either of those cities. Rome is even farther south than Florence, and Naples is even farther south than Rome in southern Italy.

MAPS

ANALYZE   What are the biggest city-states on the map? What are the smallest city-states on the map?

CONNECT   What are the seas that surround Italy and Sicily?

Do you own a Bible? Chances are you own at least one. I personally love reading a variety of versions as I study the Scripture and therefore own no fewer than seven Bibles. My very favorite one is a journaling Bible. I enjoy how I can journal, draw, and color while I read and pray my way through the Scriptures. Bibles are so readily available to us that it is easy to take them for granted. But Bibles have not always been accessible.

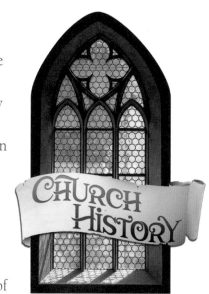

As the Renaissance moved throughout Europe, scientific discoveries and innovative inventions were much more common than in the centuries before. One such invention changed the world in more ways than I'm sure this inventor ever imagined it would. Johannes Gutenberg's movable type printing press not only changed the world of printing, but it also changed the world on a spiritual level.

You see, the first big Gutenberg printing project was a Bible. The Gutenberg Bible is also called the Forty-two line Bible because of its unique layout. It was completed in 1455 in Mainz, Germany. The Bible was a three-volume set with printing in 42-line columns ("Gutenberg Bible" 2016). Like many books of that time, the Gutenberg Bible has no page numbers ("Gutenberg Bible" 2016).

The Gutenberg Bible was the first printed book in the Western world. (The technology had existed earlier in Asia.) It paved the way for the mass production of books — like the one you are reading right now! — and did away with the centuries-old practice of copying manuscripts by hand. This made it much easier for anyone who could read to have access to books. It also gave people access to Bibles. No longer did people have to rely on what a priest said the Bible tells us. People could now read it for themselves. These changes significantly altered how people lived and worshiped.

There are approximately 40 copies of the Gutenberg Bible in existence today ("Gutenberg Bible" 2016). There are well-preserved complete ones in the U.S. Library of Congress, the French Bibliothèque National, and the British Library ("Gutenberg Bible" 2016). There are several almost complete texts in various other locations ("Gutenberg Bible" 2016).

19th century engraving of Gutenberg at work with his press

VENICE

The city of Venice is entirely surrounded by a lagoon, as this picture from space shows. Venice is made up of dozens of islands, connected by bridges and canals.

Italy

Because of Venice's location near so much water, flooding is a recurring problem. A project currently in place is trying to build flood barriers to protect the city.

When Venice was its own city-state, it was run by an elected leader called a doge (DOH-jay). This official lived in the Doge's Palace right by the water.

The main waterway through Venice is the Grand Canal. Cars are not allowed to drive in Venice. To get anywhere, people must either walk or use water-based transportation, like water taxis and water buses.

The gondola boat is a popular way to travel the canals of Venice. A gondolier (gon-do-LEER) drives the boat.

22

START HERE

In all of history, there was not another era in which the world of art changed more than the Renaissance. In this chapter, we will watch the flat characters of yesteryear's art transform and take on a whole new depth. This newly developed technique of dimension would forever affect every aspect of the art world. Individuality, coupled with the new prestige and freedom of creativity they now enjoyed, allowed each major artist to leave their legacy for the world. Come along with me as we make an acquaintance with a few of the biggest names in art history. Among them, we'll shake hands with Michelangelo, the sculptor and painter who famously painted a ceiling, and nod to Leonardo da Vinci, who exquisitely intertwined his passions for anatomy and art.

THE ART OF THE RENAISSANCE

In our last chapter, we learned about a few of the influential factors that led to the Renaissance. One of these was the rediscovery of the ancient classics. Artwork depicting these scenes had been rare before this time, but it became increasingly popular for Renaissance artists of this period to paint depictions of these characters, showing them in action at the climax of the story.

All this artwork depicting mythical creatures and characters was very different from what artwork had been like before the Renaissance. You might remember studying about this in Chapter 5. For many centuries, the Church influenced most of the culture, so most art centered around the Catholic Church. This was not a bad thing (after all, it was the Church that helped much of the population through hard times), but because of these restrictions, artists were not encouraged to express themselves freely. Instead, they were usually commissioned by the Church to create something specific that would be displayed in a church. Most paintings and statues depicted scenes of the Bible, with the most common focus being either Mary and baby Jesus (called a Madonna (muh-DON-uh) with child) or of Christ Himself as a grown man.

However, with the coming of the classics and a renewed interest in elements of life outside the Church, the art world became the pulse of the Renaissance. Although there was a fair amount of artwork still centered around religious imagery, the style of painting, the individual expression of each artist, and the overall feeling that it gave the viewer was entirely different from that of the old style of art. Formerly, art had been merely decorative or used to tell a simple story and artists were considered craftsmen, but now art was valued as an immensely important element of life — it represented a connection to the spirit and the mind of an individual. During the Renaissance, it was recognized that a truly gifted artist can touch viewers' emotions and make them feel a connection. This change in the way art is studied and viewed is still influential today.

Before the Renaissance, European artwork was more simplistic, with a distinctly underdeveloped quality. Artistic technique had remained stagnant for many centuries, causing much of the artwork produced to look remarkably similar. If you study the artwork from the Middle Ages, you will notice how flat the pictures appear, and to an untrained eye, one painting looks basically like the next, regardless of who the painter was.

Leonardo da Vinci's best-known painting, the *Mona Lisa*, c. 1503

Masaccio's painting of John and Peter healing the sick, 1400s

Improvements in depth and perspective were one of the major ways Renaissance art differed from medieval art. You may also remember learning about this in Chapter 5 when we learned about medieval art.

Though other medieval artists had experimented with the idea, it was during the early 15th century that an artist by the name of Masaccio (Ma-ZAT-cho) improved on technique, making his art less flat-looking and more like what he saw when he looked around. His paintings were not famous or even popular when he was alive, but after his death, many other artists of the time came to see his work. They were amazed at how it looked like you could walk into his paintings. The characters were painted in such a way that they looked like they were standing behind each other, and the horizon line looked like it did in the real world around them. This fascinated the other artists, and soon, they too were experimenting with bringing this element into their work.

Remember in our last chapter when we discussed how wealthy, influential individuals took great pride in sponsoring artists during the Renaissance period? The patronage of these wealthy families and individuals is responsible for the tremendous growth in the Renaissance art world, and the artists enjoyed the privilege of a highly honored position in society. They were looked upon almost as royalty, and their work was placed in prominent places.

When I am learning about something new in history, I like to connect the unfamiliar events and time periods with more familiar happenings. This type of organization helps me to see a bigger part of the whole picture, and it helps me to see connections that I may otherwise miss. Let's do that with the Renaissance. We are all familiar with this rhyme that we use as a mnemonic device to help us remember the date that Columbus (whom we'll study in Volume 3) sailed in search of a westerly route to the Indies: "In 1492, Columbus sailed the ocean blue." Columbus sailed from Spain in the same period that these Italian artists were experimenting and discovering ways to improve their methods. The Renaissance artists were more interested in studying the classics and improving their educations and lifestyles than exploring the world, but in many ways, their Renaissance ideas, philosophy, literature, and art were going to change the world as much as the explorers setting sail for places unknown did.

NARRATION BREAK:

Discuss what you read today.

 **CONNECT** Printmaking is an interesting way of creating art. Printmaking is how artists can produce images on paper or other materials but without using paint or more traditional materials (Peterdi 2018). The equipment that makes prints enables the artist to make multiple copies easily. Printmaking has many different techniques and processes.

Though printmaking had existed in China for centuries, it was not used in Europe until the Renaissance. In the Northern Renaissance, printmaking became a wonderfully unique form of art. In the 15th century, popular forms included both series of illustrations created for books, as well as a multitude of single prints. Interestingly, these prints are neither signed nor dated, making it difficult to know their origins, and because they portrayed religious figures, they were carried from place to place by religious pilgrims, making it even more difficult to trace their origins (Peterdi 2018).

There were two main techniques used for printmaking during this time. The first one is intaglio (in-TAL-yo). Intaglio prints were created by carving a design or picture into a printing plate. These indentations were then brushed with ink, and the excess is wiped away (Peterdi 2018). This process is similar to embossing (Peterdi 2018). You can think of intaglio as being a concave stamp (The ink is in the sunken area).

Renaissance-era etching by German artist Daniel Hopfer. He is believed to be the first artist to use etching with printmaking.

The second technique was relief printmaking. This technique is the opposite of intaglio. Where intaglio is a concave stamp, relief printing is convex, meaning it sticks out from the printing plate surface. This style of printing is very similar to our modern-day rubber stamping. The image is drawn in reverse on a printing surface, with the excess areas carved away, leaving the design raised (Peterdi 2018). The ink is brushed across the raised image and then stamped onto the paper or material. In both techniques, there is a variety of ways to carve the design and therefore to create shading and shadowing.

Now, we will learn about some of the most famous artists in history. These Renaissance artists spun the world on its ear, and it has never been the same again. I am sure that many of you hearing or reading this story have heard the name Michelangelo, the famous artist who painted the ceiling of the Sistine (sih-STEEN) Chapel in Rome, Italy. Michelangelo's full name was Michelangelo di Lodovico Buonarroti Simoni. History simply calls him Michelangelo (my-keh-LAN-juh-low).

Michelangelo considered himself a sculptor, not a painter. Sometimes, his paintings look more like statues for this reason. When Pope Julius II asked him to create paintings depicting famous stories from the Bible, Michelangelo initially was reluctant to do so. It took him four-and-a-half years of painstaking labor to complete the ceiling of the Sistine Chapel, but it is widely regarded as a masterpiece.

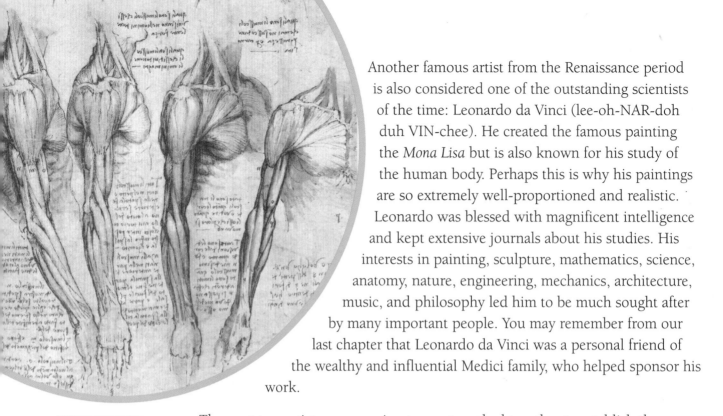

Another famous artist from the Renaissance period is also considered one of the outstanding scientists of the time: Leonardo da Vinci (lee-oh-NAR-doh duh VIN-chee). He created the famous painting the *Mona Lisa* but is also known for his study of the human body. Perhaps this is why his paintings are so extremely well-proportioned and realistic. Leonardo was blessed with magnificent intelligence and kept extensive journals about his studies. His interests in painting, sculpture, mathematics, science, anatomy, nature, engineering, mechanics, architecture, music, and philosophy led him to be much sought after by many important people. You may remember from our last chapter that Leonardo da Vinci was a personal friend of the wealthy and influential Medici family, who helped sponsor his work.

Examples of da Vinci's anatomy studies. These drawings are from one of his many notebooks.

The next two artists we are going to meet worked together to establish the Venetian school of Italian Renaissance Painting. Giorgione Barbarelli da Castelfranco was known for his "poetic" style of painting. Not much is known about Giorgione (shgee-or-GO-nee), and only six pieces of his work remain. We do know through written accounts about him that he was a significant influence on the world of Renaissance art. We also know that he was the teacher of another Italian painter, Tiziano Vecellio, better known as Titian (TISH-un). Titian is known for his use of color and his distinctive brushwork. His brushwork was less precise than that of other painters, but it was extremely expressive. Titian had much influence on the future generations of artists.

In the late 1400s, when France invaded Italy and encountered the beautifully innovative Renaissance art, the French king was enthralled. As we learned in our last chapter, this was the beginning of the spread of the Renaissance to other European countries. The Netherlands was one of the countries most influenced and changed by the Renaissance art. The Renaissance was also highly influential among the Dutch-speaking Flemish in what is now Belgium. In fact, there were advances in painting among the Dutch and Flemish before the Italian Renaissance's influence reached the area. The Northern Renaissance painters were less interested in depicting scenes from the classics than they were in making extremely detailed, realistic-looking artwork, often about everyday life.

One of the contributions of the Northern Renaissance was their pioneering use of oil paint. Italian painters often used fresco or tempera paint, but the Dutch painters from the Netherlands and the Flemish painters from Belgium quickly mastered the art of oil painting. One of these early Northern Renaissance painters was Jan Van Eyck. He used to be incorrectly credited as the inventor of oil paint, which became one of the most popular paints and remains a favorite of artists today. Though van Eyck did not invent oil paint, he was an early pioneer of its use, and his lovely, detailed paintings still hold their vivid colors well to this day. He was followed by many other talented Northern Renaissance painters.

Among them was Pieter Bruegel (BREW-gul), an artist who loved to paint crowds. In fact, it is said that he never passed up a chance to paint a throng of people in their natural habitats. He loved to paint groups of people enjoying themselves after a long week of work. He also frequently painted peasants, as well as landscapes. Pieter had taken a trip to Italy to see what the fuss was about. He saw the paintings and the statues, and then he returned home determined to be true to his own style of art. He drew more inspiration from his fellow Northern Renaissance painters but still maintained his unique style and vision. Because of this determination to stick to his individual style and view of art and life, Pieter Bruegel is considered one of the greatest Flemish Renaissance artists.

NARRATION BREAK:

Talk about the Renaissance artists you read about.

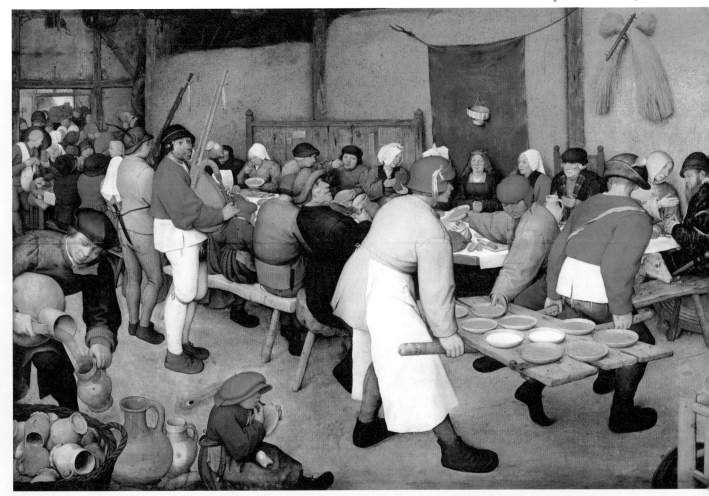

Pieter Bruegel's *The Peasant Wedding*, 1560s

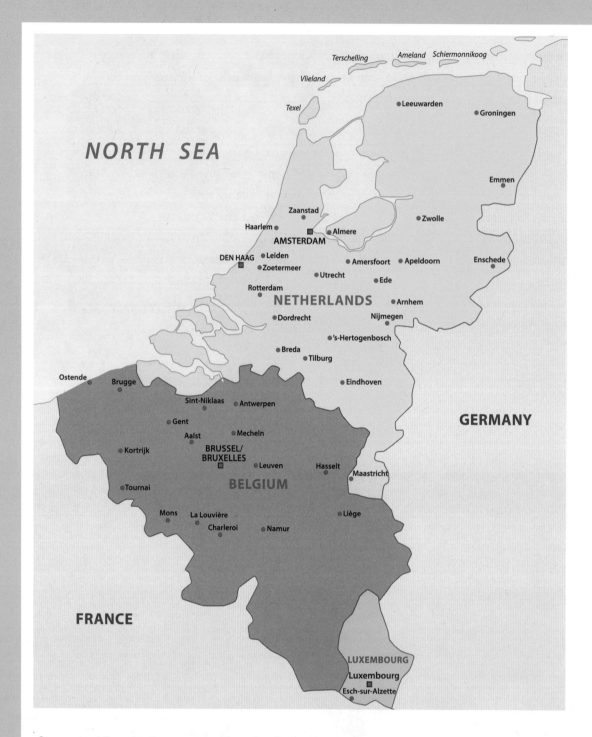

One part of Europe that was significantly affected by the Northern Renaissance is the Low Countries. This area is called that because so much of it is below sea level or right at sea level. The Low Countries are what the modern-day nations of Belgium, the Netherlands, and Luxembourg are called.

As the map shows, the Low Countries are between France and what is now Germany. This location has long affected their culture. The nation of Belgium, for instance, is divided between French speakers and those who speak Flemish, a dialect of the Germanic language Dutch.

ANALYZE	The Netherlands and Belgium border which sea?
CONNECT	What are the two major cities in the Netherlands? (Hint: They're labeled differently than the other cities.)

In our chapter, we learned about the famous sculptor and painter Michelangelo, who painted the Sistine Chapel. When you hear the word "chapel," you may think of a small church that serves as an intimate gathering place for a small number of people to worship. This is not what the Sistine Chapel is, however. Built in the years 1473–1481, the Sistine was designed by an architect named Giovanni dei Dolci on the orders of Pope Sixtus IV, and that is whom it was named after ("Sistine Chapel" 2018). The Sistine Chapel is the pope's personal chapel, used for special ceremonies. Although it is most famous for its frescoes (a type of painting on plaster) by Michelangelo, the Chapel is also home to several other artists' beautiful works.

Adorning the north wall are six frescoes showing events from the life of Christ, painted by the artists Perugino, Pinturicchio, Sandro Botticelli, Domenico Ghirlandaio, and Cosimo Rosselli ("Sistine Chapel" 2018). The south wall is painted with six more frescoes showing the life of Moses by several Renaissance artists ("Sistine Chapel" 2018). Smaller frescoes of the popes fill the space between the windows ("Sistine Chapel" 2018). During official occasions, the lower sections of the walls are covered with tapestries designed by Raphael that depict scenes from the Gospels and Acts ("Sistine Chapel" 2018).

Even today, tourists still flock to the Sistine Chapel to experience Michelangelo's artwork.

FLORENCE

Centuries after its heyday as the birthplace of the Renaissance, Florence still remains an important Italian cultural center. Some visitors are so overcome with the many artistic masterpieces in the city that local medical professionals are on the lookout for overwhelmed tourists, a condition called Stendhal Syndrome.

Italy

Though the dome of the Florence Cathedral is more famous, the entire structure is ornate. Due to Florence's reputation as an artistic center, there was never any shortage of skilled artists to work on commissions in the city during the Renaissance.

There are numerous homes in the city connected to the Medici family. This is the courtyard of one of these homes — the Palazzo Medici-Riccardi. These homes (and the city's museums) are full of classic art from the Renaissance period.

Florence is located in the central Italian region of Tuscany, which is noted for its beauty. Many Italians are proud of their local regions, especially since these regions were independent of each other for centuries.

The cathedral in Florence is well known for its famous dome.

A street in Florence

23

START HERE

When Jesus died on that Cross, He conquered death and sin. He created a way to the Father through forgiveness. He did not give us this gift to squander or misuse. In this chapter, we are going to learn about a time of purification in the Christian Church. Before we work through this section of our journey, I want you to read one of my favorite sections of Scripture, which teaches us what we should do with the amazing gift of grace and mercy bestowed on all of us who are called the adopted children of God:

Once you were dead because of your disobedience and your many sins. You used to live in sin, just like the rest of the world, obeying the devil — the commander of the powers in the unseen world. He is the spirit at work in the hearts of those who refuse to obey God. All of us used to live that way, following the passionate desires and inclinations of our sinful nature. By our very nature we were subject to God's anger, just like everyone else. But God is so rich in mercy, and he loved us so much, that even though we were dead because of our sins, he gave us life when he raised Christ from the dead. (It is only by God's grace that you have been saved!) (Ephesians 2:1–5; NLT).

As the Renaissance slowly awakened Europe, God used many people to question long-standing beliefs that had held His people captive. The Church had long been a dominant force in European society. It had achieved a lot of good in preserving scholarship and helping the poor. However, the Church had also become increasingly corrupt.

As we have studied in earlier chapters, the Christian Church at this time was divided between the Eastern Orthodox, who were mainly in Eastern Europe and Asia, and the Roman Catholics, who were dominant in Western Europe. The pope led the Roman Catholic Church, but his political influence and wealth had increased over the years. Many thought that he should not have this kind of power. This unhappiness with the pope especially increased as countries began to develop national identities. As we studied with the Hundred Years' War, people began to see themselves as English or French (and other nationalities), with their own kings. The pope's broad political power made him seem like a threat to the authority of kings.

Others were unhappy with the Church's policies. For example, as more people learned to read, people wanted to read the Bible for themselves. This was strongly opposed by the Church, which had been the center of education and scholarship. If people could read and Bibles became available in everyone's native tongue, rather than in the Latin that was reserved for scholars and priests, many clergy felt that their authority and position would be threatened. Church positions were also often sold instead of going to the person most qualified for the job. This caused corruption and meant that some high-ranking church officials were more interested in having prestige and power rather than doing the right thing.

Others were opposed to how the Church handled forgiveness of sin. The Catholic Church taught that, to ask for forgiveness, people had to confess their sins to a priest, who would absolve them after the sinner had performed penance (usually in the form of prepared prayers). Another method of obtaining forgiveness was through indulgences. You might remember learning about them when we studied the Crusades. Indulgences were certificates that exempted the owner from having to do penance. The selling of these certificates became a

Joseph Noel Paton's 1861 painting depicts Luther's realization while reading Romans.

business all over Europe. Even though this was not their original intent, the Church had become more and more corrupt.

The state of the Church was not going unnoticed by everyone, however! As always, God had His man of the hour, and He had His Word ready to cut through the darkness. John Wycliffe (WIH-cliff), a professor in England in the 1300s, believed wholeheartedly that the Church was not built on traditions, clergy, popes, and indulgences. He believed that the Church was made up of all the people who loved Jesus and followed Him with all their hearts and lives. He believed, and rightly so, that the Church needed God's Word. They needed to have and hold their own Bible written in their own language!

Of course, this didn't go well with the church leaders of the day. The church leaders were mad at Wycliffe for translating the Bible, but during his lifetime, they were not able to harm him or make him stop writing. He died before finishing his translating project, but his work was completed by his followers. As these faithful friends handed out these new Bibles, they preached hope, forgiveness, and the power of a personal relationship with God. A light had been turned on. God's Word is a bright light — a light that extinguishes the darkest night!

The teachings of John Wycliffe took root beyond his native England. People were beginning to know Jesus and follow Him instead of the Church's teachings about who controlled the Church on Earth. As the truth leaped and catapulted its way across borders, it fell on the ears of a professor and priest from the modern-day Czech Republic. Jan Hus was a brilliant man, and when he heard the teachings of Wycliffe, he readily embraced the joyful truth.

John Wycliffe

Painting of Wycliffe and his followers, who distributed copies of his Bible translations

The local church banned the teachings of Wycliffe, but Hus refused to be quiet about it. He preached the truth from the pulpit, and the Church retaliated by revoking his right to preach. Hus kept preaching the good news of the truth, anyway. He preached that people should follow God, not the Church's leaders. He told them they should study the Word of God and that if the Church was not saying the same thing as the Bible, they should obey the Bible instead of the Church. All this preaching made Hus enemy number one of the Church's officials; they turned him over to the government to be killed because they considered his preaching to be heresy.

Jan Hus, preacher of the gospel of Christ, was sentenced to be burned alive for preaching the truth of the gospel. Right up to his death in 1415, Hus prayed for those who killed him and sang psalms. As he stepped from this earth into the realms of glory, Jan Hus left behind a legacy of forgiveness and grace. The lighting of that fire sent burning embers all over Europe. The light of the truth cannot be put out! Glory! Wycliffe and Hus both wanted to change how the Church operated, and they were also forerunners of a movement that sprang up during the Renaissance — the Reformation. We will learn more about this movement and the man who started it in the next section.

NARRATION BREAK:

Discuss what you read today.

19th century Czech artist Václav Brožík depicted Jan Hus' trial in this painting.

Monument to Jan Hus in the city of Prague. Hus studied and taught for many years in this city in the modern-day Czech Republic.

CONNECT As I was preparing to write this section, I came to realize that this empire that history calls the Holy Roman Empire is difficult to explain because it is unlike any other in history. You might remember learning about Charlemagne and his empire earlier in this book. The Holy Roman Empire developed from the remnants of Charlemagne's empire.

The Holy Roman Empire itself was an assortment of hundreds of smaller kingdoms and territories, each with their own individual noble rulers (Steinberg 2016). All the various rulers and princes would meet to elect the emperor, who was then crowned by the pope (Steinberg 2016). In some ways, we can think of it this way: when a king was named the emperor of the Holy Roman Empire, he was given a major "upgrade" in authority over the other rulers.

For centuries, this was one of the most powerful titles in Europe; the Holy Roman Emperor was a powerful force in European politics. The close ties with the pope was one source of the Holy Roman Empire's power — for many, the Holy Roman Empire was unique because it was the only kingdom that seemed to operate with the pope's permission and blessing (Steinberg 2016). Due to all the turmoil and chaos after Rome had fallen, this strong, seemingly unified empire and its association with the Church was often considered desirable because it was believed to bring stability.

The Holy Roman Empire is closely identified with the modern country of Germany, though other territories were also a part of it. One reason is that most of the Holy Roman emperors came from one of the many kingdoms in modern Germany (Meagher 2002). Eventually, the Holy Roman Empire became basically hereditary like other kingdoms, with the Habsburg family ruling the empire for centuries (Meagher 2002). This family, through the brilliant strategy of marrying the right heiresses throughout central Europe, gained and maintained power at an unprecedented level (Royde-Smith 2016). This led them to not only be the Holy Roman emperors, but it also meant they eventually controlled territory far outside the Holy Roman Empire, including Spain.

We are going to step into the year 1505 and meet up with a German lawyer named Martin Luther. On this day, Martin was almost hit by lightning while traveling, so his nerves were just a wee bit rattled! You'll have to excuse the terrified expression on his usually dignified and somewhat placid face. You see, Martin was so terrified by the near lightning strike that he cried out to God to save him, and in the heat of the moment, he promised that he would become a monk if his life were spared. God saved Martin and didn't allow the lightning bolt to strike him directly. Martin, being a man of his word, worked at becoming a monk. There was a problem, however. The more Martin studied, the more he was struck by the depravity of his sin and the stark contrast made by the holiness of God. The terror of God's wrath against him, probably reminiscent of the sizzling lightning bolt, drove him to spend hours in confession.

Poor Martin was so driven by guilt and anguish that his monastery sent him away to study at the University of Wittenberg. After a while, Martin became a professor at Wittenberg, but still, he was haunted by this one question: How can anyone please a righteous God? As Martin searched the Bible for the truth, he was led to read Romans

1:17: "For therein is the righteousness of God revealed from faith to faith: as it is written, The just shall live by faith" (KJV).

Finally, Martin had an answer! Righteousness was not only a condition but also an act of God. God declares those who come to repentance through Jesus' death and Resurrection righteous. Grace and mercy through the forgiveness of sin, by the blood of Jesus shed on the Cross, brought former sinners to righteousness. Martin's spiritual eyes were opened, and as the Scripture says, the truth set him free.

As is usually the case when God enlightens the mind and heart of someone who seeks Him, Martin's great transformation annoyed many who liked things just the way they were. His opposition to selling indulgences caused problems. The selling of indulgences was a long-running tradition that made a lot of money for some high-ranking church officials. Greed and selfishness fueled many abuses against the common man. Martin detested this practice and was appalled to see a monk selling his wares on the streets of his town. Martin scowled whenever he saw the monk Tetzel selling indulgences to the people. Tetzel would sing out, "As soon as the coin in the coffer rings, the soul from purgatory springs!" The Catholic Church taught that purgatory was between heaven and hell and where souls performed penance before going to heaven.

Martin Luther statue in his hometown of Eisleben, Germany. At the time, this city was part of the Holy Roman Empire, as was all of Germany and many other neighboring areas.

Martin's blood boiled until, finally, he could stand it no longer. In October 1517, Martin scribbled a list of 95 topics that he wished to debate and nailed them to the door of the local church. Little did he know what his Ninety-Five Theses would do to the world. The Catholic Church was extremely upset by his challenge. The pope declared Martin Luther a "drunken German" (Bainton 2013, 72), and three years later, when Martin was still speaking out about his convictions, the pope published a bull (a statement written in the pope's name) entitled "Arise, O Lord." In his bull, the

Ferdinand Pauwels' *Luther Posting the 95 Theses*, 1872

Martin Luther nails the 95 Theses to the church door in this 1878 painting by German artist Julius Hübner. This dramatic moment has frequently captivated the attention of painters.

pope called Luther a "wild boar" who had invaded the Lord's vineyard, the Church (Bainton 2013, 140). Luther threw his copy of the pope's bull in a bonfire.

Two months after Luther's bonfire, he received a letter from the Holy Roman Emperor himself. The Holy Roman Emperor was the powerful ruler of much of Central Europe. Because he was German, Luther was a subject of the Holy Roman Emperor. The letter told Martin to come under the protection of the emperor and answer questions regarding his books. We call this meeting the Diet of Worms. No, Martin was not made to eat worms because of his books! "Diet" is the Latin word for an imperial meeting, and the meeting took place in the German city of Worms (VURMZ). Thus, the Diet of Worms.

Martin fully expected to lose his life at this meeting. There had been others who had been ordered "under the protection of the Holy Roman Emperor" to attend a diet and had never been seen again. As he stood there with sweat glistening on his brow, Martin was filled with the conviction of the truth he had learned. When asked if he defended what he had written, Luther responded, "[M]y conscience is captive to the

This is the cathedral door that Luther nailed his 95 Theses on in 1517. Today, the actual text from the 95 Theses is engraved on the doors themselves.

Due to the Gutenberg press, Reformers like Luther could quickly spread their teachings and message anywhere people could read. In 1534, he printed the first complete translation of the Bible into German, which also included his own commentary.

Word of God. I cannot and I will not recant anything, for to go against conscience is neither right nor safe. God help me" (Bainton 2013, 182). God safe-guarded Martin's life that day.

There had been other reformers before Martin Luther, but he was the first to identify the theological challenges behind the Church's practices, rather than just condemning those issues on their own. His protest resonated with many and sparked a movement that spanned numerous countries throughout Western and Northern Europe: the Protestant Reformation. Luther's actions inspired others and still have a significant impact on Christianity today.

Narration break:

Discuss what you read about Martin Luther.

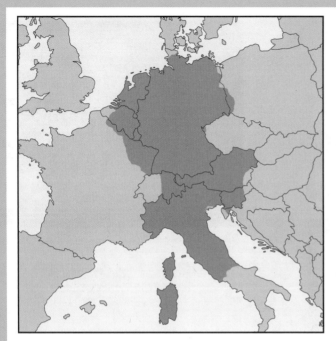
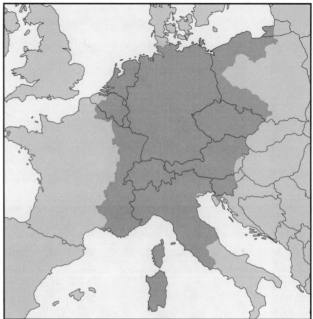

The Holy Roman Empire

- 962: Foundation
- 1200: Greatest Extent
- 1806: Dissolution

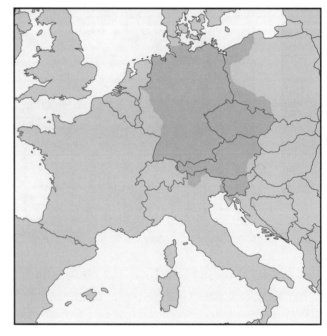

This series of maps shows what the Holy Roman Empire looked like when it was founded, at its height, and when it ended. As the maps show, it was an extensive empire, covering multiple modern European countries.

ANALYZE — Can you recognize any of the modern countries on the map? If so, how many? (Check your answers on a globe or atlas.)

CONNECT — How long did it take the Holy Roman Empire to reach its greatest extent after its foundation? (Hint: Look at the map key.)

The inside of the fish barrel was cramped and horribly smelly. It didn't matter to Katie because she knew that freedom awaited her along with the fresh air at the end of her journey. She had spent most of her life in Catholic convents for nuns, and while she appreciated the roof over her head and the care of the nuns, she wanted a different life. Her father had brought her to the convent after the death of her mother, when she was a tiny child of 5 years of age (Tucker 2017, 15–18). Now she was a woman of 18, and she longed for freedom.

She thought of the preaching that had made its way into the convent. Martin Luther's Reformation preaching had made her long even more for life outside the walls of the cloister. When Luther had heard that Katie and others wanted freedom, he had arranged for a merchant friend of his to deliver herring to the convent in 12 barrels. On his return trip, 12 nuns occupied the empty fish barrels. Luther helped the nuns to return to their homes, find husbands, or find a position of work. Only Katie was left.

Luther's friends helped persuade him to take Katie as his wife. Thus, 26-year-old Katherina von Bora married 42-year-old Martin Luther. Katie gladly took on the role of wife and keeper of Luther's house. She efficiently managed not only the home but also the family finances. She cared for the garden, orchard, fishpond, and barnyard animals (Tucker 2017, 121–122). The Reformer's family served as a beautiful role model for Christian families for centuries afterward. The Luthers had problems just like every other real-life family, but together they worked through them and raised their children (Tucker 2017, 119). Katie lived six years longer than her husband. It is often said that her last words were "I will cling to Christ like a burr on a velvet coat" (Tucker 2017, 169).

This portrait of Luther's wife Katherina was painted in 1526, a year after their marriage.

19th century painting of Martin Luther and his family

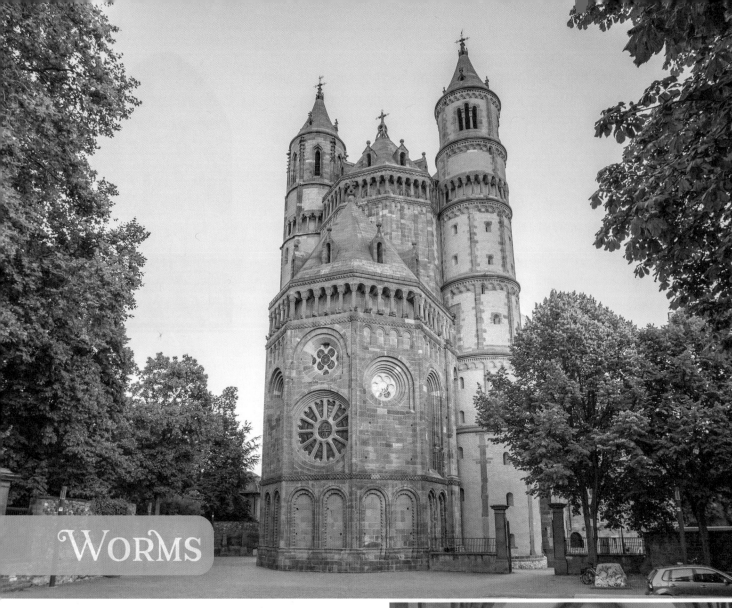

WORMS

Worms Cathedral. In the Holy Roman Empire, Worms was an Imperial Free City. That meant the city was not under the control of local princes and answered directly to the emperor. Free cities were wealthy and powerful.

Germany

Inside the Worms Cathedral. Just as Worms was an Imperial Free City, the local cathedral was considered an Imperial Cathedral for the Holy Roman Emperor's use.

Worms is home to the oldest Jewish cemetery in Europe and had a large Jewish community for centuries. The tombstone shown here has stones on it because Jews place rocks rather than flowers on graves.

In the city where Luther appeared before the Imperial Diet, the largest Reformation memorial in the world commemorates Luther and other early Protestant leaders and thinkers.

Worms' location on the Rhine River has long made it an important city. The Rhine was a major transportation and trade route through Europe. In World War II, the first American troops to cross the Rhine River into Germany crossed at Worms.

This sign in Worms honors the city's sister cities. In the 20th century, cities around the world began to unite with other places (called sister cities) to promote international friendships and connections. Worms' sister cities are in Italy, Israel, France, England, Germany, and America.

24

START HERE

Can you imagine not owning a Bible written in the language you read? How would it affect your life to not have access to the Word of God on a daily basis? I don't know about you, but I couldn't live without my dog-eared, tear-stained copy of the God-breathed Scriptures. I was a wee girl of four years old the very first time I read a Bible, and I was hooked. Throughout my painfully difficult childhood, the Word of God became an anchor for my soul. Even though I did not understand it well, and the evil spiritual influences around me were strong, there is life in the truth of God's Word, and the little seeds of truth that were planted then have grown into big trees now. In this chapter, we are going to continue learning about those who were instrumental in bringing reform to the Church. As you read through this section of our story, I encourage you to think deeply about the sacrifices these brave people made to reform the powerful institution that the Catholic Church had become.

THE COUNTER-REFORMATION REACTS

Luther may be the most famous person involved in the Reformation, but he was hardly the only one. Another was a Swiss priest named Ulrich Zwingli (OOL-rik ZWEENG-lee), who was born in 1484, one year after Luther. Like Luther, Zwingli argued for Scripture as the sole source of doctrine, strongly believed in the necessity of Bibles translated into the people's own languages, and opposed Catholic teachings like indulgences, confession, and purgatory. The citizens and local city council of Zurich, where Zwingli lived, supported him. Zwingli's teachings also spread to other cities in the Swiss Confederacy (modern-day Switzerland).

Since Luther and Zwingli both worked for reform in the Church, their followers wanted to unite them. The two men agreed to meet and discuss uniting in the German city of Marburg. Luther did not agree with the Roman Catholic or Eastern Orthodox Churches about how Christ is present at communion services. These two churches believe that the wine and bread physically become the blood and body of Christ. This is called transubstantiation. Martin Luther instead believed that the wine and bread remained present but also included Christ's blood and body. This became known as consubstantiation. Zwingli, on the other hand, held the belief that Jesus' words at the Last Supper — "this is My body" and "this is My blood" (Matthew 26:26, 28) — were symbolic and that the wine and bread used during communion did not change form. For these two reformers, this and different views on other theological matters were enough to keep them from uniting.

Our next reformer is well known as the father of the Reformed Church. John Calvin started his journey as a Renaissance leader. He was one of the men who encouraged people to think for themselves concerning the Bible and what God said through the Scriptures. As we studied when we learned about the Renaissance, the word "humanist" in modern times means someone who worships human thinking, completely excluding God from the picture. However, during this time, a humanist was someone who emphasized personal human involvement with their relationship with God. Erasmus, a Dutch scholar, was a leading Renaissance humanist whose work influenced the Reformation. Humanist ideas about a personal relationship with God was a big part of the growing Protestant movement, especially the belief that the

Illustration of Ulrich Zwingli bidding his family farewell shortly before he is killed in battle in 1531

Martin Luther

Ulrich Zwingli

John Calvin

mediation of a priest was not necessary. Christianity was starting to move from being a religion about Christ to a relationship with Christ.

John Calvin was a Renaissance humanist. What John Calvin preached rattled the government of Calvin's homeland, France, and he was forced to flee for his life to the Swiss Confederacy. He wrote the first systematic summary of Protestant theology, a book called *Institutes of the Christian Religion*. Calvin's message met with acceptance in some circles and resistance in others, but he would go on to become one of the leading reformers of the Church.

Eventually, there developed a divide between so-called Magisterial Protestants like Luther, Zwingli, and Calvin, and Radical Protestants, called Anabaptists. The Magisterial Protestants had their disagreements with the Catholic Church, but they still placed a strong emphasis on the authority of their own reforming leaders and rulers. After centuries of the government and the Church being so intertwined, it seemed natural to continue that tradition, even if the church in question was no longer the Catholic Church.

The Magisterial Protestants also benefited from rulers who approved of their disagreements with the Catholic Church. For some of these kings and officials, their approval derived from a genuine belief in the doctrine these reformers taught. For others, they were chiefly motivated by the desire to strengthen their political independence and authority without the interference of the powerful pope. Regardless of the government's motivations, Zwingli and Calvin both benefited from the support of the city councils in Zurich and Geneva, respectively, and Luther himself was protected from the Catholic Church and the Holy Roman Emperor by Frederick III, his local prince.

The Anabaptists, however, strongly opposed any government interference in religion. Most Anabaptists also went further and rejected mandatory military service and swearing oaths of any kind, including to rulers and government officials. They also held what were considered radical beliefs concerning baptism. At the time, people were always baptized as infants by the Catholic Church. Adult baptism only occurred if they had not already been baptized as infants; if so, re-baptism was not allowed. Other reformers in the Protestant movement maintained the Catholic teaching on infant baptism, but Anabaptists rejected it and performed baptisms on adult believers. The Anabaptists faced persecution from both Catholic and Protestant leaders. For the Catholics, the Anabaptists were regarded as heretics (someone in defiance of Catholic belief), just like the other Protestants. For the Magisterial Protestant political leaders, however, the Anabaptists represented a political threat.

NARRATION BREAK:

Talk about what you read today.

CONNECT

In our chapter, we have learned a little about a group called the Anabaptists. In this Connect section, we are going to take a look at two groups who grew out of the Swiss Brethren, an Anabaptist group. You may be somewhat familiar with the Amish and the Mennonite churches. The Mennonites came from the Anabaptists and are named for Menno Simons, a Dutch priest who helped to institutionalize the work started by the Anabaptist leaders. There are many Mennonite communities around the world but especially in the United States and Canada.

Mennonites immigrated to North America to seek religious freedom and economic opportunity. They also wanted to escape from European militarism. Because they are pacifists, they do not believe in fighting. For several centuries, the Mennonites mostly lived in farming communities and used their ancestors' German language. Even to this day, many Mennonites still wear their unique plain clothing and strive to keep to themselves, separate from the rest of society.

The Amish church came from the Mennonites when there was a rift in the group. The Amish preferred to be stricter in how separate they were from the world. In the early 18th century, the Amish also began immigrating to North America to find a place to live and grow peacefully. Like the Mennonites, they live in their own communities, separated from the world. The Amish practice shunning as their most severe punishment for extreme disobedience. This punishment uses social separation and what may be called "the silent treatment" to punish the one being shunned. Over their years in America, the Amish have experienced rifts over whether to accept technological innovation or not. Those who do not are called the Old Order Amish.

As a general rule, Mennonites are more receptive to some modern technology than the Amish, though individual groups differ. For instance, many Mennonites have electricity in their homes and own cars, though most Amish have neither.

The Amish continue to farm as their ancestors did, largely avoiding modern conveniences, such as tractors.

This picture depicts Calvin in Geneva. At one point, he was forced to leave the city but was eventually able to return.

As we have traveled together through the last couple of chapters of our story, we have seen the Roman Catholic Church starting to lose its influence on the world. A wave of reform had begun to build. Martin Luther's writings garnered the attention of many, and change was imminent. We have learned about the group who became known as the Protestants, but there were also those inside the Catholic Church who wanted things to be different. These Catholic reformers had wanted change even before Martin Luther's Ninety-Five Theses were nailed to the church door. Their plans for reform had to be rethought, however, when the Protestants came along.

At first, the Catholic reformers wanted to reunite with the Protestant reformers who had left the Church. A split in the Church was the last thing they wanted to happen. Remember, the Church and the European kingdoms were closely linked together. What affected one affected the other; therefore, it affected the entire continent. In 1541, Protestant leaders (including John Calvin) met Roman Catholic reformers with the hopes of ironing out their differences. Their efforts to reconcile and find a middle ground, however, did not work. Both sides ended up not agreeing to the proposals put forth. It was the last effort to prevent a split.

The failure to reconcile the two groups of Christians frightened many people. What would happen to the worldwide Christian Church if everyone had their own Bible and could read and interpret the Scriptures for themselves? What would happen to the truth? Would the Church fall apart, shattered into a thousand separate pieces? Did Christ come just to have His followers divide and turn on each other? And what about the rest of the world? How could a shattered Church reach those who were lost? How could reform be good if it was going to lead to the demise of the Church?

All these questions led the Roman Catholic Church leaders to speak out strongly against the Protestants. The pope condemned all Protestants as heretics. However, many within the Catholic Church recognized that some of the things Protestants were unhappy about were problems that needed to be addressed. As a result, the Catholic Church did institute several responses to the Reformation. One was the Council of Trent, held from 1545–1563, which affirmed their doctrinal opposition to Protestant theology but also provided reform from within the Church. For instance, the Council of Trent instituted better educational standards for clergy and banned the worst of the abuses of the indulgence system.

The Catholic Church also instituted an inquisition for dealing with heretics, called the Roman Inquisition. You may recall studying the Spanish Inquisition in Chapter 18. That involved the persecution and expulsion of people who were not Catholic from Spain, including Jews and Muslims, as well as Christians deemed heretics. The Roman Inquisition operated in any Catholic country and was specifically aimed against Protestants. One of its activities was banning books that were authored by Protestant theologians like Martin Luther and John Calvin.

Another change was the focus on missionary work in foreign lands. If Catholicism was losing ground in Europe, that didn't mean it couldn't gain followers around the rest of the world. As exploration, which we will study in-depth in Volume 3, opened areas previously uninhabited by Europeans, the Catholic Church focused on converting the native peoples of the Americas, Asia, and Africa to Catholicism. The Jesuits were a Catholic missionary society founded in the 1500s that was responsible for greatly expanding the reach of the Catholic Church beyond Europe.

Cristiano Banti's *Galileo Facing the Roman Inquisition*, 1857.

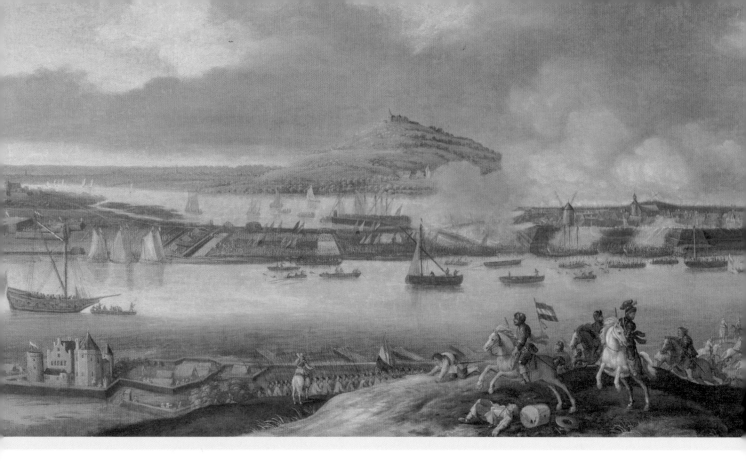

Gerrit van Santen's *Siege of Schenkenschanz,* 17th century. This painting depicts a famous siege during the Eighty Years' War.

The Catholic Church may have been devoting resources to converting peoples who had never been Christian, but they also still tried to convert Protestants back to Catholicism. The Reformation had begun, and the Counter-Reformation had responded. This idea of reform in the Catholic Church, and therefore reform throughout the world, would be fuel for wars in the years to come. Country would fight against country, brother against brother. This would become one of the bloodiest eras in history.

As a result, several bitter wars over Christianity plagued Europe in the 1500s and 1600s. One of the most brutal occurred in the Netherlands. Calvin's Reformed teachings had taken hold here, but there remained a substantial Catholic population. In addition, the area was under Spanish control, and the Spanish government ruthlessly persecuted Protestants. Eventually, after a long conflict known as the Eighty Years' War, the northern parts of the area became the independent Protestant Dutch Republic (modern-day Netherlands) while the southern portion (modern-day Belgium and Luxembourg and parts of northern France) remained under Spanish Catholic control.

France was the scene of further persecutions against Protestants. In France, Protestants were heavily influenced by Calvin's Reformed teachings and were known as Huguenots (HEW-guh-nos). They faced hundreds of years of persecution, mistreatment, and violence at the hands of the French Catholic kings. Many of the Huguenots eventually left France and immigrated to other Protestant lands where they could practice their religion freely.

The Counter-Reformation strengthened the Catholic Church, especially in places that had remained relatively free of Protestant influence, such as Spain and Italy. However, it did not eliminate Protestantism, especially in places where these teachings had initially gained popularity. By about 1600, only a few decades after the split between the Catholic and Protestant faiths, Catholicism remained strong in the Western European countries of Ireland, Spain, Portugal, France, and Italy, as well as in certain parts of Eastern Europe, such as Poland. (Much of the rest of Eastern Europe remained Eastern Orthodox.) Protestantism, however, had firmly taken root in a large portion of modern-day Germany, as well as throughout the Netherlands, Scandinavia, Scotland, and England. How England became Protestant is an unusual story and will be the focus of our next chapter.

NARRATION BREAK:

Discuss the Counter-Reformation.

Reformation Wall in Geneva. This memorial commemorates early Protestant Reformers with ties to Geneva. In addition to depicting Calvin, the statues also portray John Knox (a leading Scottish Calvinist) and two of Calvin's fellow French Calvinists, Guillaume Farel and Theodore de Beza.

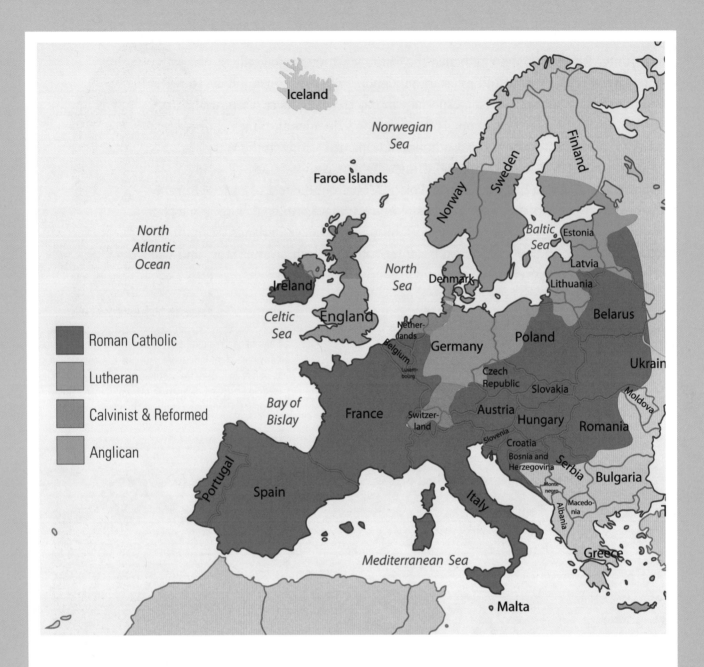

Roman Catholic

Lutheran

Calvinist & Reformed

Anglican

Not quite 50 years after Luther issued his 95 Theses and appeared at the Imperial Diet of Worms, Protestantism had spread to numerous countries in Northern and Central Europe. As the map indicates, Roman Catholicism retained its hold in the parts of Eastern Europe that were Catholic and not Eastern Orthodox (Poland, Lithuania, Hungary, etc.). Catholicism also held firm in Italy, Spain, Portugal, France, and most of Ireland.

Three different branches of Protestantism predominated. The Lutherans, who followed Martin Luther's teachings, predominated in Scandinavian countries like Norway, Sweden, and Denmark, as well as parts of Germany. Calvin's Reformed teachings were most popular in parts of Switzerland, as well as the Netherlands and Scotland. The Anglican Church, which we will learn about later in this book, arose in England and what is now Northern Ireland.

ANALYZE   Which branch of Protestantism occupied the smallest area?

CONNECT   Which different branches occupied Germany?

MAPS

In the study of church history, the most fascinating characters come to light. Some, such as Martin Luther, are big and bold with well-known names, and others are somewhat quieter in nature. I have discovered that these quieter, more obscure characters are highly intriguing and powerfully influential on the historical scene. Such is the case of the man we will focus upon in this section. Desiderius Erasmus (des-ih-DEER-ee-us eh-RAZ-mus) was a Dutch scholar who, like Luther, wanted to see reform in the Catholic Church. Unlike Luther, Erasmus did not break from the church; instead, he sought to reform it from within. Although these two men respected each other and agreed about the need of church reform, they did not agree with each other on how this reform should come about.

Erasmus wanted to bring reform by teaching people to study the original manuscripts of the Scripture. He didn't like what I call "fluffy" Christianity. He believed that if a Christian would study and learn, like he did, to read the original biblical languages, they would reap deeper rewards for their efforts. After studying the works of Origen, an early Christian scholar who wrote biblical commentary and compiled various translations, and St. Paul in Greek, Erasmus set about consolidating his thoughts into a book of his own: *Handbook of a Christian Knight*. His book encouraged readers to study and meditate on the Scriptures and to apply them to their lives on a practical level.

It seems that history is more thrilled with the big, bold, highly vocal world changers, and sometimes the quieter ones are either misunderstood, underappreciated, or — depending on the current cultural school of thought — overlooked. I like this quote about Erasmus: "Only in the past several decades have scholars given due recognition to the fact that the goal of his work was a Christianity purified by a deeper knowledge of its historic roots" (Tracy 2016). I feel like Erasmus and I would get along well; I, too, appreciate discovering historic roots.

Engraving of Erasmus, 16th century

GENEVA

Geneva from the nearby Mont Salève in France. Geneva is nestled on the enormous Lake Geneva and surrounded by mountains from the Jura range.

Switzerland

One of Calvin's other legacies is the University of Geneva, which he founded. It remains a leading Swiss university.

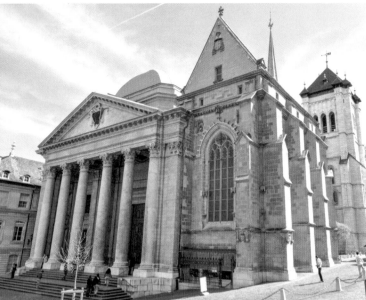

During Calvin's time, Geneva was known as the Protestant Rome. He preached from St. Peter's Cathedral, which is now a Reformed church. Despite Geneva's history as a Protestant city, only about half of the city's residents are Christian now. Catholics currently greatly outnumber Protestants. Growing numbers of residents now consider themselves as having no religion, which is sadly becoming more common across Europe.

Geneva has long been a center for international diplomacy. At various times in its history, it has served as headquarters for international organizations, including the Red Cross, the League of Nations, and the United Nations (U.N.). The Geneva Conventions, rules that are intended to protect soldiers, prisoners of war, and civilians during war, were drafted in the city.

Nearly 500 years after his death, John Calvin's influence on Geneva is still felt. Here is a street named after him. The sign is in French because Geneva is a French-speaking city. Each part of Switzerland has its own language. Geneva is in the Swiss French western side of the country. Swiss Italian is spoken in the north while Swiss German is spoken across much of the rest of the country. A unique native local language called Romansh is spoken in parts of the southeast.

25

START HERE

Welcome to the extremely strange and somewhat confusing story of Henry VIII. Henry, whose real name was Harry, married his brother's widow and was instrumental in the establishment of the Church of England, although his motivations were purely fueled by evil. His story is an extraordinary tale of selfishness, greed, and disregard of the legacy he was leaving for his children. Come along with me as we take a tour through the House of Tudor's most infamous king. First, read and think carefully through these verses about greed:

Greed brings grief to the whole family, but those who hate bribes will live (Proverbs 15:27; NLT).

Whoever oppresses the poor shows contempt for their Maker, but whoever is kind to the needy honors God (Proverbs 14:31; NIV).

The greedy stir up conflict, but those who trust in the LORD will prosper (Proverbs 28:25; NIV).

Due to the Renaissance and the Reformation, the world was changing. As is usually the case when change happens, there were those who fought against it and, even worse, those who tried to use the new way of thinking to their own selfish advantage. King Henry VIII of England was guilty of the last one.

This story is rather unusual and will take some extreme concentration to keep straight in your mind. First, do you remember when we learned about the War of the Roses? Richard, King Edward IV's brother, took the throne away from 12-year-old King Edward V. Edward and his younger brother disappeared without a trace, and Richard crowned himself Richard III. His reign didn't last long, however, when a distant cousin laid claim to the throne. Henry Tudor ushered in the Tudor age of England and was crowned Henry VII.

After all the chaos over who would be king, Henry VII was concerned about his royal heirs. He wanted to ensure that his son would become king, followed by his grandson, and so on. To make sure his own son would have heirs and strong political connections, Henry VII orchestrated a wedding between his son and the princess of Spain. (Her parents were Ferdinand and Isabella, the Spanish rulers we learned about in Chapter 18.) This probably doesn't seem like that big of a deal, but what if I told you that the groom, Prince Arthur, was two years old, and his bride, Catherine of Aragon, was only three? These two weren't legally married, but this wedding ceremony, which is called a proxy (because adults had to stand in for the toddlers), ensured that these two had to get married just as soon as they possibly could. When Arthur and Catherine were 15 and 16 years old, they got married again; this time, they stood up for themselves. Unfortunately, Arthur died not long after their wedding, leaving Henry VII to pass the crown to his next oldest son, Harry.

This left Henry VII in a predicament, indeed! He wanted his son Harry to marry Arthur's young widow. Just as he had with Arthur, the king wanted to make sure that Harry had heirs and a good political alliance. This was an unusual situation, so King Henry VII went to the pope for help — special permission was necessary for Harry and Catherine to marry since she had been married to Harry's brother. The pope gave his approval, and the wedding took place.

Joos van Cleve's portrait of Henry VIII, circa 1530s

This painting depicts Catherine of Aragon crying after Henry ends their marriage while he talks in the background with his new wife Anne Boleyn. Many of the English people sympathized with her over the way Henry treated her.

When Henry VII died two months later, Harry was placed on the throne, and he became Henry VIII. Years passed by, and Catherine and Henry VIII did not have a son. Instead, they had a daughter, Mary. Henry VIII was becoming desperate! Catherine was getting too old to have children. Instead of accepting the situation, Henry wanted to get rid of Catherine and marry another woman. This is not what the Bible teaches us, but Henry did not care.

At the time, the only way to end a marriage when both people were alive was to get an annulment. That means the marriage would be considered invalid, and he would be free to marry again. He asked the current pope, Clement VII (a member of the famous Medici family), to annul the marriage because Catherine had been his brother's widow. Annulling it would have meant that he was free to marry again. The pope refused because Henry had been granted special permission to marry her all those years earlier. Granting the annulment would make it look like the Catholic Church had made a mistake when it gave permission the first time.

Another reason the pope refused to agree to the annulment is that Catherine's nephew was the Holy Roman Emperor. That made him one of the most powerful leaders in all of Europe, and the pope did not want to make him mad. As far as the pope was concerned, it was better to make the king of England mad rather than the Holy Roman Emperor. The fight stretched on for several years.

It was about this time that Reformation teachings were also spreading across Europe. Henry VIII personally did not care about their intended reforms, but he did selfishly see this as an opportunity to end his marriage to Catherine. At the king's urging, the English Parliament broke from the Roman Catholic Church in 1533 and established the Church of England, with Henry VIII as its leader. His new church then allowed his annulment to take place. In Catherine's place, Henry married a young woman from his royal court named Anne Boleyn. He hoped that she would give him a son and heir.

Because Henry VIII was uninterested in the actual Reformation, the church he formed was, essentially, Catholic in every way except one — they did not accept the pope's authority. Henry VIII's motivations were very different than those of Luther, Calvin, Zwingli, or the Anabaptists. He was not interested in furthering the cause of the Reformation. He was simply trying to get rid of his wife! He was also demonstrating his power to the pope. By doing this, Henry was saying, "I am the king of England, and no Italian pope is going to tell me what to do!"

NARRATION BREAK:

Talk about what you read today.

THE TUDORS

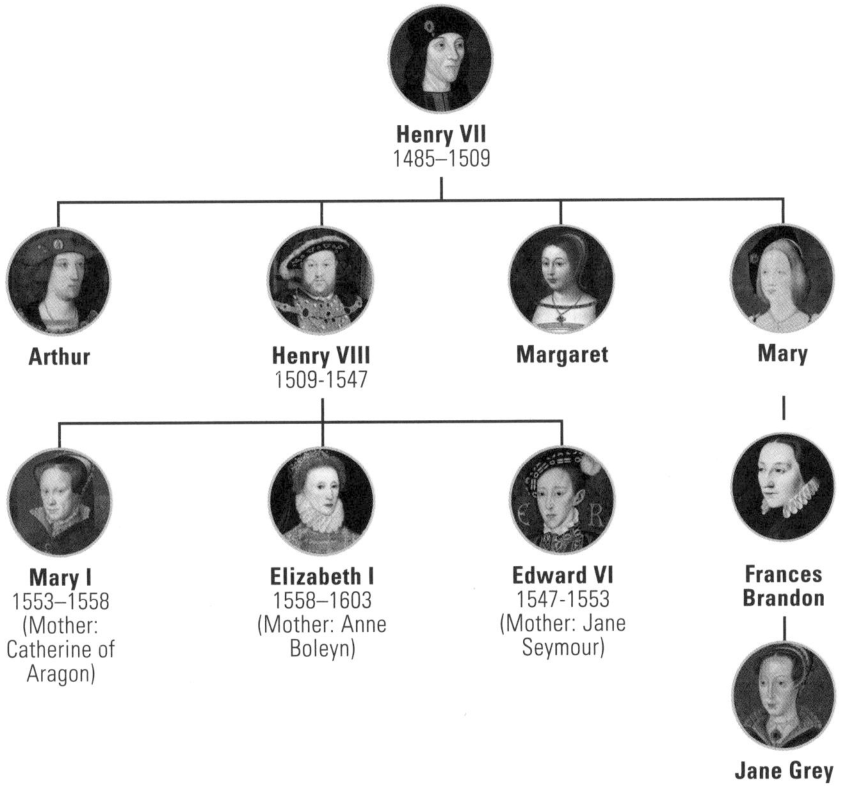

Henry VII
1485–1509

Arthur

Henry VIII
1509-1547

Margaret

Mary

Mary I
1553–1558
(Mother: Catherine of Aragon)

Elizabeth I
1558–1603
(Mother: Anne Boleyn)

Edward VI
1547-1553
(Mother: Jane Seymour)

Frances Brandon

Jane Grey

After marrying Anne, Henry was excited to find out that he was going to be a daddy again. He thought he finally would have his son, but he didn't. A little girl named Elizabeth was born to Anne and Henry instead. Henry was furious. By 1536, Henry no longer wanted to be married to Anne and ordered Anne beheaded and had their marriage declared invalid. Henry married wife number three within two weeks of the unfortunate end of wife number two.

Wife number three was a lady named Jane Seymour. As providence would have it, Jane gave Henry the son he had so desperately wanted. Sadly, Jane herself died soon after the baby was born. Henry did not spend much time grieving for Jane. He decided to marry the sister of a Protestant German noble. It would make a good alliance, and the painting he was shown of her was beautiful. When Anne of Cleves arrived for the wedding, Henry was rather startled; it seems the portrait artist's depiction did not quite capture the princess' true appearance. King Henry VIII did not want to anger the lady's family, so he went through with the marriage. Afterward, however, he decided that he could not live with her, and because he was the head of the Church of England, he also had this marriage annulled. With that, wife number four gladly ran out the door!

Hans Holbein the Younger's portrait of Anne of Cleves, Henry's fourth wife

Depiction of Henry with his third wife Jane and their son Edward

CONNECT Have you ever heard the expression, "With friends like that, who needs enemies?" This is what comes to my mind as I prepare to tell you the story of a man named Thomas Cromwell. Though he was born into poverty, Thomas became a successful merchant and lawyer in his early career before becoming a member of Parliament. It seems that Thomas' political abilities in Parliament attracted the attention of King Henry VIII (Elton 2017). For the next three years, Thomas worked to gain favor with Henry, and in 1530, he entered the service of the king (Elton 2017). Within a short time, he had reached the inner circle of confidential advisers and established an important position in Parliament (Elton 2017).

Hans Holbein's portrait of Thomas Cromwell, circa 1530s

Thomas was appointed to a string of prestigious and influential jobs by the king and made himself indispensable to King Henry VIII. When the pope denied Henry an annulment from his first wife, Catherine, it was Thomas who proposed that the king should create his own church to restrict the influence of the Catholic pope in England (Elton 2017). When the king followed through with his plan, establishing the Church of England in place of the Roman Catholic Church, it was Thomas who was given the power to reform all the monastic institutions in the country. Within four years, all the monasteries had been reformed or closed, and their fortunes turned over to the king (Elton 2017).

Everything seemed to be going well for Thomas: he had the power of the kingdom second only to the king, and his prestige and influence were unmatched. Then his favor changed. In 1539, the king was looking for his fourth wife. Who would the not-so-lucky lady be? Thomas Cromwell decided that the king should marry Anne of Cleves. This would help form a Protestant alliance between the English following the Church of England and German Lutherans (Elton 2017). The king, however, was not a staunch Protestant and actually preferred Catholicism, minus the influence of the pope. He had only formed his own church to divorce his wife. As a result, he hated his fourth wife and resented Thomas for arranging his unsavory marriage (Elton 2017). This disagreement was the beginning of Thomas Cromwell's fall from the favor of the fickle king. His enemies seized the opportunity to convince Henry that Thomas was a heretic and a traitor (Elton 2017). Thomas was arrested, condemned without a trial, and executed within a few short weeks.

This drawing shows the monks being expelled after Henry's break with the Catholic Church.

Henry was on the lookout for wife number five. It did not take him long to find her. Catherine Howard was around only a little while before the self-centered king also had her beheaded. Catherine Parr was wife number six and, if I may say, very brave! By this time, Henry VIII was old and ill, and Catherine took care of him for the last few years of his life. She was also a good mother to his three children and encouraged him to reconcile with Mary and Elizabeth, despite how he had treated both daughters' mothers.

Henry VIII is most famous for his troubled personal life, but other developments also happened during his rule. He is often considered the "Father of the English Navy" because he established navy dockyards in England and substantially increased the size and strength of the country's navy. In later centuries, England would be well known for the power of its navy, and that started with Henry VIII.

Henry also strengthened England's position in relation to neighboring Wales and Ireland. He increased English domination of Wales, which was already under the kingdom's control. As we learned earlier, the English had controlled Ireland since the 1100s, though their power there had significantly weakened over the centuries. Following an Irish revolt in 1534, Henry VIII re-established control, having himself declared the country's king in 1541. Though Ireland remained staunchly Catholic, Henry tried to impose his Church of England on the country.

Despite other events that occurred during his reign, Henry VIII's most significant act as king was the establishment of the Church of England (also called the Anglican Church). Though Henry's motivation to split from the Catholic Church was selfish, the decision set England on the same track as other Protestant countries in Europe in the wake of the Reformation. In the future, disputes over religion in the country were also political and caused many problems for his successors and the people of England. Because of Henry's selfishness, his actions negatively affected his family and country for years.

Another of his actions after splitting from the Catholic Church was to close the monasteries. He enriched himself by either keeping the valuable land or selling it off for a profit. The traditional role of the monasteries for centuries had been providing charity and education, but that ceased when they closed, which hurt the local communities. Henry did not care because this also solidified his control over his new Church of England, which helped him strengthen his general power as king.

Henry VIII was continuing the Tudor tradition started by his father of strengthening the monarchy at the expense of the English nobles. In centuries past, the nobles (and, eventually, Parliament) had been a powerful force in English politics. They would and could threaten a king's position. However, that was not true with Henry VIII and other Tudors. The land he gained from closing the monasteries and his actions toward Wales and Ireland, as well as his tendency to ignore and dominate Parliament, all increased the king's power.

Henry VIII died in 1547, leaving the throne to his beloved son, Edward VI. Edward was a little boy when his father died, so his mother's brother helped him rule before that uncle was executed and replaced by another powerful adviser. King Edward VI was a sickly child; he wasn't very strong or big, and he had a bad cough that wouldn't go away. He died when he was only 15. Edward had not been very old when he died, but he had been a devout Protestant. Instead of leaving the throne to his Catholic sister Mary, Henry VIII's daughter with Catherine of Aragon (which was what Henry VIII and Parliament had both wanted), he tried to leave the throne to his Protestant cousin, Lady Jane Grey. She was the granddaughter of one of Henry VIII's sisters. She ruled for only nine days before handing the crown over to Mary. We will learn more about Mary and her half-sister Elizabeth in our next chapter; theirs is a story that, like their father's, also changed the course of history.

NARRATION BREAK:

Discuss Henry VIII and his reign.

Portrait of Edward VI, Henry's only son

England and Wales are both noted for their historic counties. Some of the boundaries have changed over the years, but these historic counties have formed an important aspect of local culture for centuries, each having their own distinct regional histories and customs.

Many of the English counties date back to medieval times, though some existed under Roman rule. The counties have been as important to their residents as states are to many Americans. Just as many Americans also consider themselves New Yorkers or Texans or Californians, many English are proud to come from Yorkshire, Cornwall, Shropshire, etc.

The Welsh have their own separate counties, but they also form their own nation within the United Kingdom (the name for England when it is combined with Wales, Scotland, and Northern Ireland). The Welsh are proud of their national culture, which is noted for its music and unique language.

ANALYZE — Look at the county names. Do you recognize any of them from other things you have read, watched, or studied?

CONNECT — Are you proud of your state or your town? What makes you proud of it?

During Henry VIII's time, there was a man who wanted everyone in England to have a Bible that they could read. His name was William Tyndale (tin-DL). He had studied Greek and Renaissance humanism at Cambridge University in England and became obsessed with interpreting the New Testament into English from Latin.

CHURCH HISTORY

There was only one problem, though: Tyndale's bishop would not give his permission for the project. This was several years before England broke away from the Catholic Church. Church leaders did not want private parties to translate the Scriptures. They believed that this job should be done by an authorized group of scholars who could combine their knowledge. They feared that any single translator could easily pass their own personal opinion and prejudices into the translation.

William Tyndale, however, believed that God would guide his efforts in the translating process. When he realized the bishop was going to try to stop him from translating the New Testament into English, Tyndale ran away to Germany to complete the publishing process. In the year 1526, a printer in Worms, Germany, published and printed 6,000 copies of Tyndale's New Testament. When the New Testaments poured into England three months later, English bishops bought thousands of them. Why would they do this? Had they inexplicably and unexpectedly become extremely interested in Tyndale's English translations? Hardly!

The bishops bought the Tyndale New Testaments to fuel a huge bonfire. They were so determined to keep this "inferior" translation out of the common people's hands that they bought and burned literally thousands of these Testaments. The Bible bonfires failed to stop William Tyndale. He simply used the money to update his New Testament. The bishops' purchases paid for the revised Testaments, which ran off the printing presses by the thousands.

Sketch of William Tyndale

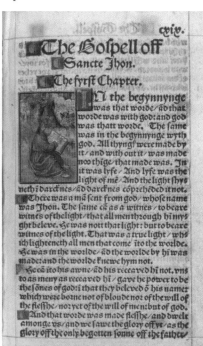

The Gospel of John in Tyndale's printing of the Bible. This page dates to 1526.

LONDON

View of London and the River Thames (pronounced TEMS). Though London is a modern bustling city and world center, some remains of its Tudor past still exist. The river itself is a big part of that past. During Tudor times, the Thames functioned as a sewer and transportation and trade route. At the time, there was only one bridge over the river, so many people boated across instead. In fact, it was such a major route that there were frequent traffic jams caused by all the boats on the water.

United Kingdom

One of Henry VIII's London homes, Hampton Court Palace, still stands, looking much as it did during his lifetime. This photo shows what the kitchen would have looked like. In addition to preparing lavish feasts for the royal family, the kitchen staff also prepared meals for the servants.

Yeoman (YO-man) warders (commonly called Beefeaters) are part of the Royal Bodyguard and still wear dress uniforms like what they would have worn during the Tudor period. Their nickname comes from their privileged position during Tudor times, which allowed them to eat as much beef as they wanted. Meat was a very expensive treat unavailable to the poor.

The Globe is a reproduction of what the theater associated with famed playwright William Shakespeare would have looked like during Tudor times. People who viewed the play from the area right next to the stage were called groundlings and stood for the entire performance. People who could afford more expensive tickets sat in the balconies.

The Tower of London is currently the home of the British royal family's crown jewels. Built by William the Conqueror, it also long served as a prison for the royal family. Famous prisoners included two of Henry VIII's wives — Anne Boleyn and Catherine Howard — and his daughter Elizabeth.

The Tower of London is noted for other famous residents, especially its ravens. Traditionally, it is believed that ravens must guard the tower, so ravens are kept on hand and even cared for by a special Raven Master. Some ravens have been dismissed from their position for "[c]onduct unsatisfactory," like attacking television equipment!

26

START HERE

We have learned that the legacy of Henry VIII was defined by his greed and lust for power. Before we move forward in our story, I would like all of us to remember what Jesus said about being greedy for things of this world. We find the story in Luke 12:13–21. Take the time now to read these verses that tell "The Parable of the Rich Man." What does Jesus call the person who focuses more on things of this world than what is eternal?

In this chapter, we will continue the story of the Tudor family. Henry VIII's daughters had survived their extraordinarily dysfunctional childhoods, and regardless of their father's insane efforts to have a long-lasting male heir to the throne, his son's reign was cut short by an early death. It would be Henry's eldest daughter who would become one of the most infamous monarchs of England, with one of the bloodiest reigns. These were sad and uncertain times for the English Protestants. Henry's younger daughter would also rise to the throne for her turn at ruling the empire.

Henry VIII's oldest child, Mary, became Queen Mary I in 1553 after the death of her younger half-brother, Edward VI. Mary's chief interest was in returning the country to Catholicism after her father had broken with the Catholic Church and formed the Church of England 20 years earlier. This is one reason why Edward VI unsuccessfully tried to block her from becoming his replacement. Regardless of the religious division in the country, the people were enthusiastic about their queen at first.

Why was Mary so strongly Catholic? Think back to the story of King Henry VIII and his many wives. Henry's first wife was Catherine of Aragon from Spain. This was Mary's mother and the woman Henry sent away after they had been married for years. Henry VIII broke away from the Catholic Church precisely because it would not permit him to end his marriage to Mary's mother. After her parents' marriage ended, Mary was separated from her mother, was no longer a princess, and was no longer an heir to the throne. Even after Henry had established the Church of England, married Anne Boleyn, and had another daughter with her, Mary and her mother remained Catholic and refused to acknowledge Anne as the queen and Elizabeth as a princess. Henry would not even let Mary visit her mother or attend her funeral. Eventually, Henry changed his mind and agreed to let Mary be an heir, but you can be sure she still remembered how her father had treated her and her mother and why!

When Mary first came to power, she promised that she would respect the fact that the country was both Catholic and Protestant. However, she really did want the country to become Catholic again. This made Parliament nervous, and her desire also was not popular with the nobles, many of whom had benefited when her father had shut down the monasteries and sold off the land. To make matters even worse as far as they were concerned, Mary arranged to marry her Catholic cousin, Philip. His father was the Holy Roman Emperor, and Philip himself was heir to the Spanish throne. English Protestants were concerned that the alliance would confirm a return to Catholicism, and they feared the interference of Spain in the affairs of the country.

An unsuccessful revolt called Wyatt's Rebellion broke out in response. Mary successfully ended the rebellion, but she became deeply suspicious and angry afterward. Elizabeth, Mary's younger half-sister, was a bit nervous

Byam Shaw's *Entry of Queen Mary I with Princess Elizabeth into London in 1553,* 1910. This painting shows Mary I arriving in London after she is queen. At this time, the English people were excited for her reign.

Queen Mary of England and her husband, King Philip II of Spain

and with good reason. Mary did not like her younger sister. She felt that Elizabeth was a threat to her reign. Mary had her sister arrested on suspicion of plotting against her. Elizabeth was thrown into the Tower of London, where she stayed for months. Princess Elizabeth, however, was not plotting against her sister, and eventually, Queen Mary had to let her leave the tower. After her stay in the tower, Elizabeth was banished to a small cottage in the countryside. Mary appointed guards to watch her sister's every move and to search the cottage often.

In response to the failed rebellion, Mary also attempted to return the country to Catholicism, ruthlessly persecuting Protestants in the process. This was a very dark period of history in England. Mary's persecution of Protestants was so severe that she was nicknamed "Bloody Mary." Hundreds of Protestants were burned at the stake, and others were imprisoned. Many fled to Protestant areas in Europe, like Geneva, Switzerland, where John Calvin's influence was especially prominent.

Meanwhile, Mary wanted to be sure that her Protestant sister Elizabeth would not take the throne after her. Queen Mary was overjoyed when she learned that she and her husband were going to have an heir to the throne. Nine months came and went, and no baby was born. This happened twice, and even though Mary was exhibiting all the signs of pregnancy, there was never a baby born. How strange! Each time these instances of "false pregnancy" occurred, Mary became weaker and sicker. Finally, in 1558, at the age of 42, Mary died, leaving no heir to the throne. Modern medicine would have probably revealed that the queen had cancer, which would have caused all the symptoms mistaken for pregnancy.

Mary's hated half-sister Elizabeth was now Queen Elizabeth I. People danced and sang in the streets. Mary was the first woman to rule England in her own right, but she had not been a good queen. Her cruelty to Protestants had terrified her subjects and made her deeply unpopular. What kind of queen would Elizabeth be?

NARRATION BREAK:

Discuss Mary I and her reign.

THE SPANISH MONARCHS

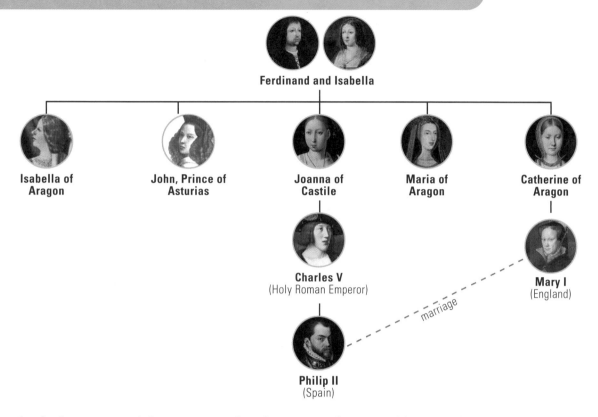

Ferdinand and Isabella

Isabella of Aragon

John, Prince of Asturias

Joanna of Castile

Maria of Aragon

Catherine of Aragon

Charles V
(Holy Roman Emperor)

Mary I
(England)

marriage

Philip II
(Spain)

Elizabeth was a much better queen than her sister. She wanted her people to love her, not be terrified of her. Her reign would last 45 years and is called the Elizabethan Age. Under her reign, England became stronger, richer, and much more influential than ever before. Elizabeth was also a popular queen. Her subjects called her "Good Queen Bess." In these years, England also became a land of cultural prominence. Artists painted beautiful masterpieces, composers wrote exquisite music, and playwrights, including the famous William Shakespeare, penned famous plays.

Though Elizabeth had a very different personality than her sister, they did have one thing in common: their father had gotten rid of both of their mothers. Elizabeth's mother Anne had been beheaded when Elizabeth was a small child. Henry VIII had also had that marriage annulled, just like he did with Mary's mother. And just like with Mary, after Henry VIII remarried again and had another child, Elizabeth lost her position as an heir before her father was convinced to change his decision years later. As you can see, Mary and Elizabeth had a rather rocky childhood because of their father's actions. The religious divisions that arose from her father's decision to break from the Catholic Church also still fueled many of the important events in Elizabeth I's reign.

When Elizabeth came to the throne, she returned the country to the Church of England. This decision caused some disagreement, though. Do you remember learning in the last section that many English Protestants fleeing Mary's persecutions

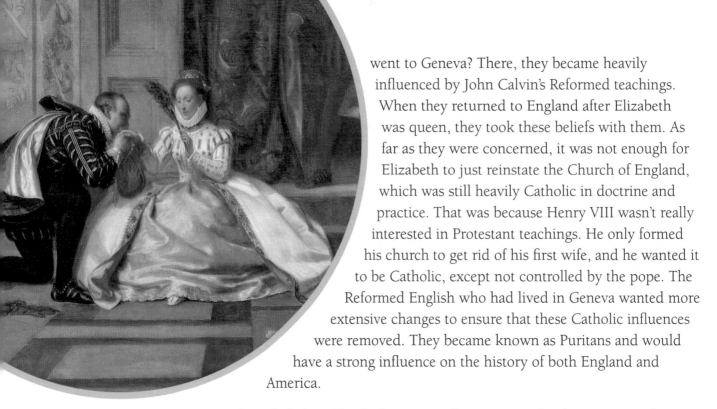

went to Geneva? There, they became heavily influenced by John Calvin's Reformed teachings. When they returned to England after Elizabeth was queen, they took these beliefs with them. As far as they were concerned, it was not enough for Elizabeth to just reinstate the Church of England, which was still heavily Catholic in doctrine and practice. That was because Henry VIII wasn't really interested in Protestant teachings. He only formed his church to get rid of his first wife, and he wanted it to be Catholic, except not controlled by the pope. The Reformed English who had lived in Geneva wanted more extensive changes to ensure that these Catholic influences were removed. They became known as Puritans and would have a strong influence on the history of both England and America.

William Frederick Yeames' 1865 painting of Elizabeth I and her close adviser Robert Dudley, the Earl of Leicester. He wanted to marry her, but she always refused to accept his proposal.

Regarding Catholics, Elizabeth was initially content to let them practice their faith quietly at home. Some attended Church of England services, which were mandatory for everyone, under protest. Others, alongside Puritans, were fined for not attending these official church services. However, tension increased after Elizabeth's life was threatened by a series of Catholic assassination attempts. For hardline Catholics, Elizabeth would never legitimately be queen because they refused to acknowledge Henry VIII's marriage to her mother.

Many of these Catholic supporters favored the Catholic granddaughter of one of Henry VIII's sisters, who was named Mary. Despite growing up in France, she became queen of Scotland, so she is known as Mary, Queen of Scots. This Mary was Elizabeth's heir, but they did not get along. Mary lost control of Scotland and fled to England. Because Elizabeth did not trust her, Mary spent years in captivity in various castles with noble families until she became involved in one of the conspiracies to assassinate Elizabeth. For her involvement, she was beheaded in 1587. Her son James, who was raised as a Protestant Presbyterian in Scotland, now became Elizabeth's heir. Around this same time that Mary's plot was uncovered, Catholics experienced more persecution in England, especially priests.

Elizabeth was urged to marry and have children to ensure that the throne went to a Protestant heir. However, Elizabeth never did marry. She believed she could do a good job ruling by herself, and she did not want the power going to someone else. Philip, the Spanish prince who had married her half-sister Mary, was now the Spanish king and offered to marry Elizabeth, but she steadfastly refused. Eventually, Elizabeth and Philip went to war with each other. He still wanted England to be Catholic, and he resented Elizabeth's interference in aiding Dutch Protestant rebels against the Spanish throne during the Eighty Years' War. In addition, English pirates had been robbing Spanish ships in the Americas.

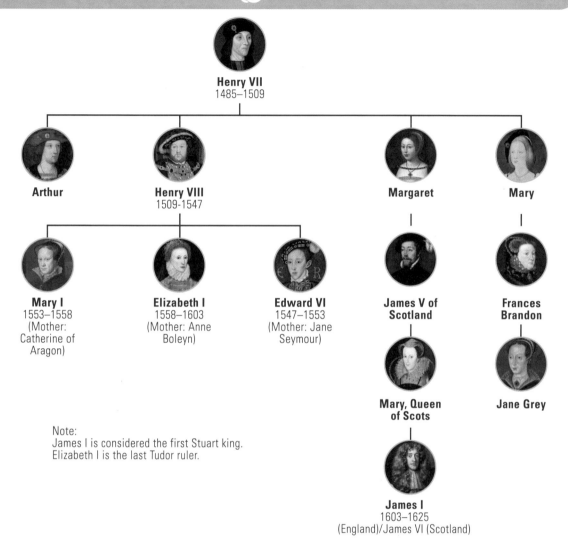

Henry VII
1485–1509

Arthur

Henry VIII
1509-1547

Margaret

Mary

Mary I
1553–1558
(Mother:
Catherine of
Aragon)

Elizabeth I
1558–1603
(Mother: Anne
Boleyn)

Edward VI
1547–1553
(Mother: Jane
Seymour)

James V of
Scotland

Frances
Brandon

Mary, Queen
of Scots

Jane Grey

Note:
James I is considered the first Stuart king.
Elizabeth I is the last Tudor ruler.

James I
1603–1625
(England)/James VI (Scotland)

Philip decided to solve the problem by invading England. He built a fleet of 130 giant, well-armed warships. He planned to use them and 30,000 men to overwhelm England's ships and invade England. This invasion force was called the Spanish Armada. When the Armada came into the English Channel in 1588, however, the English were prepared. Their ships were much smaller and faster than the floating fortresses of the Armada. The English warships sailed circles around the massive Spanish ships, shooting holes up and down the sides. Even though the Spanish had larger ships with more guns, the agility of the English warships proved to be too much for the Armada. At least half of the Armada's ships and men were lost. England had won the battle, and from that point on, the country would be known for the strength of her navy.

Just as during the time of Henry VIII, revolts in Catholic Ireland against Protestant English control continued. The unrest continued for decades, with Catholic land being seized and given to English nobles instead. Elizabeth finally re-established control over Ireland shortly before her death, but the Irish bitterly resented Protestant English rule and putting down the rebellions was expensive for the English government.

When Elizabeth I of England died, her heir was James, the king of Scotland. Though he was the son of Elizabeth's Catholic rival, Mary, Queen of Scotland, James himself was a Protestant. Now, England, Ireland, and Scotland were all ruled by the same Protestant monarch, though they were not officially joined for another century.

NARRATION BREAK:

Talk about Elizabeth I and Mary, Queen of Scots.

CONNECT

Of all the English playwrights ever to write plays, one Elizabethan stands head and shoulders above the rest — William Shakespeare. William Shakespeare was born five-and-a-half years after Queen Elizabeth came to the throne. William started acting at a young age, and soon, he had a troupe of actors working with him. Though we  often only think of him as a writer of plays, Shakespeare also acted and was part-owner of several theaters. His plays were written for his own troupe, who called themselves "Lord Chamberlain's Men" and later "The King's Men" when they received patronage from King James I. They traveled around England, performing at inns and in courtyards, and were among the most popular theater companies in the country. Eventually, they performed in the Globe Theatre, a large outdoor theater with rows of balconies, which gave the audience an unobstructed view of the play. There's a picture of a reproduction of it on the feature page for Chapter 25.

The plays William wrote made people laugh and cry; he wrote tragedies, comedies, and historical dramas, especially about the English kings. He performed for rich people and for poor people, and soon, William's name was on everyone's lips. Queen Elizabeth even called on William Shakespeare to perform for her, as did her successor James I. For these royal fans, the troupe went to their palaces to perform, so that the royal audience did not have to visit the theater. Shakespeare's plays are still performed today. They have been published in books and made into movies. Out of all the playwrights in history, William Shakespeare's plays are undoubtedly some of the most famous, most popular, and most quoted of all time.

This 19th century painting shows numerous well-known characters from Shakespeare's plays. Some of his works are histories while others are comedies or tragedies.

1. Stage
2. Backstage
3. Gallery for balcony scenes
4. The Heavens
5. The Hell
6. The Yard
7. The audience galleries
8. The main entrance for audience
9. The backstage door for performers and crew

Diagram of what the Globe likely looked like during Shakespeare's time. The stage is where most but certainly not all of the action occurred. In the rooms behind the stage, the performers got ready, the props were stored, and the musicians played. Sometimes the open gallery was used for balcony scenes. High above the stage was the place known as "The Heavens." A trap door here allowed performers to be lowered to the stage when the play called for it. Below the stage was called "The Hell." A trap door here also allowed performers to be lowered below the stage when required to do so. The open area in front of the stage is called the Yard and is where the cheapest seating was. Poorer members of the audience stood here to watch the play. Wealthier members of the audience paid for seating in the galleries.

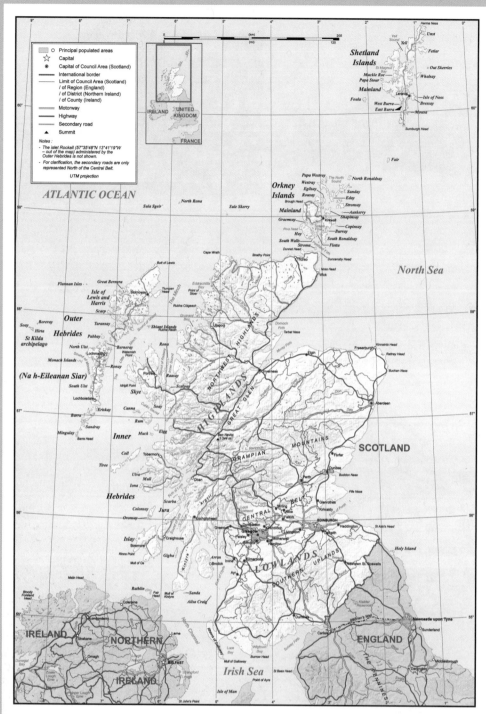

Scotland, the nation north of England, has a lengthy, rich history of its own. Culturally, the nation is often divided between the rugged mountainous Highlands in the north and the Lowlands of the south.

In ancient times, it was the home of several tribes, including the Picts. They resisted the Romans, though the Anglo-Saxons and Vikings invaded and raided Scotland, much as they did neighboring England. During the Middle Ages, Norman influences from England entered the Scottish royal family. In the 1200s, there was a dispute over who was rightfully ruler of Scotland.

The English king at the time, Edward I, tried to install someone loyal to him, but when that backfired, he invaded and claimed Scotland as his own.

The Scots fought back and won their independence, though warfare between the two countries continued periodically. The Protestant Reformation had a profound impact on Scotland. The key figure was John Knox.

It might be difficult to understand the importance of James I becoming king of both Scotland and England without understanding the often bitter history between the two countries. Even after they were united under one throne, the disagreements, rebellions, and warfare continued well into the 1700s. For the past few hundred years, Scotland has been part of the United Kingdom, alongside England, Wales, and Northern Ireland.

ANALYZE Study the map. What do you notice about Scotland's geographic location?

CONNECT What bodies of water surround Scotland?

When Henry VIII decided to break England away from the Catholic Church in 1534, he established the Church of England, with himself as the head. This break was done for selfish reasons, as we have learned, and Henry really did not have any interest in starting a new type of church. Henry's motives were purely to remove the pope from a place of authority over him, and he intended that the Church of England would remain Catholic in practice.

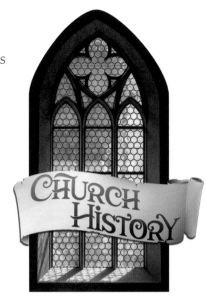

Throughout the reign of Henry's daughter Mary, the Protestants suffered through intense persecution. When Elizabeth became queen, she reestablished the Church of England, which was still very Catholic in practice but also technically Protestant because it refused to recognize the pope. This led to the development of various groups who were in opposition to the Church of England. They were often referred to as Separatists, Dissenters, or Nonconformists.

It was these remnants of Catholicism that the Puritans rebelled against. They wanted to bring reform to the Church to purify it of these remnants. They scorned the Church of England's rituals, believing that they were contrary to what the Bible teaches (Curtis 2010). These Puritans would eventually break from the Church of England. Many Puritans eventually immigrated to New England in America to practice their faith freely.

Another of the Separatist groups to develop were the Quakers. The Quakers placed great importance on having a personal relationship with God, believing God was present in every person, and did not have organized services or official ministers, which horrified Puritans and other Protestants (Vann 2017). Their public testimonies were very important to the Quakers, also called the "Friends." Because of this, they dressed and spoke plainly and refused to take any oaths or worldly comforts. The Quakers faced much persecution from just about everyone else in the Christian churches around them. Like the Puritans, the Quakers immigrated in large numbers to America, especially to Pennsylvania.

This 18th century illustration shows a Quaker meeting in England. By this time, many Quakers had moved to America, seeking religious freedom.

Other groups that broke with the Church of England either at this time or later in history included the Presbyterians (who followed John Calvin's teachings and were especially prominent in Scotland), Baptists, and Methodists.

SCOTLAND

Scottish royalty ruled from Edinburgh Castle in the city of Edinburgh (ED-in-burr-ah). It remains the capital of Scotland and an important Scottish cultural center.

The Scottish Highlands are well known for their stunning scenery and soaring mountains.

United Kingdom

The largest city in the country is Glasgow (GLAZ-go). This city rose to importance in the 1800s because it had many factories and became a Scottish industrial center. The city has its own distinctive accent and slang, which many outsiders have difficulty understanding.

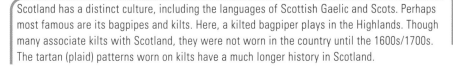

Scotland has a distinct culture, including the languages of Scottish Gaelic and Scots. Perhaps most famous are its bagpipes and kilts. Here, a kilted bagpiper plays in the Highlands. Though many associate kilts with Scotland, they were not worn in the country until the 1600s/1700s. The tartan (plaid) patterns worn on kilts have a much longer history in Scotland.

Scotland has numerous islands off its coasts. One of its most famous lies to the north — Shetland. Settled by Norwegian Vikings, Shetland was heavily influenced by Scandinavian culture, including its language, and wasn't even part of Scotland until the 1400s. Some of its most famous residents are its Shetland ponies.

27

START HERE

It's time to fill your canteen — we are going on an African safari! Our journey will take us through several major African empires that grew wealthy because of resources they pulled from the ground. Africa is a beautiful continent, blessed with a vast abundance of wildlife and natural resources.

Also in this chapter, we will sail up the west coast of Africa to the country of Portugal, where we will learn about a prince named Henry who didn't care to become king. Instead, Henry wanted to contribute to the world of navigation and trade. Sadly, the trading establishments and routes would eventually lead to Portugal's involvement in the horrible African slave trade.

The beauty of Africa and her people would forever bear the incredibly painful scar of the cruel slave trade. I do not want to spend too much time focusing on this topic, but I do want to give you something to think about concerning it. Horrible practices like this occur when humankind forgets or ignores the God-given worth of all human life. Before reading this chapter, I encourage you to read these verses and think about how they are related to the value of life: Genesis 2:7, Psalm 139:13–16, and Isaiah 46:3b–4.

AFRICA DURING THE MIDDLE AGES

We've spent the past several chapters focusing on Europe as we study the Renaissance and Reformation, but now we're going to turn our attention to another important part of the world — Africa. We'll spend quite a bit more time learning about Africa and how European explorers affected the people (and not always for the better) in our next volume, but it's essential that we also study these regions and cultures to learn more about what life was like before the time of the explorers.

What do you think of when you hear the name "Africa"? Do you think of the hot desert? Or maybe the windy savanna teeming with lions and wildebeests? If you thought about either of these things, you would be right! Africa is a beautiful and diverse continent, with a huge variety of ecosystems. When you think of Africa, you might also think of all the wonderful wildlife that roam these areas and are amazing examples of God's creativity. African animals vary greatly from place to place. You might see monkeys and parrots — similar to those you would see in the Amazon rainforest in South America — or zebras and elephants roaming through the grasses of the savannas. You might even be fortunate enough to catch sight of a mob of meerkats, standing at attention like a small group of soldiers.

During the Middle Ages and the ancient period before that, most visitors to Africa didn't make it any farther south than the Sahara Desert, which is in North Africa and inhabited primarily by Muslim Arabs and Berbers. So, for a long time, that's what most people knew about Africa. They didn't know how diverse the land, the animals, or the people were on the rest of the continent.

During this time, there were numerous African kingdoms and empires across the continent, but we are going to focus on the ones in northwest Africa, right where the Sahara (suh-HAIR-uh) Desert transitions into the savanna. This was the site of three well-established, powerful empires. They were the empires of Ghana (GAW-nuh), Mali (MAH-lee), and Songhai (sohn-GUY).

Let's look a little more closely at each of these empires, starting with the Ghana Empire. Though it shares the name of the modern country of Ghana, the Ghana Empire was actually located in what is now Mauritania and Mali. Most of the people in Ghana lived in red,

Africa is well known for its wide variety of animals, including the elephant. This illustration is from the 18th century when Europeans were colonizing the continent.

clay-brick houses with reed roofs. They were farming people who also hunted and fished. The Ghanaian people were known for their skill in iron working. Ghanaians may have been good farmers and excellent metal workers, but that is not how they made their fortunes. They became wealthy on gold — not just their gold, mind you, but also their neighbors' gold.

You see, this part of Africa had lots of gold in the ground. The Ghana Empire had its own gold mines, but their neighbors to the south did, too. Since these tribes with the gold had to go through the Ghana Empire to trade the gold, the Ghana Empire took advantage of the situation. They charged a hefty "passage tax" on the gold going through their land. Since this gold was in great demand, the Ghana Empire made quite a fortune on the gold that was simply traveling through their country. Many of these gold pieces and gold jewelry were sold to merchants who carried it to Europe and across North Africa.

Another interesting aspect of this story is the "currency" that the southern tribes used when selling their gold. The Arab and Berber lands to the north were rich in salt, while the southern tribes were short on it. The northern people had so much salt that they used it to buy gold. Since the Ghana Empire was in the middle, they taxed

Salt caravans are still a part of life in Africa today. This caravan is traveling in the country of Chad. Their salt will be traded for grain.

The area between the Sahara desert and the savanna in West Africa is called the Sahel. The trading empires covered in this chapter were all located in the Sahel.

both the gold going north and the salt coming from the north. By 800, the empire had become extremely wealthy and powerful! The Ghana Empire did not last forever, though. It is not entirely clear what happened, though attacks from the North African Muslims weakened the empire. Little by little, the Ghana Empire crumbled and was no longer in existence by the early 1200s.

As the Ghana Empire became weaker and weaker, the neighboring empire of Mali took over the salt and gold trade. Like Ghana, Mali lay between the gold in the south and the salt in the north, and their empire eventually included the Ghana Empire, as well as lands farther south. Mali grew stronger, and by the 1200s, they had become the dominant empire in West Africa.

The Mali kings were extremely powerful and controlled their people's lives. The most powerful of these kings, Mansa Musa, became famous throughout the Middle East when he took the Muslim pilgrimage to Mecca. Muslims had served in the government and been important in trade before, but he is believed to have been the first or one of the first Mali emperors who was Muslim. Many of the people in the empire still practiced their traditional religion, but Islam was increasingly the religion of the upper and ruling classes. Eventually, the Mali Empire became too big to govern effectively. Several areas either revolted and declared independence or were seized by neighboring states. The Mali Empire was no longer a powerful force in West Africa by the mid-1500s.

NARRATION BREAK:

Discuss the African trading empires.

 Maps have been around a very long time. The early people groups scratched out maps depicting their hunting and fishing territories ("Cartography" 2017). The Egyptian scientist Ptolemy, who lived during the time of the Roman Empire, crafted a world map that depicted a spherical earth ("Cartography" 2017). The maps produced during the Middle Ages followed Ptolemy's geographical guide, with one major difference: they place east at the top of their maps, with the city of Jerusalem as the focus. These maps are sometimes called T-maps because they only show the continents of Europe, Asia, and Africa, with the Mediterranean Sea and Nile River forming a T ("Cartography" 2017). It wasn't until the 1300s that more realistic maps were created for navigation ("Cartography" 2017).

In modern times, cartography (the science and art of creating a map) mostly involves using aerial and satellite photographs as a base for maps and charts. Such technology allows us to obtain a close-up view of anywhere on earth. Cartography is a highly scientific profession, which takes both the ability to focus on tiny details and the skill of thinking about the big picture. I want to tell you the story of a man who did just that. His attention to the details led him to look at the bigger picture to make an important discovery, which greatly contributed to the world of cartography.

Example of a 15th century map

Many centuries ago, around the year 240 B.C., an Egyptian librarian named Eratosthenes (er-uh-TAS-tho-nees) made an important discovery. This man, who liked to think big thoughts about many subjects, had heard that the sun could be seen shining at the bottom of a certain well in a town called Syene on the longest day of the year. After thinking about this for a while, he surmised that this must mean that the sun was directly over the well. He knew that if the sun was directly overhead, it did not cast a shadow on upright pillars, yet he knew that in his city, the pillars did cast shadows on the longest day of the year. This

Many ancient and medieval texts of Timbuktu have been kept for centuries in people's homes. Work is underway to locate and preserve them.

The next empire that arose in Western Africa was the Songhai Empire. It started to become powerful in the late 1300s and eventually included much of the Mali Empire, as well as points west and north. Have you ever heard the expression, "We got lost and ended up in Timbuktu"? In the Middle Ages, you could literally do this. Timbuktu was a major city in the Songhai Empire (and had been a major city of the earlier Mali Empire, too). In addition to being a major trade city, it also became a center of Islamic culture. As with the Mali Empire, the Songhai Empire had Muslim rulers, and Islamic scholars flocked to Timbuktu, where there were numerous schools. The Songhai Empire, and especially Timbuktu, was fascinating to the visitors from the north. We know that some of these visitors were explorers who came to Africa and then returned to Europe to write books about it. The Songhai Empire eventually collapsed in the late 1500s, when Muslim soldiers from Morocco came in and took control of this area.

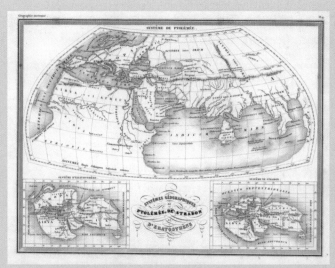

This 19th century map recreates three different maps of the world by the ancient Greeks.

Bernardo Strozzi's 17th century painting of Eratosthenes teaching

puzzled Eratosthenes, so he decided to travel the 800 kilometers (about 500 miles) to Syene to see for himself.

Sure enough, the sun did reflect in the well as he had been told, and the pillars did not cast a shadow on the longest day of the year. Eratosthenes thought about this information. Why did the pillars in his home city of Alexandria, Egypt, cast shadows when the pillars in Syene did not? By this time, the ancient Greeks knew the world was not flat. But Eratosthenes wanted to know exactly how round it was. Using his math skills, Eratosthenes calculated the size of the earth by measuring the angles of the shadows to find that they were approximately 7.12 degrees. He knew that this was about one-fifth of a circle, and he also knew that the distance between Syene and Alexandria was 800 kilometers, so he simply multiplied 50 x 800 to find 40,000 kilometers as the circumference of the earth (Maxwell 2011, 16–17). I find this amazing! Today, we have more advanced methods for making these measurements, but the figure that Eratosthenes came up with is still only a mere 8 kilometers (4.97 miles) off. (Maxwell 2011, 16–17).

Our next stop in our story takes place in a small country called Portugal, which runs along the west coast of Spain. Portugal has a very long coastline because its entire western border lies on the Atlantic Ocean. This country is known for its numerous picturesque bays and harbors, where many ships and sailboats bob in the blue water. Portugal may be small in size, but it holds an important place in history.

Earlier, we learned about the famous King Ferdinand and Queen Isabella of Spain. They are often mentioned when we read stories of Christopher Columbus, the explorer credited for discovering America. In this chapter, however, we will learn about a famous prince of Portugal, who also encouraged exploration. Henry was one of the younger sons of the Portuguese king, so he grew up knowing that he would probably never have the throne. This did not bother Henry, however, because he was more interested in being a soldier.

When Henry was a young man, he was part of a Portuguese group that seized the Moroccan town of Ceuta. This was an important trade city that was one of the destinations of the trading routes controlled by the West African empires we have studied in this chapter. This experience is likely what interested Henry in exploring West Africa further. He realized that if Portugal wanted to trade directly with the merchants of West Africa, they needed to control these areas. Despite his nickname, Henry the Navigator (which he was never called during his lifetime), Henry himself was not an explorer, sailor, nor navigator. But he famously invested the wealth and power he had as a member of the royal family into promoting exploration and expansion of trade.

Henry favored a new type of ship called a caravel for conducting these explorations. They were light but fast and easy to maneuver. Unfortunately, Henry had a new problem. Most people were afraid to travel down into what they called "The Sea of Darkness." Sailors of that day were convinced that as they went farther south, the sun would get so hot that the water would boil, cooking them on their ships.

Finally, in 1434, Henry found someone who was brave enough to face the certain peril of the Sea of Darkness — Gil Eanes. What this brave sailor found was water conditions no different than those along the Portuguese coastline. After this discovery was made, other sailors decided they were brave enough to try it, too. Under Henry's sponsorship, Portugal claimed several islands in the Atlantic and off the coast of West Africa, including the Azores, Madeira, and Cape Verde. These all boosted trade and were the sites of sugar plantations that the Portuguese had established.

Henry had fond hopes of his ships finding their way all the way around the southern tip of Africa and up the other side to India. This did not happen during Henry's lifetime, however. The maps of the Middle Ages did not show how truly huge the continent of Africa is. Henry the Navigator had helped Portugal become a leader in exploration and trade, but he did not reach India. It would be much later before an explorer would come along and discover how truly immense Africa is.

Illustration of Henry the Navigator

One of Henry's other legacies led to a much more brutal and tragic aspect of world history. The exploration and trading activities he promoted also led to the Atlantic slave trade. Before the Portuguese became involved in trade in West Africa, slaves had been part of the gold/salt trade that the West African trading empires conducted with North

The Monument to the Discoveries in Portugal commemorates Henry the Navigator and the country's explorers.

African merchants. In the 1440s, Portuguese explorers commissioned by Henry purchased gold and slaves in an African market. It was only a matter of years before Portugal was heavily invested in the slave trade and was capturing their own slaves in Africa. The slaves were then transported to the newly acquired islands and forced to work on the sugar plantations. The conditions they lived in were terrible. Portugal started Europe's involvement in the Atlantic slave trade, but other European countries soon participated. Its cruel legacy has still left an imprint on the world today and will affect a lot of the events we study in the next volume.

It seems in the telling of human history, I often feel deeply troubled at the end of my writing a chapter. I do not want to end this segment of our story on such a sad and grim note. Before I close this particular chapter, I would like to refocus on the sovereignty and love of God. I want you, my friend, to know that even as the slave trade was beginning, God was raising up men and women who would stand against it. Evil never goes unpunished by our Holy God. In the end, Satan will be thrown into the abyss. You can read about this in Revelation 20:2–3.

NARRATION BREAK:

Talk about Henry the Navigator.

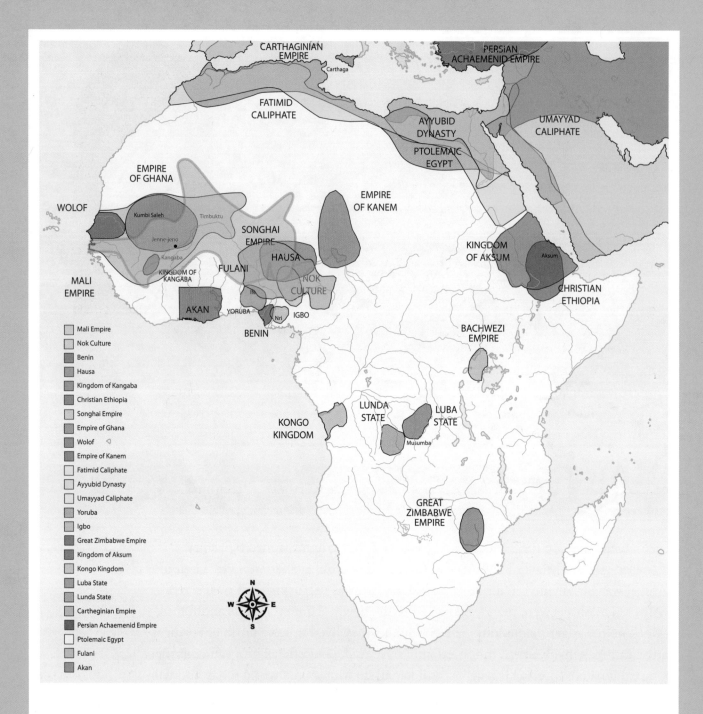

Map Legend:
- Mali Empire
- Nok Culture
- Benin
- Hausa
- Kingdom of Kangaba
- Christian Ethiopia
- Songhai Empire
- Empire of Ghana
- Wolof
- Empire of Kanem
- Fatimid Caliphate
- Ayyubid Dynasty
- Umayyad Caliphate
- Yoruba
- Igbo
- Great Zimbabwe Empire
- Kingdom of Aksum
- Kongo Kingdom
- Luba State
- Lunda State
- Carthaginian Empire
- Persian Achaemenid Empire
- Ptolemaic Egypt
- Fulani
- Akan

In our chapter, we focused on a small number of African kingdoms, primarily in the northwestern part of the continent. However, as this map shows, there were numerous kingdoms and civilizations throughout Africa. This map shows the pre-colonial period before European nations began to become involved in Africa. Some of these kingdoms were in existence then while others had long since ceased to exist.

Some of those in North Africa are ones we have already studied in either this book or Volume 1. But many of the other civilizations may not be familiar to you. Take some time to study this map. Remember, not all the civilizations were in existence at the same time, so in any given century, the map would not always look the same.

ANALYZE   Which parts of the map have multiple civilizations?

CONNECT   Which empire was the largest in northwest Africa?

MAPS

Africa was a major center of Christianity in the first three centuries A.D. Many Early Church Fathers, such as Origen, Tertullian, and Augustine, were originally from North Africa (Sigg 2010). Unfortunately, the Christian faith all but disappeared in North Africa with the advance of Islam (Sigg 2010). Only in Egypt and in Ethiopia had Christianity been fully established enough that it survived and continues to this day (Sigg 2010).

Although Catholicism was introduced by the Portuguese to the Kongo Kingdom in central Africa between the 1500s and 1700s, it did not truly take root there (Sigg 2010). Finally, at the end of the 18th century, Evangelical Revival missionaries came to invest in Africa. Their work finally brought an enduring Christian presence in Sub-Sahara Africa. Unfortunately, the missionaries from the Western civilization were not the only ones who came to Africa at this time. Transatlantic slave traders brought with them their greed and desire to plunder the great continent of Africa, not only of its people to be sold as slaves but also of its abundant natural resources to sell for a profit (Sigg 2010). Africa would become a war zone between those who wanted to spread the love of Jesus and stop the vile slave trade and those who wielded almost limitless power and resources.

The seed of Christianity had been planted, but would the Christian church in Africa grow? Slowly but surely, the gospel spread throughout the remote areas of the continent. Reformers called for change in the missionary-established churches, which led to both reform and new churches — including churches started by Africans. These are called the African Initiated Churches (AICs) (Sigg 2010).

One of the oldest African Initiated Churches is the Ethiopian church. Here, Ethiopian priests celebrate Timkat, which commemorates Jesus' baptism.

TIMBUKTU

At its peak, Timbuktu benefited in trade from its location on the edge of the Sahara Desert. Now, the city, which is in the modern country of Mali, has been threatened by desertification. That means land that was not a desert is becoming a desert. Timbuktu has endured devastating droughts in recent decades. Its streets are made of sand.

Mali

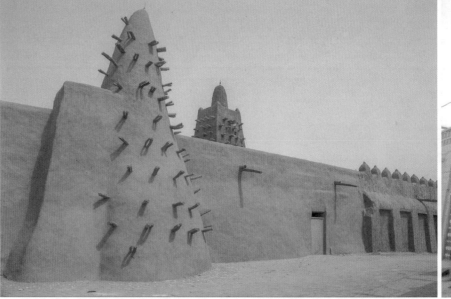

Built in the 1300s, the Djinguereber Mosque is one of the most famous sites in the city.

The mosque is made of mud and must be frequently repaired. The pegs on the side are to make it easier for repair crews to work. Many of the buildings in the city are made from the same material and also require careful maintenance.

Donkeys on the streets of Timbuktu

During its heyday, Timbuktu was the home of many scholars and schools. It was also famous for its libraries and manuscript collections. This building is a reproduction of one of the city's famous libraries. It was destroyed during recent political turmoil but is being rebuilt.

28

START HERE

Our journey together through the Middle Ages is coming to a close. Before we say goodbye (and see you soon in *The World's Story 3*), we are going to make one more stop. Any study of the Middle Ages would not be complete without a look at what was happening in the great continents of North and South America during this period. I need to warn you, however, that our stop in the Americas is not going to be a completely positive and enjoyable experience; some of the cultures of the peoples during this time were extremely dark, pagan, and full of cruelty and oppression. Please remember, though, that there were bright spots of godly love and service even in these dark places. In our Church History section at the end of the chapter, we will be learning the story of one of these servants of God, who bravely shined the light of Jesus into the world. Come with me one more time as we learn about the civilizations of these two land giants and what was happening on the eve of European exploration.

If we continued west after visiting Africa and Portugal, we would be traveling over the great Atlantic Ocean, toward the continents of North and South America and the stretch of land connecting these two giants. This connecting piece of land, Central America, is part of North America and is the focus of the first part of this chapter. A large part of this area is also called Mesoamerica (MESS-o-a-MER-i-ca) and is the site of several important civilizations.

If you were with me in Volume 1 of this series, you might remember how we learned about some of the interesting ancient tribes of the Americas. We discovered the Olmecs, who left behind some extremely intriguing artifacts and ruins of ancient temples and pyramids in Central America. We also learned about the fascinating, gigantic ground drawings that the Nazca left etched in the earth farther south in South America and the magnificent, deserted city of Machu Picchu, which the Inca left high in the Andes Mountains. Two other major civilizations that we did not study were the Aztecs and the Maya.

Our first stop will be in Central America in what is now Mexico. No one knows for sure where the Aztecs originally came from, but during the Middle Ages, roaming tribes of Aztecs lived in this area. The area in which the Aztecs roamed had other residents, but the Aztecs conquered them. Aztec legend tells the story of how they finally found a home. It is supposed that one day the Aztecs were wandering around as usual when they came upon a huge lake with soft, muddy shores. Out in the middle of the lake was an island, and on that island grew a huge cactus, which had an enormous eagle perched upon its branches. The Aztecs gaped in astonishment when they saw that the eagle was grasping a giant snake in its talons.

The Aztecs took this as a sign from their false gods that this was to be their permanent home. The lake, Tenochtitlan (teh-NOCH-teet-lan), and the island needed a lot of work. The Aztecs used mud and timbers to build up the island; they used logs and rocks to make pathways and roads out to their floating city. They became adept at making floating "mat-gardens." These gardens were planted in soil that was loaded on woven mats of grass or reeds. The seeds sprouted, sending their roots down through the mat and into the water. This amazing gardening

This 16th century manuscript illustration depicts the Aztecs building Tenochtitlan.

technique guaranteed the Aztecs would have food even in a drought and helped them transform swampy land unsuitable for agriculture into productive soil.

Warfare was an important part of Aztec society. Every man received some military training, and elite warriors belonged to special warrior societies. The Aztecs had many enemies — and for a good reason! They were always raiding their neighbors' villages to kidnap their next human sacrifice. This is why the Aztecs placed a higher priority on their warriors taking captives than killing the enemy. What an absolutely terrible and depraved way to live!

We can, however, thank the Aztecs for one thing — chocolate. Yes, it was the Aztecs who discovered the delicious taste of the cacao (kuh-KAY-oh) bean. They liked the taste so much that they made bars from it and even drank it as a hot drink. Only the wealthy could afford it, but it was a great favorite. The next time you come in from playing in the cold to a cup of hot chocolate, you can thank the Aztecs for it! They also ate other foods you probably recognize, including tortillas, corn, tomatoes, avocados, and turkey.

Aztec calendar

Aztec Codex. The Aztecs recorded their history and culture in their own forms of books. They called such a book a codex. They are one of our best sources about Aztec life.

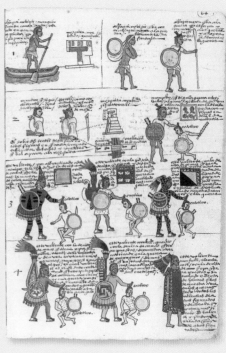

Children were educated at home but were sent to school as teenagers. There were two types of schools that they could attend. One focused on practical topics, including agriculture, crafts, and warfare. Poorer people usually went to this school, and graduates ended up in the Aztec military or went home to farm and work. Teenagers from wealthier families went to a more advanced school that taught writing and astronomy, as well as other subjects. The boys who went to this kind of school grew up to be scholars, priests, and government officials.

We will learn more about when the Aztecs encountered the Spanish explorers in the next volume, but the Spanish were impressed with how advanced Aztec society was. Their cities of stone buildings were clean and well-built, and the culture had advanced knowledge of astronomy, mathematics, city planning, architecture, and agriculture. However, the Spanish were also greatly alarmed and confused by the Aztec practice of human sacrifice.

NARRATION BREAK:

Talk about what you read today.

Aztec sculpture of a man carrying a cacao pod. Chocolate is made from these pods.

Diego Rivera's mural of Tenochtitlan, 1945

The next civilization we are going to study is the Maya. They lived slightly to the south of the area where the Aztecs lived in southern Mexico and modern Central American countries like Guatemala, Belize, Honduras, and El Salvador. Most of this civilization was located on the Yucatán (yew-kuh-TAN) Peninsula, which separates the Gulf of Mexico and the Caribbean Sea. It is not clearly understood when the Maya civilization began, but many historians believe that the first of their settlements was established sometime before 1500 B.C.

Many of the Maya records were destroyed many hundreds of years later, at the time of the Spanish invasions, which we will learn more about in our next volume. However, the artifacts and ruins left behind give us a glimpse into the lives of these people. Their artwork and pottery have been found in many locations hundreds of miles from their homeland. Written inscriptions in Maya hieroglyphics date back hundreds of years and give us a look at their written language and their rather lavish culture.

19th century lithograph of Uxmal, an ancient Maya city

The Maya were even more advanced than the Aztecs (and the Europeans) in science, especially astronomy, and they also were excellent mathematicians. Science and astronomy were very important to the Maya because they were closely linked to their religious practices. As they studied the moon, stars, and planets, they developed a complicated calendar for counting the days and years. They also kept impeccable records of what they studied in the heavens, charting the paths of celestial bodies and recording events like eclipses, solstices, and equinoxes.

Why did the Maya create such elaborate calendars predicting when catastrophic happenings would occur? Just like everyone else at that time, the Maya did not have access to charts of the stars or written documentation of when solar eclipses would take place. In fact, they did not even understand what an eclipse was. Remember, at this time, there were no high-powered telescopes with which to study the universe. All they had were the records they kept of the obvious paths of certain bright "stars" or other heavenly bodies. They even speculated about certain heavenly features that were not discovered until much later.

These records show that the Maya were surprisingly accurate in their predictions, but of course, they did not know when the end of the earth would happen. The Bible tells us that only God knows this information. At the time of the Maya, people thought the earth was the center of the universe. No records show that the Maya believed any differently about the position of the earth in relationship to the sun.

Even though they were excellent record-keepers, the Maya believed in mythology, which kept them from really understanding what they saw when they studied the heavens. For instance, they believed the heavens were held up by four jaguars, one at

 If you were to visit the Yucatán Peninsula, which includes part of Mexico, Belize, and northern Guatemala, you might hear someone speaking a language that has changed very little from its beginning in the 16th century. The Yucatec language is one of the languages that the Maya spoke. Some of the ancient Maya stories and knowledge were written in Yucatec with Spanish spelling in the 1600s and 1700s ("Yucatec Language" 2017). There are some additional written materials from the 16th century that are also thought to be the written form of the classical form of Yucatec, but they have not been deciphered yet ("Yucatec Language" 2017). Today, approximately 750,000 people on the Yucatán Peninsula still speak Yucatec.

A little to the north of where the Maya lived were the Aztecs. The Aztecs, too, had a language that is still spoken today in an altered form. Nahuatl (NAW-wat-uhl) has undergone some phonetic changes through the centuries ("Nahuatl Language" 2016). Like Yucatec, it uses Spanish spelling ("Nahuatl Language" 2016). The classic form of the language had a noticeable *tl* sound that has been lost in two of the modern forms of the language. One form of the language, the eastern Aztec dialects, have replaced the *tl* sound with *t*, thus they are called Nahuat ("Nahuatl Language" 2016). In the western dialects, called Nahual, the *tl* has been replaced with *l* ("Nahuatl Language" 2016). The remaining form, the northern and central dialect, keeps the *tl* sound and is called Nahuatl as a result ("Nahuatl Language" 2016). There are approximately 1,500,000 Nahuatl speakers in Mexico today.

Names of Maya Days, 1-20

each corner. They worshiped the rain, earth, plants, and animal gods. Because of this, when they studied the heavens, they believed they were actually watching distant gods that might intend to either "bless" them or "curse" them.

The Maya civilization was organized into city-states. Their palaces, cities, and monuments were elaborate in design. Perhaps the most famous of all the Maya monuments is the stepped pyramids, which they built in their religious centers. These pyramids stand over 100 feet tall and, in many cases, were built near the palaces of the rulers. Information about the rulers' genealogy and military accomplishments were inscribed in hieroglyphics on rock slabs and placed near the palaces and pyramids. All these amazing architectural feats were accomplished without the help

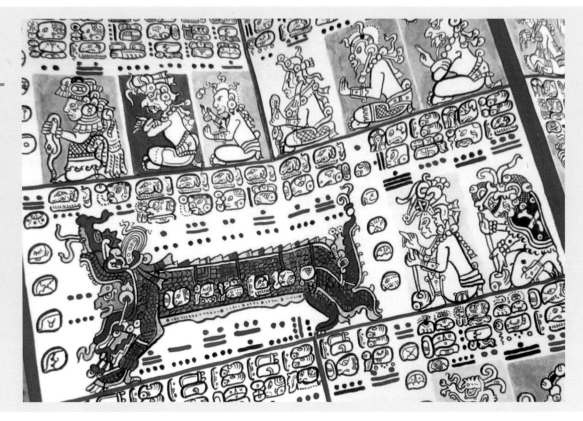

The Dresden Codex is the oldest Maya manuscript known to exist, dating to before the Spanish invaded.

of metal tools or even the wheel! Instead, they used sheer manpower, logs rolled onto stones, and chisels made from a mineral called jadeite to create these impressive buildings.

The great Maya civilization would thrive for hundreds of years before declining. There are many theories why the civilization finally collapsed, but we do know that the complete and final ruin came when the Spanish conquistadors came across the Atlantic Ocean to conquer them in the 1500s.

We learned about them in the last volume, but just as a recap, to the south of the Maya, way down on the western coast of South America, was the Inca civilization. The Inca kept records through an elaborate system of knots called quipu, but they did not have a written language. For this reason, they did not leave many records behind, and scholars can't always decipher what they did leave.

However, we do know that the great Inca civilization stretched about 2,000 miles down the west coast of South America. This is truly amazing! That is comparable to the width of our great country from the East Coast to the West Coast, which is about 2,800 miles. We can also piece together what life was like for the Incas. We know by seeing the solid, well-built streets that the Incas were skilled masons. In many instances, the streets were paved with large stones so carefully fitted together that there was no need for mortar! We also know that merchants used llamas to transport goods along the cobbled streets. The Inca empire stayed strong for many years. However, as we will learn in the next book, European explorers came into Central and South America and conquered the Aztecs, Maya, and the Incas.

The Inca Trail. This road leads to the famous Inca city of Machu Picchu (mah-chew-PEE-chew).

Inca quipu (KEE-poo), an Inca method of documentation. Modern scholars are still not sure how to decode what most of the quipu mean.

Throughout our study of this fascinating time period from the fall of Rome to the Renaissance, we have seen many changes around the world, and we have come face to face with the fact that much of human nature chooses to pursue power and affluence. I think this would be a wonderful time to revisit the quote from C.S. Lewis' book *Mere Christianity*, which I included in the Introduction of this book, along with the Scripture I also included. Lewis said, "[H]uman history [is] . . . the long terrible story of man trying to find something other than God which will make him happy" (2009, Book 2, Chapter 3).

Let's not be discouraged, though! Instead, let's focus again on what Jesus says in John 16:33: "I have told you all this so that you may have peace in me. Here on earth you will have many trials and sorrows. But take heart, because I have overcome the world" (NLT).

In our next volume, we will see even more change as we move into the modern era. Just as with all the kingdoms and historical figures and developments we have studied in the Middle Ages, we will continue to see how God is always in control in the modern era, too.

NARRATION BREAK:

Discuss the Maya and their civilization.

MESOAMERICA

Tenochtitlan   Chichen Itza

SOUTH AMERICA

Cuzco

- ■ Maya: 1500 B.C.-A.D. 900
- ■ Aztec: Circa A.D. 1200-1521
- ■ Inca: Circa A.D. 1200-1533

This map shows the relative locations of the three major Central and South American empires we studied in this chapter. The Maya civilization was the earliest, with the Aztec and then Inca following, though there was overlap in time between the last two.

The Aztec were located in what is now modern Mexico. The range of the Maya included Mexico, as well as Central American countries like Guatemala, Belize, El Salvador, and Honduras. The Inca Empire was massive, spanning the modern South American countries of Columbia, Ecuador, Peru, Bolivia, Chile, and Argentina.

ANALYZE   What do you notice about the three empires and their locations on the map?

CONNECT   How many years after the Maya civilization ended did the Aztec and Inca civilizations begin? (Hint: Look at the map key.)

MAPS

For our last Church History section, I want to tell you the story of a man named Bartolomé de Las Casas (bar-toe-luh-MAY dey las cah-sas). To tell you this story, we will need to jump ahead just a little to learn the setting in which it takes place. Beginning in the late 1400s and early 1500s, Spanish colonists established lavishly rich plantations in the Americas. (We'll learn more about this time period in Volume 3.) Many of these plantations were run by natives who had been turned into slaves. Bartolomé de Las Casas was one of these plantation owners (Graves "Bartolomeo de Las Casas" 2010). In 1509, a Dominican monk named Father Montesinos scolded the Spanish colonists for the horrible treatment of these natives. He challenged them by asking them how men who called themselves Christians could be that vile toward a fellow human being. The monk's words cut to the heart of 24-year-old Bartolomé, and he released his slaves immediately (Graves "Bartolomeo de Las Casas" 2010).

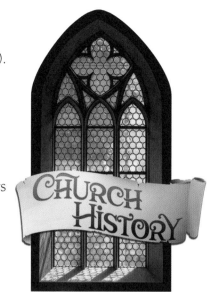

This did not stop the anguish in Bartolomé's heart, though, and he sought advice from Father Montesinos to know what else he could do. The monk gladly trained the young man to be a priest, and Bartolomé became the first Spaniard to be ordained as a priest in the New World (Graves "Bartolomeo de Las Casas" 2010). God's love for the natives had set a fire in Bartolomé's spirit, and he devoted his life to exposing the evils being perpetrated against them. He traveled five times across the ocean to appeal to the king, reminding him that the pope had granted Spain land in the New World to evangelize the Indians, not terrorize them (Graves "Bartolomeo de Las Casas" 2010)!

Although Bartolomé's work was scoffed at by most of the other Spaniards, the natives saw and appreciated his work on their behalf. On July 31, 1566, Bartolomé died (Graves "Bartolomeo de Las Casas" 2010). When the news of his passing reached the villages of the natives he had fought so hard to protect, they honored him by lighting fires and lamenting his death (Graves "Bartolomeo de Las Casas" 2010). Although the story of Bartolomé de Las Casas is not well known (I honestly had never heard mention of him until I stumbled across his account in a rather obscure article), I love knowing that God knew him. Moreover, I would venture to say that He was well pleased with this man, who chose to stand against all odds to show kindness to those who were oppressed. He's a wonderful inspiration to us all to think about ways we can spread the love of God and stand up for those in need.

16th century portrait of Bartolomé de Las Casas

CHICHEN ITZA

There are several ancient Maya cities still in existence. The largest and one of the best known is Chichén Itzá (chee-chin eet-ZAH) in modern-day Mexico. The most famous building in Chichén Itzá is The Castillo, a pyramid with a temple on top.

Mexico

Goal at Chichén Itzá Ball Court. Modern scholars are unsure of how exactly the game was played but suspect it was like modern volleyball without a net. It was not all fun and games, though. The games were used to settle disputes or to punish prisoners of war. The losers were killed. A non-deadly variation called ulama is still played in parts of Mexico today.

The Maya liked taking steam baths, and the ruins of the bath houses at Chichén Itzá still remain. The steam was created by pouring hot water over rocks.

The Caracol was probably used as an observatory tower to study astronomy.

When the Spanish found the city, they called this building complex The Nunnery because it reminded them of the monasteries back home. It is believed, however, that these buildings actually served as a palace.

Cenotes (sinkholes) served as water sources in Chichén Itzá. They were important because Chichén Itzá was in Mexico's Yucatán Peninsula, which is prone to droughts. One of the most famous is called Ik-Kil and is only a couple of miles from the city's ruins.

BIBLIOGRAPHY

Appleyard, Ernest Silvanus. 1850. *Eastern Churches: Containing Sketches of the Nestorian, Armenian, Jacobite, Coptic and Abyssinian Communities.* London: James Darling.

"Auto-da-fé." 2014. *Encyclopaedia Britannica.* July 14, 2014. Accessed May 3, 2018. https://www.britannica.com/topic/auto-da-fe.

Ayduz, Salim. n.d. "Ottoman Contributions to Science and Technology." *Muslim Heritage. Foundation for Science, Technology, and Civilisation.* Accessed April 12, 2018. http://www.muslimheritage.com/article/ottoman-contributions-science-and-technology.

Bainton, Roland H. 2013. *Here I Stand: A Life of Martin Luther.* Nashville, TN: Abingdon Press.

BBC. 2015. "New Rules on Royal Succession Come into Force." *BBC News.* March 26, 2015. Accessed April 18, 2018. http://www.bbc.com/news/uk-32073399.

Black, Annetta. n.d. "Elephant Clock." *Atlas Obscura.* Accessed April 18, 2018. https://www.atlasobscura.com/places/elephant-clock.

Bosworth, Joseph. 2010. S.v. "Engla Land." *An Anglo-Saxon Dictionary Online.* Edited by Thomas Northcote Toller and others. Faculty of Arts, Charles University. March 21, 2010. Accessed April 16, 2018. http://bosworth.ff.cuni.cz/009427.

Brooks, Sarah. 2009. "The Byzantine State Under Justinian I (Justinian the Great)." *In Heilbrunn Timeline of Art History. Metropolitan Museum of Art.* April 2009. Accessed April 16, 2018. https://www.metmuseum.org/toah/hd/just/hd_just.htm.

Burman, Thomas E. 1994. *Religious Polemic and the Intellectual History of the Mozarabs, c. 1050–1200.* Leiden: E.J. Brill.

Centers for Disease Control and Prevention. 2015. "History of Plague." *CDC.* September 14, 2015. Accessed April 12, 2018. https://www.cdc.gov/plague/history/index.html.

Chickering, Howell D. 2006. "Introduction." *Beowulf: A Dual-Language Edition.* New York: Anchor Books.

Child, John, Nigel Kelly, and Martyn Whittock. 1992. *The Crusades.* Oxford, England: Heinemann Educational.

Cohen, Doron B. 2013. *The Japanese Translations of the Hebrew Bible.* Leiden: BRILL.

Collins, Father Michael; Alexander Black, Thomas Cussans, John Farndon, and Philip Parker. 2017. *Remarkable Books: The World's Most Beautiful and Historic Works.* New York: DK Publishing.

Corning, Caitlin. 2006. *The Celtic and Roman Traditions: Conflict and Consensus in the Early Medieval Church.* New York: Palgrave Macmillan.

Curtis, Ken. 2010. "Who Were The Puritans?" *Christianity.com.* April 28, 2010. Accessed May 14, 2018. https://www.christianity.com/church/church-history/timeline/1601-1700/who-were-the-puritans-11630087.html.

"Cyrillic Alphabet." 2015. *Encyclopaedia Britannica.* November 16, 2015. Accessed May 4, 2018. https://www.britannica.com/topic/Cyrillic-alphabet.

D'Emilio, Frances. 2004. "Vatican Looks Back At Inquisition." *CBS News.* June 15, 2004. Accessed September 18, 2019. https://www.cbsnews.com/news/vatican-looks-back-at-inquisition/.

Department of Asian Art. 2001. "Southern Song Dynasty (1127–1279)." In *Heilbrunn Timeline of Art History. Metropolitan Museum of Art.* October 2001. Accessed April 11, 2018. https://www.metmuseum.org/toah/hd/ssong/hd_ssong.htm.

Department of Asian Art. 2001. "Yuan Dynasty (1271–1368)." In *Heilbrunn Timeline of Art History. Metropolitan Museum of Art.* October 2001. Accessed April 11, 2018. https://www.metmuseum.org/toah/hd/yuan/hd_yuan.htm.

"Edward II." 2018. *Encyclopaedia Britannica.* April 18, 2018. Accessed May 3, 2018. https://www.britannica.com/biography/Edward-II-king-of-England.

Elton, Geoffrey R. 2017. "Thomas Cromwell." *Encyclopaedia Britannica.* December 20, 2017. Accessed May 14, 2018. https://www.britannica.com/biography/Thomas-Cromwell-earl-of-Essex-Baron-Cromwell-of-Okeham.

Esposito, John L. 2004. "Caliphate." In *The Islamic World: Past and Present, Vol. 1.* New York: Oxford University Press.

"False Dmitry." 1998. *Encyclopaedia Britannica.* July 20, 1998. Accessed May 4, 2018. https://www.britannica.com/topic/False-Dmitry.

Frayer, Laura. 2014. "After 522 Years, Spain Seeks to Make Amends for Expulsion of Jews." *NPR.* December 25, 2014. Accessed May 3, 2018. https://www.npr.org/sections/parallels/2014/12/25/371866778/after-522-years-spain-seeks-to-make-amends-for-expulsion-of-jews.

Goldschmidt, Debra. 2015. "15 Cases of Human Plague This Year, CDC Says." CNN. October 22, 2015. Accessed May 3, 2018. https://www.cnn.com/2015/10/22/health/plague-cases-2015-cdc/index.html.

Gramley, Stephan, and Kurt-Michael Pätzold. 2004. *A Survey of Modern English, 2nd edition.* Routledge: London.

Graves, Dan. 2010. "Bartolomeo de Las Casas, Father to the Indians." *Christianity.com.* April 28, 2010. Accessed May 14, 2018. https://www.christianity.com/church/church-history/timeline/1501-1600/bartolomeo-de-las-casas-father-to-the-indians-11630011.html.

Graves, Dan. 2010. "Henry's Love for Becket Became Hatred." *Christianity.com.* April 28, 2010. Accessed April 24, 2018. https://www.christianity.com/church/church-history/timeline/901-1200/henrys-love-for-becket-became-hatred-11629803.html.

Graves, Dan. 2010. "Leo III Attacked in a Processional." *Christianity.com.* April 28, 2010. Accessed April 10, 2018. https://www.christianity.com/church/church-history/timeline/601-900/leo-iii-attacked-in-a-procession-11629757.html.

Graves, Dan. 2010. "The Venerable Bede." *Christianity.com.* April 28, 2010. Accessed April 16, 2018. https://www.christianity.com/church/church-history/timeline/601-900/the-venerable-bede-11629735.html.

"Gutenberg Bible." 2016. *Encyclopaedia Britannica.* January 27, 2016. Accessed May 4, 2018. https://www.britannica.com/topic/Gutenberg-Bible.

Hain, Kathryn. 2012. "Devshirme is a Contested Practice." Abstract. Historia: *Alpha Rho Papers. Utah Historical Review.* Vol. 2. June 21, 2012. Accessed April 11, 2018. http://epubs.utah.edu/index.php/historia/article/view/629.

BIBLIOGRAPHY

Hajar, Rachel. 2013. "The Air of History Part III: The Golden Age in Arab Islamic Medicine An Introduction." *Heart Views* 14, no. 1 (Jan–Mar): 43–46. *Gulf Heart Association.* Accessed April 18, 2018. https://dx.doi.org/10.4103%2F1995-705X.107125.

"Henry IV." 2018. *Encyclopaedia Britannica.* March 13, 2018. Accessed May 3, 2018. https://www.britannica.com/biography/Henry-IV-king-of-England.

Highfield, J.R.L., and Thomas Frederick Tout. 2018. "Edward III." *Encyclopaedia Britannica.* April 24, 2018. Accessed May 3, 2018. https://www.britannica.com/biography/Edward-III-king-of-England.

Highley, Christopher. 2008. *Catholics Writing the Nation in Early Modern Britain and Ireland.* Oxford, England: Oxford University Press.

History.com. 2010. "Black Death." *History.* Accessed April 11, 2018. https://www.history.com/topics/black-death.

History.com. 2011. "Taj Mahal." *History.* Accessed April 23, 2018. https://www.history.com/topics/taj-mahal.

Hughes, Kathleen. 1977. "The Early Irish Church, from the Coming of Christianity to the End of the Viking Era." In *The Irish World: The Art and Culture of the Irish People.* Edited by Brian de Breffny. New York: Harry N. Abrams.

"Isabella of France." 2017. *Encyclopaedia Britannica.* November 30, 2017. Accessed May 3, 2018. https://www.britannica.com/biography/Isabella-of-France.

"Janissaries." 2011. *GlobalSecurity.org.* November 7, 2011. Accessed May 3, 2018. https://www.globalsecurity.org/military/world/europe/ot-janissaries.htm.

"Janissary." 2014. *Encyclopaedia Britannica.* April 24, 2014. Accessed May 3, 2018. https://www.britannica.com/topic/Janissary-corps.

Jones, Timothy Paul. 2009. *Christian History Made Easy.* Torrance, CA: Rose Publishing, Inc.

"Kana." 2016. *Encyclopaedia Britannica.* March 4, 2016. Accessed April 23, 2018. https://www.britannica.com/topic/kana.

"Kanji." 2017. *Encyclopaedia Britannica.* September 26, 2017. Accessed April 23, 2018. https://www.britannica.com/topic/kanji.

"Kievan Rus." 2016. *Encyclopaedia Britannica.* February 22, 2016. Accessed May 4, 2018. https://www.britannica.com/topic/Kievan-Rus.

"Knights Templars and Philip the Fair." *Christianity.com.* April 28, 2010. Accessed April 24, 2018. https://www.christianity.com/church/church-history/timeline/1201-1500/knights-templars-and-philip-the-fair-11629854.html.

Kuhn, Anthony. 2015. "Driven Underground Years Ago, Japan's 'Hidden Christians' Maintain Faith." *NPR Weekend Edition.* October 11, 2015. Accessed April 25, 2018. https://www.npr.org/sections/parallels/2015/10/11/446865818/driven-underground-years-ago-japans-hidden-christians-maintain-faith.

Kuiper, Kathleen, ed. 2011. *The Culture of China.* New York: Britannica Educational Publishing.

Lechêne, Robert. 2018. "Printing." *Encyclopaedia Britannica.* April 5, 2018. Accessed April 23, 2018. https://www.britannica.com/topic/printing-publishing.

Lee, Cheuk Yin, and Ying-kit Chan. 2016. "China, imperial: 7. Ming dynasty period, 1368–1644." Abstract. *The Encyclopedia of Empire, 1. Wiley Online Library.* January 11, 2016. Accessed April 11, 2018. https://onlinelibrary.wiley.com/doi/abs/10.1002/9781118455074.wbeoe326.

Lewis, C.S. 2009. *Mere Christianity.* San Francisco: Harper One. Kindle.

Liberman, Anatoly. 2009. *Word Origins . . . And How We Know Them: Etymology for Everyone.* New York: Oxford University Press.

Maxwell, John C. 2011. *How Successful People Think Workbook.* New York: Center Street.

McFall, J. Arthur. 2006. "First Crusade: People's Crusade." *Military History. HistoryNet.* July 12, 2006. Accessed April 26, 2018. http://www.historynet.com/first-crusade-peoples-crusade.htm.

McGurkin, John Anthony, ed. 2014. *The Concise Encyclopedia of Orthodox Christianity.* Chichester, England: John Wiley & Sons.

Meagher, Jennifer. 2002. "The Holy Roman Empire and the Habsburgs, 1400–1600." In *Heilbrunn Timeline of Art History. Metropolitan Museum of Art.* October 2002. Accessed May 14, 2018. https://www.metmuseum.org/toah/hd/habs/hd_habs.htm.

Merriam-Webster. n.d. S.v. "dog," under "Origin and Etymology of dog." Accessed April 10, 2018. https://www.merriam-webster.com/dictionary/dog.

Merriam-Webster. n.d. S.v. "gold," under "Origin and Etymology of gold." Accessed April 10, 2018. https://www.merriam-webster.com/dictionary/gold.

Meyendorff, John. 2018. "Eastern Orthodoxy." *Encyclopaedia Britannica.* February 28, 2018. Accessed May 3, 2018. https://www.britannica.com/topic/Eastern-Orthodoxy#ref59584.

Morrill, John S., Bentley Brinkerhoff Gilbert, et al. 2018. "United Kingdom." *Encyclopaedia Britannica.* April 29, 2018. Accessed May 3, 2018. https://www.britannica.com/place/United-Kingdom/John-1199-1216#ref44792.

Morrison, Heidi. n.d. "Devshirme System [Gravure]." Annotation. *Children and Youth in History, Item #464. George Mason University's Center for History and New Media. University of Missouri-Kansas City.* Accessed April 11, 2018. http://chnm.gmu.edu/cyh/primary-sources/464.

Mote, Frederick W. 2003. *Imperial China 900–1800.* Cambridge, MA: Harvard University Press.

"Nahuatl Language" 2016. *Encyclopaedia Britannica.* March 22, 2016. Accessed May 14, 2018. https://www.britannica.com/topic/Nahuatl-language

"Nestorian." 2014. *Encyclopaedia Britannica.* March 28, 2014. Accessed April 23, 2018. https://www.britannica.com/topic/Nestorians.

"Old Church Slavonic Language." 2018. *Encyclopaedia Britannica.* May 3, 2018. Accessed May 4, 2018. https://www.britannica.com/topic/Old-Church-Slavonic-language.

Online Etymology Dictionary. n.d. S.v. "Viking." Accessed April 16, 2018. https://www.etymonline.com/word/Viking.

BIBLIOGRAPHY

Örsi, Tibor. 2015. "*Cow verses Beef:* Terms Denoting Animals and Their Meat in English." *Eger Journal of English Studies* 15 (2015): 49–55. http://anglisztika.ektf.hu/new/english/content/tudomany/ejes/ejesdokumentumok/2015/Orsi_2015.pdf.

Peterdi, Gabor F. 2018. "Printmaking." *Encyclopaedia Britannica.* March 9, 2018. Accessed May 10, 2018. https://www.britannica.com/art/printmaking.

"Plague." 2018. *Encyclopaedia Britannica.* March 22, 2018. Accessed May 3, 2018. https://www.britannica.com/science/plague#ref253271.

"Rightly Guided Caliphs." n.d. *The Oxford Dictionary of Islam,* edited by John L. Esposito. *Oxford Islamic Studies Online.* Accessed April 10, 2018. http://www.oxfordislamicstudies.com/article/opr/t125/e2018.

Roberts, Steve. 2017. "Reconquista." *Military History. HistoryNet.* July 11, 2017. Accessed April 11, 2018. http://www.historynet.com/reconquista.htm.

Robinson, Richard McCaffery. 2006. "Fourth Crusade." *Military History. HistoryNet.* July 31, 2006. Accessed April 11, 2018. http://www.historynet.com/fourth-crusade.htm.

Royde-Smith, John Graham. 2016. "House of Habsburg." *Encyclopaedia Britannica.* July 27, 2016. Accessed May 14, 2018. https://www.britannica.com/topic/House-of-Habsburg.

Ryan, Edward A. 2017. "Spanish Inquisition." *Encyclopaedia Britannica.* December 18, 2017. Accessed April 11, 2018. https://www.britannica.com/topic/Spanish-Inquisition.

Saul, Nigel. 2017. "Richard II." *Encyclopaedia Britannica.* March 7, 2017. May 3, 2018. https://www.britannica.com/biography/Richard-II-king-of-England.

"Schism of 1054." 2017. *Encyclopaedia Britannica.* August 22, 2017. Accessed April 24, 2018. https://www.britannica.com/event/Schism-of-1054.

Shan, Mark Chuanhang. 2011. "The Kingdom of God in Yurts: Christianity among Mongols in the Thirteenth and Fourteenth Centuries." *Africanus Journal* 3, no. 2 (November 2011): 29–41. *Gordon-Conwell Theological Seminary.* Accessed April 23, 2018. https://www.scribd.com/document/74284784/Africanas-Journal-Volume-3-No-2#fullscreen.

Sigg, Michèle. 2010. "An Historical Overview." In "The Dictionary of African Christian Biography." *Christianity.com.* April 28, 2010. Accessed May 14, 2018. https://www.christianity.com/church/church-history/timeline/2001-now/the-explosion-of-christianity-in-africa-11630859.html.

"Sistine Chapel." 2018. *Encyclopaedia Britannica.* January 31, 2018. Accessed May 10, 2018. https://www.britannica.com/topic/Sistine-Chapel.

Smith, Catherine Delano, John Frederick Haldon, and et al. 2018. "Greece." *Encyclopaedia Britannica.* May 2, 2018. Accessed May 4, 2018. https://www.britannica.com/place/Greece/Athens-Thebes-and-Corinth#ref26402.

Spielvogel, Jackson. 2012. *Western Civilization, Eighth Edition.* Boston: Wadsworth Cengage.

St. Patrick. 2017. *Patrick's Confessions and Breastplate.* In Great Christian Classics Vol. 1. Edited by Kevin Swanson and Joshua Schwisow. 181–209. Green Forest, AR: Master Books.

Steinberg, Jonathan. 2016. "The Holy Roman Empire Has Been Much Maligned." Review of *The Holy Roman Empire: A Thousand Years of Europe's History* by Peter H. Wilson. The

Spectator, January 23, 2016. Accessed May 14, 2018. https://www.spectator.co.uk/2016/01/the-holy-roman-empire-has-been-much-maligned/.

Stockwell, Robert, and Donka Minkova. 2001. *English Words: History and Structure.* Cambridge, England: Cambridge University Press.

"Taj Mahal" 2018. *Encyclopaedia Britannica.* April 19, 2018. Accessed April 23, 2018. https://www.britannica.com/topic/Taj-Mahal.

Tracy, James D. 2016. "Desiderius Erasmus." *Encyclopaedia Britannica.* December 16, 2016. Accessed May 14, 2018. https://www.britannica.com/biography/Desiderius-Erasmus.

Treharne, Reginald Francis. 2018. "Edward I." *Encyclopaedia Britannica.* April 20, 2018. Accessed May 3, 2018. https://www.britannica.com/biography/Edward-I-king-of-England.

Tucker, Ruth A. 2017. *Katie Luther: First Lady of the Reformation.* Grand Rapids, MI: Zondervan.

Turnbull, Stephen. 1998. *The Kakure Kirishitan of Japan: A Study of Their Development, Beliefs and Rituals to the Present Day.* Richmond, England: Japan Library.

"Umayyad Caliphate." n.d. *The Oxford Dictionary of Islam,* edited by John L. Esposito. *Oxford Islamic Studied Online.* Accessed April 10, 2018. http://www.oxfordislamicstudies.com/article/opr/t125/e2421.

Usselman, Melvyn C., and Alan J. Rocke. 2017. "Chemistry." *Encyclopaedia Britannica.* October 23, 2017. Accessed April 16, 2018. https://www.britannica.com/science/chemistry.

Van Helden, Albert. 2018. "Galileo." *Encyclopaedia Britannica.* February 14, 2018. Accessed May 4, 2018. https://www.britannica.com/biography/Galileo-Galilei.

Vann, Richard T. 2017. "Society of Friends." *Encyclopaedia Britannica.* April 21, 2017. Accessed May 14, 2018. https://www.britannica.com/topic/Society-of-Friends.

Vincent, Nicholas. 2015. "The Origins of Magna Carta." *British Library.* March 13, 2015. Accessed May 3, 2018. https://www.bl.uk/magna-carta/articles/the-origins-of-magna-carta.

Weiner, Rebecca. n.d. "Judaism: Sephardim." *Jewish Virtual Library.* Accessed May 3, 2018. http://www.jewishvirtuallibrary.org/sephardim.

Whelan, Christal, ed. and trans. 1996. *The Beginning of Heaven and Earth: The Sacred Book of Japan's Hidden Christians.* Honolulu: University of Hawai'i Press.

Wood, Michael. 2011. "King Arthur, 'Once and Future King.'" *BBC.* February 17, 2011. Accessed April 26, 2018. http://www.bbc.co.uk/history/ancient/anglo_saxons/arthur_01.shtml.

Yapp, Malcolm Edward, and Stanford Jay Shaw. 2017. "Ottoman Empire." *Encyclopaedia Britannica.* December 29, 2017. Accessed April 11, 2018. https://www.britannica.com/place/Ottoman-Empire.

"Yucatec Language." 2017. *Encyclopaedia Britannica.* August 20, 2017. Accessed May 14, 2018. https://www.britannica.com/topic/Yucatec-language.

Zacharia, Paul. 2016. "The Surprisingly Early History of Christianity in India." *Smithsonian Magazine.* February 19, 2016. Accessed April 23, 2018. https://www.smithsonianmag.com/travel/how-christianity-came-to-india-kerala-180958117/.

INDEX

All images are public domain (PD-US, and PD-Art), except for:

Shutterstock: Cover, p 36 R, P 46 R, p 70 T, p 160 T, p 200, p 220, p 224, p 228, p 230 T, p 231 BL, p 232, p 233, p 235, p 241, p 243 TR, p 244, p 250, p 252 (2), p 253 (4), p 254, p 256 L, p 257 R, p 259 TR, p 262, p 264 T, p 265 TL, p 266, p 267, p 272, p 273, p 276 T, p 278, p 279, p 286, p 288 (T0, p 289 BL, p 290, p 299, p 300 (2), p 301 T, p 302, p 304, p 308, p 309, p 312 (2), p 313 R, p 314, p 316 L, p 319, p 321 (2), p 324 (2), p 325 CR, CL, BL

iStock: p 6, p 12, p 18, p 28, p 38 T, p 40, p 44 R, p 48 T, P 49 L, p 50, p 60 (2), p 61 TL, BL, p 62, p 64, p 72 T, p 74, p 76, p 78 R, p 80, p 81, p 83, p 84 (2), p 86, p 90, p 94 T, p 96, p 99 R (5), p 100 (2), p 101, p 102, p 103, p 106 T, p 108, p 118 T, p 119 CL, p 120, p 125, p 128 (2), p 129 TL, BL, p 130, p 133 BL, p 140 T, p 141 CL, CR, p 142, p 145 T (3), p 149, p 150 BR, p 152, p 164, p 168 TL, p 169 R, p 171, p 173, p 174 (2), p 176, p 182, p 186 B, p 188, p 190 B, p 222 BR

Super Stock: p 8 BL, p 9, p 10, p 13, p 22, p 31 L, p 32, p 42 BL, p 47, p 56, p 67, p 68, p 75, p 77 R, p 79, p 109, p 111, p 112 T, p 131, p 139, p 143, p 144, p 155 T, p 156 TL, p 157, p 166, p 168 TR, p 181, p 183, p 189, p 196, p 201, p 204, p 229, p 239, p 247, p 248, p 251, p 270, p 271, p 275, p 280, p 284, p 315

dreamstime.com: p 105

Flickr: p 17 C (Jorge Láscar), p 17 BL (Dennis Jarvis), p 119 T (Christopher Michel), p 119 BR (Al Jazeera English), p 175 TL (Esther Westerveld), p 208 T (Neticola Sny), p 231 TL (Katya), p 288 BR (Timitrius)

Pixabay: p 30, p 33 TR, p 45 TR, p 210, p 289 TL

geograph.org: p 33 BR

Wikimedia Commons:Images from Wikimedia Commons are used under the CC0 1.0, CC BY-SA 2.0 DE, CC-BY-SA-3.0 license or the GNU Free Documentation License, Version 1.3.

p 7, p 8 BR, p 14, p 15 (2), p 16 (2), p 17 TL, p 17 BL, p 19, p 20 (5), p 21, p 26 (2), p 27 (3), p 29, p 31 R, p 33 TL, p 34 (2), p 36 L, p 37 (2), p 38 BR, p 39 (3), p 41, p 42 T, p 43, p 44 L, p 45 TC, p 46 L, p 48 BR, p 49 R(2), p 51, p 52, p 53 (2), p 54 (2), p 55 (2), p 57, p 58, p 59, p 61 CR, BR, p 63, p 65, p 66, p 71, p 72 B, p 73 (4), p 77 L, C, p 78 L, C, p 85 (4), p 87, p 88-89, p 89, p 92 (4), p 94 BR, p 95 (4), p 97, p 98 (3), p 99 BL, p 104, p 106 BR, p 107 (4), p 110 (2), p 112 B, p 113 (2), p 114, p 117, p 118 BR, p 119 BL, p 121, p 122, p 123, p 124, p 127, p 129 CR, BR, p 132 (2), p 133 BR, p 134 (2), p 135, p 136-137, p 137 B, p 138 (2), p 140 BR, p 141 T, BL, p 145 BR, p 146, p 147, p 148 T, p 150 T, p 151 (4), p 153, p 154, p 155 BR, p 156 TR, p 158, p 159, p 161, p 162 (2), p 163 (3), p 165, p 167, p 170, p 172, p 175 CR, CL, BR, BL, p 177, p 178, p 179, p 180 (2), p 184, p 185, p 186 T, C, p 187 (3), p 190 T, p 191, p 194, p 195, p 197, p 198 (2), p 199 (4), p 202, p 203, p 205, p 206, p 207, p 208 BR, p 209 (4), p 211, p 212, p 213, p 214, p 215, p 216, p 217 (3), p 218 (2), p 219 (4), p 221, p 222 BR, p 223, p 225, p 226, p 227 (3), p 230 B, p 231 C, p 234, p 236 (2), p 237 (2), p 238 (2), p 240, p 242 (2), p 243 C, B, p 245, p 247, p 249, p 255, p 256 R, p 257 L, p 259 B, p 260, p 261 (2), p 263 (2), p 264 BR, p 265 TR, C, BL, BR, p 268 (3), p 269, p 276 BR, p 277 (3), p 289 C, BR, 281 (10), p 282 (2), p 283, p 285, p 287 (2), p 291, p 292, p 293 (10), p 294, p 295, p 296 (2), p 297 (2), p 298, p 301 BL, BR, p 303, p 305, p 306 (2), p 307 (2), p 310, p 311, p 331 TL, BL, p 316 R, p 317 (2), p 318, p 320, p 323, p 325 T

L	left
R	right
T	top
C	center
B	bottom
CL	center left
CR	center right
TL	top left
TR	top right
BL	bottom left
BR	bottom right
BC	bottom center

BEGINNING 1
GRADE 5-8

Students will master basic writing with unique exercises on dialogue, reporting, interviews, role playing, persuasion, story writing, organizing and grouping ideas.

BEGINNING 2
GRADE 5-8

Students will learn how to effectively master using sentences and paragraphs, main and supporting ideas, process of rewriting, point of view, and creating characters.

INTERMEDIATE 1
GRADE 6-9 *[1 YEAR / 1 CREDIT]*

Students will learn about effective paragraphs, descriptive writing, narrative voice, and tense usage, as well as how to analyze plots in literature.

INTERMEDIATE 2
GRADE 6-9 *[1 YEAR / 1 CREDIT]*

Students will study writing strong arguments, dialogue, papers, and letters, as well as literary elements like theme, genre, point of view, and tone.

ADVANCED 1
GRADE 7-10 *[1 YEAR / 1 CREDIT]*

Students will practice writing reports, short stories, essays, and other forms of writing and learn about literary devices, including imagery, symbolism, and rhetorical language.

ADVANCED 2
GRADE 7-10 *[1 YEAR / 1 CREDIT]*

Students will refine their writing and research skills and study John Bunyan's classic *Pilgrim's Progress* in-depth.

TEACHING COMPANION

Teachers will find this an invaluable resource, not only for using the *Writing Strands* curriculum but also for teaching any course that includes writing and literature as a component. The *Teaching Companion* provides a helpful overview of the *Writing Strands* system, as well as additional information on a range of writing, grammar, and literature issues that a teacher may face at any level of the program.

Available at MasterBooks.com & other places where fine books are sold.
800-999-3777